"Gary Johns' book is a must read ..."
- Helen Hughes, *Spectator*.

"Johns' book is a challenge ... an antidote to the idealism of young lawyers, social workers ..."
- Stephen Gray, *The Weekend Australian Review*.

"A book which will find its place in Australian history."
- Mal Brough, former Commonwealth Minister for Indigenous Affairs.

"This book is a game changer."
- Keith Windschuttle, *Quadrant*.

"An important new book, a challenging and confronting work."
- Paul Comrie-Thomson, ABC Radio National, Counterpoint.

"The book ... is the best diagnosis I have seen of the causes of the massive plight of some of the Aboriginals living in remote settlements or on the fringes of towns like Alice Springs."
- Henry Thornton, blog.

ABORIGINAL
Self-Determination
THE WHITEMAN'S DREAM

GARY JOHNS

FOREWORD BY BESS NUNGARRAYI PRICE

connorcourt
PUBLISHING

Published in 2011 by Connor Court Publishing Pty Ltd.

Copyright © Gary Johns 2011.

Not to be reproduced without the permission of the Copyright holders.
All rights reserved.

Connor Court Publishing Pty Ltd.
PO Box 1
Ballan VIC 3342
sales@connorcourt.com
www.connorcourt.com

ISBN: 9781921421860 (pbk.)

National Library of Australia Cataloguing-in-Publication entry
Subjects: Aboriginal Australians--Government policy.
Aboriginal Australians--Legal status, laws, etc.
Aboriginal Australians--Politics and government.

Dewey Number: 323.119915

Cover design by Ian James.

Picture of Aborigine sitting on the flag by Paul Newman, first published in *The Australian* on 11 November 2010, used with permission.

Printed in Australia.

Table of Contents

Author's Dedication	1
Foreword	3
Dedication	5
Introduction	15
1 Competing strategies in Aboriginal advancement	**39**
Integration	41
Self-determination	44
The strategies compared	50
Costs and benefits of self-determination	62
Exit strategy	67
2 Identity at any price	**75**
From race to identity	76
Aboriginal programs fuel identity	82
Governance obsession	86
3 Defensibility of Aboriginal culture	**99**
Explanations of violence in Aboriginal society	104
Traditional violence	110
Culture inhibits adjustment	118
Folly recognising law and custom	124

4 Inquiries into white morality   **131**
   Royal Commission into Aboriginal Deaths in Custody (1991) 132
   Hindmarsh Island Royal Commission (1995)   141
   Separation of ATSI Children from Their Families (1997)   148
   Cubillo and Gunner (2000)   154
   Rudd Government Apology (2008)   162

5 Inquiries into black morality   **165**
   Five Inquiries into Aboriginal violence and sexual abuse:
   Robertson - Queensland (1999)   166
   Gordon - Western Australia (2002)   170
   Ella-Duncan - New South Wales (2006)   175
   Wild and Anderson - Northern Territory (2007)   179
   Mullighan - South Australia (2008)   188
   New directions despite the Inquiries   192

6 Pretend economy   **205**
   Promise of land rights   209
   Iconic land rights battles   218
   NT Land Rights Act mining veto   223
   Cape York Wild Rivers   230
   Community Development Employment Projects   237

7 Real economy   **249**
   Back to the mission   253
   No job, no house   262
   Using culture in education   289

Conclusion   **301**
Bibliography   **303**
Index   **315**

Author's dedication

I have worked with and through the Bennelong Society on Aboriginal policy for more than a decade. I would like to thank all members of the Society for their assistance, but especially the board with whom I have met on a monthly basis throughout the period. In writing this book, I have drawn on a number of the papers presented at Bennelong conferences and acknowledge these throughout the text. Most important are the insights of Pastor Paul Albrecht, formerly of Hermannsburg, and Rev Dr Steve Etherington, formerly of Oenpelli.

For their encouragement in the project and many and detailed comments on the book, I would like to thank Dr Ron Brunton, John Dawson, Rev Dr Steve Etherington, Dr Stephanie Jarrett, and John Nethercote.

I would also like to thank Dr Anthony Cappello and his team at Connor Court Publishing for encouragement in the project and professional competence in publishing.

Recently, I have befriended Bess Nungarrayi Price and Dave Price of Alice Springs. They have taught me a great deal about the ongoing struggle of Aboriginal people in remote areas to achieve equality with other Australians. Bess is an Aboriginal woman of exceptional strength. I hope that this book will assist her cause. Bess has been kind enough to write a Foreword.

In the early stages of preparing this book I asked my friend Peter Howson, vice-president of the Bennelong Society, to write of his thoughts and involvement in Aboriginal policy. I felt time was of the essence and that it would be a record of his part in development of Aboriginal policy. It would also provide me with an opportunity to show my indebtedness to his work.

I have taken the liberty of sharing Peter's thoughts by way of a Dedication.

Peter Howson died on 1 February 2009, aged 89. We miss him greatly but we are secure in the knowledge that his work was not in vain.

I am a lucky man. I have a wonderful and caring family. They have listened to my arguments and ideas for so long, and love me still. Thank you, Catherine, Elena, and Greta.

Gary Johns
President
Bennelong Society
December 2010

Foreword

Bess Nungarrayi Price

My mother and father were born in the desert. They taught me the old, sacred Law that our people lived by. It worked when we were living in tiny family groups taking everything that we needed from the desert. It was strong for sacred business and for marriage. Men had the power of life and death over their wives. Young girls were forced into marriage with older men. There was no law for property except that everything must be shared. There was no law for money, houses, cars, grog, petrol or drugs: we didn't have any. The only way to punish was by beating or killing the law breakers. We had no army, police, or courts and only our family to defend us. Law Men used magic to heal or harm and kill.

Now we have a new law that is not sacred and doesn't believe in magic. We have property, houses, cars, grog, drugs, pornography. We live off welfare or we need to get a job to live. We still share everything. We can't say 'no' to kin even if they waste our money or destroy themselves with it. Too many men still want the power of life and death over their wives. We don't plan for the future, budget or invest.

Too many of our kids are at terrible risk. There's too much drunkenness, feuding, sickness, suicide, unemployment and despair. Our kids are not being educated properly in either law.

The old Law was not about human rights. It was about unconditional loyalty and obedience. Wise old people tried to make sure that there was justice. But even they couldn't deal with grog, drugs and violence. It all happened too quickly.

We still respect and honour our ancestors and want to keep our culture. But my people are confused. If they go the blackfella way they break whitefella law, if they go whitefella way they break blackfella law. Our young men are caught in the middle, that's why they fill up the jails. My parents understood that things were falling apart. My mother outlived eight of her eleven children. They understood the difference between the letter of the Law and its spirit.

We now need to change the letter of our Law to keep its spirit alive. We need to do this ourselves but with the support of governments and our fellow citizens. The time for shouting slogans and waving placards is over. We need to do some tough thinking and honest debating.

I don't agree with everything that Gary Johns says in this book but he is honest and believes in what he says. I am happy to write this foreword and to encourage and praise him for the contribution he is making to the debate we need to have.

Alice Springs
December 2010

Dedication

The Honourable Peter Howson, CMG

I have been actively concerned with Aboriginal affairs for 47 years, perhaps longer than any other person in government circles. Looking back it is clear that Aboriginal policy took a wrong turn in the 1960s. One group of Aborigines, those who were last to have contact with white society, have been cruelled by the experiment in Aboriginal self-determination.

I was first involved in Aboriginal policy as a member of the Parliamentary Voting Rights Committee in 1961; second, as Minister for Aboriginal Affairs from 1971 to 1972; and third, from May 1993 when I was asked by a Shadow Minister of the Federal Opposition to take a particular interest in formulating policy on Aboriginal affairs.

In gathering my thoughts I have been greatly assisted by several former Commonwealth public servants who have been in the Northern Territory for much longer than I have. I should single out two particularly. The first is Les Penhall, who joined the Northern Territory Public Service in 1940 as a patrol officer. He conducted his first patrol from Alice Springs to the Western Australian border on a camel in 1940. He had been in the department for over 30 years during which time I had known him. He saw a lot of hunter-gatherers as they were before they had really caught up with the movement of

Australians into the remoter parts of the Northern Territory. He has been able to furnish me with a real idea of what the hunter-gathering existence was like. The other is Dr Ted (E P) Milliken, a psychologist, recruited Deputy Director of the newly-formed Welfare Department of the Northern Territory Administration under Harry Giese. He took up that job in 1954 and not only has a wealth of information at his fingertips, but he has also been able to explore the archives of that period, at least those archives that survived the 1974 cyclone in Darwin. I have been able to get access to the archives of that period to refresh my memory of all that took place between 1954 and 1971.

In 1961 I was appointed one of the seven members of the Parliamentary Voting Rights Committee established to decide whether the Aborigines should be eligible for voting in federal elections. The first thing the committee did was to consult the Chief Commonwealth Electoral Officer to tell us the definition of an Aborigine. It varied from state to state. The Chief Electoral Officer told us that for the purpose of his decision as to who voted and who did not, he used the current definition of an Aborigine in the Northern Territory. That definition was that an Aborigine is a person who is of full-blood Aboriginal descent, or at least has 50 per cent Aboriginality. Anybody who had less than 50 per cent was not an Aborigine. We used that definition in all our hearings. Because we had to go to places where there were Aborigines who conformed to the definition, we had to go to the really remote communities of Australia at that time.

We visited 39 separate communities from Cape Leeuwin to Thursday Island. It included places like Kalumburu in the far north of Western Australia and Hooker Creek on the edge of the Western Desert in the Northern Territory. We had with us Hansard reporters so there is a full Hansard report of about 500 pages which has been a very useful source of material. The main advantage of our hearings was that we were talking to a large number of people who had recently been hunter-gatherers, or at least whose parents or grandparents remembered what hunter-gathering life was like. These people realised that the new opportunities envisaged by converting to our way of life were much less arduous.

As well as recommending that the Aborigines should have the right to vote, although it was not compulsory to enrol, the report also had these words:

> The declared policy of the Commonwealth Government towards the Aboriginal people is that they should gradually be integrated into the European community. Over the past five years the majority of the remaining nomads have, of their own volition, come to the settlements and missions scattered throughout the Commonwealth, and your committee considers that there are now fewer than 2,000 Aborigines living in their traditional tribal cultures. As the nomadic Aboriginal adults are moving to the settlements and missions, gradually renouncing their nomadic and semi-nomadic lives, their children attend schools where their integration commences. It was demonstrated to your committee that any policy other than integration of the Aboriginal people into one Australian society, would be impracticable.

And,

> As a situation of complete integration is inevitable, your committee considers that the aim of the Commonwealth should be to assist integration to continue as smoothly and speedily as possible. The Aborigines need a considerable capital investment in education, including technical and agricultural education in industries, land tenure and housing.

It is interesting to note that in the whole of the 500 pages of evidence, not once was there the words 'land rights', or 'self determination', or 'separate development'. Those were all concepts that appeared later. I should add that once every two years from 1961 until 1967 there was a meeting of ministers of the Commonwealth and of the States. For the whole of that time the policies endorsed in our report were those followed by government.

The report that I have just outlined has been foremost in my mind for the past 47 years because I believe that these people, who were the last to give up hunter gathering, were the people who never got a decent education or training for a decent job. Their needs were forgotten by ministers and Aboriginal leaders who came in subsequently. And it is their descendants who had to endure more than 30 years of living on welfare, having no ability to get employment or receive a decent education. Their education was halted half-way through and has never resumed. In fact these are the people whose descendants are now the subject of the intervention that began in June 2007.

My next real opportunity to handle Aboriginal Affairs came in June 1971 when I was appointed to be Minister for Aboriginal Affairs. I was the first Minister for Aboriginal Affairs. Prior to that, between the 1967 Referendum and my appointment, the responsibility for Aboriginal Affairs had rested in the Prime Minister's Department, where for a time the Prime Minister was assisted in Aboriginal Affairs by Bill Wentworth, the Minister for Social Services.

About 1963 we first heard about the words 'land rights' and, soon after, those of 'self determination' and the concept of 'separatism'. I should add that those who were activating the need for a referendum were the Federal Council of the Aborigines and Torres Strait Islanders, and it is interesting when we look at the membership of that council and of the adherents from which they were drawn. They were people who in 1963 would not have been classified as Aborigines using the 1961 definition. They had all had the opportunity of a decent education and were able to hold down employment in Australian society. People like Faith Bandler, a South Sea Islander whose forebears were horticulturalists, and Aborigines who had no recollection of a hunter-gathering existence. They were at least two or three generations separated from that time and had really a rather mystical idea of what

Aboriginal culture was like. These were the people who clamoured for the referendum to be held in 1967.

The movement was also strongly assisted by several white activists who introduced concepts from overseas, many of them from United Nations' resolutions and from even the Communist Comintern of 1931. So that the ideas were not those of the Aborigines concerned, but of a new concept coming from post colonial times.

Anyway, the referendum was carried and so the Commonwealth now became responsible, in some ways, for Aboriginal affairs. The Government really failed to come to grips with the way in which they should carry out their new responsibilities. The government of the day never really decided the role of the Minister for Aboriginal Affairs as it related to the ministers in the States and the ministers responsible for the territories.

A Council for Aboriginal Affairs was also created. It had no defined duties and responsibilities. It only provided advice when it felt that it needed to, and was not prepared to advise on questions put to it by the government.

These were the issues that confronted me when I was appointed Minister for Aboriginal Affairs. One of the first issues that arose was when the Council for Aboriginal Affairs recommended that we needed a new definition of who was an Aborigine. They came up with the concept that an Aborigine was any person who had some evidence of descent from an Aborigine or who had been associated with Aborigines for such a time that they felt they were a part of their society. This considerably increased the number of Aborigines in Australia and so, while in the 1950s the total number of Aborigines in the census was in the order of 50,000, 50 years later the number was nearer 500,000.

This also meant that we now had in effect two sets of Aborigines: those who had been defined in accordance with the 1961 definition; and those who were defined in the 1971 definition, and their needs were very different. But the people in the 1971 definition were much better educated and had a greater ability to define their needs and to clamour for funds to advance their ideas. Those who were still in the 1961 definition were not able to express their needs adequately, and so they were forgotten and the people responsible for training them, such as the missions and the patrol officers, were gradually dismissed.

The new issues of 1971 were chiefly related to land rights. The Council for Aboriginal Affairs recommended that Aborigines should be granted the right to run pastoral properties and they were recommending that pastoral companies be bought from owners or lease-holders and handed to Aboriginal groups. How these new owners of pastoral properties were expected to run the properties was never defined. They had had no training as pastoralists. They had never had any idea as to how they could exist on a property as hunter-gatherers – that was two or three generations away from them. And all they could do was to sit on those properties either leasing them to the former owners who then ran them, and paid them a pittance for living there, or they existed on those lands receiving welfare from the government. This whole idea of land rights had never been properly defined and caused so much trouble in the years ahead.

Alcohol was another issue beginning to appear in 1971. I asked the Council for Aboriginal Affairs to advise me as to what should be our policy in regard to alcohol, because there were issues with the United Nations that said the Aborigines should have the same rights to alcohol as other Australian people. My own view was that suddenly to introduce alcohol to communities that had been alcohol-free should be carefully considered. But I never got an answer from the Council and some States were introducing things like wet canteens in which light beer only was served.

This was a time of great change from the idea that we had in 1961 of certainty, and we now had a period of uncertainty and of new ideas of Commonwealth responsibility. These were undefined and were the seeds of problems that were to arise when I ceased to be Minister at the end of 1972. For the next 20 years I was away from any contact on Aboriginal affairs and could only sit on the sidelines watching the destruction of all the ideas and projects that I and others had set in place. I saw the way in which many Aborigines were going downhill and living in misery.

But in 1993, following five consecutive election losses by the Liberal Party, a shadow minister approached me and invited me to formulate a new policy on Aboriginal affairs for the Liberal Party. This meant that I first had to think out new aims that I had formulated back in 1961 and in 1971, setting out in my own mind the principles on which a policy should be based. It also involved assembling a team of like-minded people who could provide us with a committee to conduct our policies, and one prominent amongst them was Ray Evans.

I then managed to take a trip to Darwin where I was able to get Harry Giese, who had been the Director of Welfare in the Northern Territory for many years, especially when I was Minister, to collect a team of former patrol officers. We had an all-day seminar in Darwin to get some idea of what was wrong in the present situation and what needed to be changed.

Following that we were able to establish groups that held annual conferences. First the Galatians Group; secondly, for a short time, *Quadrant*, and then the Bennelong Society. From 1994 until 2008 there have been annual conferences which have gradually established the aims that we have been trying to get Australians to understand, particularly the real needs of Aborigines. My trip to Darwin also enabled me to recruit speakers from the remote communities who knew exactly what was going on and were able to bring their needs to light through the conferences.

Through the Galatians Group we were able to recruit Dr Geoffrey Partington to write a book, *Hasluck versus Coombs*, which set out clearly the different approach to Aboriginal affairs by Hasluck in the 1950s and 1960s, and by Coombs in the 1970s and 1980s. We were fortunate that one of the first acts of John Herron as Minister for Aboriginal Affairs in the Howard Government was to launch the book.

I think I can sum up the aim of our policy as set out under the heading really of 'Dignity'. Many anthropologists have attested to the innate dignity of an Aboriginal man as a hunter-gatherer. When that man decided to cease hunter-gathering and to join our society, he lost that dignity because he was dependent on welfare. The only way in which he could regain that dignity was to be able to become independent of welfare. This meant that it was necessary for him to be educated, and to acquire a skill that would enable him to get employment in our society. Once he was independent of welfare, his dignity was restored, but while he was dependent on welfare there was no dignity and he sank into misery.

This has been the aim that has been at the back of all our policies now for the last 15 years. Jobs are more important than any other consideration. What is the use of land rights if you cannot make use of the land on which you are sitting? What is the use of separatism if you were living in a separate state in which you could do nothing to exist without outside help? And what is the use of retaining a culture which was related to hunter-gathering which was no longer part of your activities? These slogans of the late 1960s were shown to be worthless.

Our aim to achieve change in Aboriginal affairs was delayed by two related bodies, Ronald Wilson's Inquiry which produced *Bringing them Home*, the so-called Stolen Children report, and the establishment of the Council for Reconciliation. The flaws in the report had to be exposed by the subsequent Cubillo and Gunner trial which only came to an end in 2000. At the same time, in 1988, Bob Hawke had set up the Council for Reconciliation as an attempt to head off the demands for a treaty, and its implied separation of Aborigines from other Australians, which were prominent in the bicentenary year. That Council finally reported in the year 2000 so that, for the years of the Howard Government from 1996 until 2000, any attempt at change was impossible. But following 2000, gradually, there was a succession of changes to bring down the edifice that had been created during the 30 years from 1973 to 2000.

What was needed were amendments to the *Land Rights Act*, the end of the Aboriginal and Torres Strait Islander Commission, the end of sit-down money, abolition of Community Development Employment Projects, and limitations on the sale of alcohol. All these things had to take place before any real change could be effected. Finally, in June 2007, Mal Brough engineered the intervention in the Northern Territory which heralded the essential change that was needed in order to restore dignity to Aborigines in the remote communities.

It is my fervent hope that this intervention be allowed to continue. To my mind it is the only way in which the Aborigines who live in the remote communities and have suffered the indignity of welfare dependence since 1973, can finally hope they will be removed out of their misery and given hope of living a meaningful life. It has taken me 47 years to achieve this goal. I believe now I can see the end in sight.

Barwon Heads
February 2008

Introduction

The dream of whiteman, that Aborigines could live collectively and separately from the rest of Australia, has turned sour. The Christian missionaries, for example, were right to protect Aborigines[1] from the worst of the rapacious whiteman's world, and right to prepare Aborigines for the modern world. They were wrong, however, to abandon those efforts in favour of self-determination. In doing so, they, and many others, condemned Aborigines to playing out a whiteman's dream — Aborigines living in ancient ways in an ancient landscape. Now, many years on, it is time to make amends. Noel Pearson urges policy-makers to move beyond what he terms the 'campaign Aboriginal', an Aboriginal fighting to protect land for recognition.[2] With some exceptions, for example, the Wild Rivers legislation in Cape York, Aborigines do not have to campaign for their rights, or land, or recognition; these have been assured for years. And yet recent visits by the president of Amnesty International and the United Nations Special Rapporteur to Alice Springs town camps and elsewhere are given prominent coverage in the media as if there was some profound remedy for Aboriginal strife in their pre-digested

---

1 The following spelling conventions are used throughout: Aborigine(s) (noun), Aboriginal (adjective) and Indigenous (Aborigine and Torres Strait Islander), except where used in quotes. Where Indigenous is used, it represents Aboriginal and Torres Strait Islander populations.
2 ABC television transcript, *Australian Story*, 'Cry Me a River', 2007.

human rights policy medicine. Aborigines do not lack rights. Their struggle is with their past, the ingrained habits of generations that prevent some from getting a foothold in the Australian economy. Aborigines do not need new homes so much as new lives; they need to change their behaviour. Unfortunately, many Aboriginal leaders misdiagnose their peoples' dilemma. Galarrwuy Yunupingu boasts:

> I have maintained the traditions, kept the law, performed my role yet the Yolngu world is in crisis; we have stood still. I look around me and I feel the powerlessness of all our leaders. All around me are do-gooders and no-hopers... Whitefellas. Balanda.
>
> Although the wealth of the Australian nation has been taken from our soil, our communities and homelands bear no resemblance to the great towns and metropolises of the modern Australian nation.[3]

Yunupingu wants the whiteman's economy and the blackman's culture – what could be simpler? But does Yunupingu seriously suggest that Aborigines could build cities and economies, and remain the skill-less people of the Yolngu tribes? To argue that wealth was taken from Aboriginal soil is to assume that civilisation does not exist and that wealth was sitting there waiting to be plucked. Wealth is not plucked or stolen – it is created – and Galarrwuy Yunupingu would be a poorer man if it were not so. Aboriginal tribal life was radically different to modern life in both culture and economy. Tribal Aborigines had no real understanding of how the world worked; their profound lack of understanding was masked by ritual as a means of explaining events, whether abundance or absence of food, or life and death. Tribal Aborigines no longer exist but, if they did, public policy would dictate that either they be assisted to enter the modern world, which would destroy their belief system and consequentially their

---

3 Yunupingu, G. 2008. *The Monthly*, December 2008-January 2009, No. 41, p. 7.

authority system, or they would be left to fend for themselves.

Policy has swung between these two views for more than two hundred years. Realistically, any Aborigines looking at their neighbours' comparative wealth would be curious enough to want the same. Wanting the same, it would be incumbent on the neighbours to teach Aborigines how to obtain the benefits, lest they steal it. The 19th century reserves for tribal Aborigines were in one sense meant to leave Aborigines well enough alone and, in another sense, to control their every move to prevent them from becoming modern. Indeed, the sentiment was based on respecting difference but it was pessimistic about bridging the gap between Stone Age people and modern people. The opposite urge, assimilation, would have made Aborigines modern and undermined their entire way of life. Either way, they were never going to survive as Aboriginal people living an ancient culture. In the modern society it is impossible to ignore cause and effect in life. Weather changes for a reason; food is abundant or scarce for a reason; people die for a reason. Such rationality does not preclude religious belief, but the Stone Age culture offered Aborigines only belief.

What, then, do we make of present experiments in Aboriginal policy in a rational world, where Stone Age belief is dead, tribal mores are dead, and many Aborigines do not look or act like tribalised Aborigines? Where is the public policy sting? Indeed, the recent and most welcome work by Peter Sutton, *The Politics of Suffering*,[4] reads as a lengthy apology on behalf of anthropologists for their encouragement of the dream of difference. Anthropologists and others in the field confused their needs with those of Aborigines. In terms of policy debate their work implicitly and, often times, explicitly gave comfort to those who wanted to continue with government programs to 'respect difference'. These programs are essentially designed to keep

---

4 Sutton, P. 2009. *The Politics of Suffering: Indigenous Australia and the End of the Liberal Consensus*. Melbourne University Press.

some Aboriginal spokespersons happy. Their argument is based on the notion that Aboriginal culture is defensible as a functioning guide to life in the modern world. Alternatively, there are those who want to use programs and incentives to change behaviour among those Aborigines (and, indeed, anyone else) who at present cannot cope in modern society. The latter want to change inappropriate behaviour and use the best tools available for the job; the former wants to preserve political power among a small group of advocates. It is heartening that Sutton will no longer allow his work to be used for the former, and for improper purposes; he now realises that 'goodwill can destroy as well as heal'.[5]

The improper purposes are the continued maltreatment of Aboriginal children by Aborigines. The much loved and enduring image of happy Aborigines is a young girl with a wide smile peeping out from the water lilies floating in a beautiful tropical billabong. The chances of that girl getting to a ripe old age are remote. She is much less likely to learn about the world outside of her community or get a job and much more likely than other Australians to be sexually abused, beaten, most likely by someone in her extended family. She buys food at a local government-owned store, not by hunting and gathering. These common truths have been well illustrated by the recent Aboriginal-directed film, *Samson and Delilah*.[6] Who is to blame for ruining the native child in her pristine environment? The whiteman? Indeed, it may have been the whiteman of settler fame brandishing a gun. But it is as likely the whiteman brandishing a laptop or a television camera who would have us believe that the young girl was treated differently before the whiteman came. Witness the social worker disciplined for failing to protect a 10-year old Aboriginal girl repeatedly raped at Aurukun in 2005. Her defence was that such children should be

---

5 Sutton, P. 2007. 'The worst of good intentions?' *ABC The Drum Unleashed*. 11 December.
6 *Samson and Delilah*, directed by Warwick Thornton, an Aborigine, won the Camera d'Or at the Cannes film festival in 2009.

reunited and returned to the community for the sake of their 'cultural, emotional and spiritual identity.'[7] All appeals to save 'the Aborigine' founded on the idea of a pristine original state and a fall from grace are doomed to fail. They are not only wildly inaccurate, they provide no answers to the present predicament, and they get in the way of saving the children.

All Australian Aborigines live in the modern world and most thrive in that world. A minority do not. They have been led to believe that they can avoid it by living on 'country', or possibly in cities, living their culture and avoiding the realities of the non-subsidised economy. The belief has irreversibly damaged thousands of Aborigines causing them to fail. Successful Aborigines – those who do not unduly rely on others for their well-being – are, by and large, descendants of those who were prepared for the modern world, often by missionaries and government patrol officers. These people knew a great deal about Aboriginal culture and its shortcomings. Successful Aborigines have language and skills sufficient to get a job and support a family. To all intents and purposes successful Aborigines are integrated into the economy and society. A minority of Aborigines live in a world of faux culture, faux economics, degradation and violence. The latter group, overwhelmingly, although by no means exclusively, living on their lands in discrete and remote communities, is being excluded from the economy. The question is, why?

Success and failure of the relationship between Aborigines and the whiteman litter the entire history of Australia, Bennelong of the Eora people at Sydney Cove being among the first, in 1789.[8] Bennelong was unsuccessful because, although his habits and language became like the whiteman, ultimately he could not bridge the immense gap between the requirements of a hunter-gatherer and a modern

---

7 *The Australian*, 18 December 2007, p. 1.
8 Smith, K. 2001. *Bennelong: the coming in of the Eora: Sydney Cove 1788-1792*. Kangaroo Press.

European. He drank himself to death, though at an age greater than many of his contemporaries who had no contact. But this is history, so why, more than 200 years later, do some Aborigines continue to fail? The answer lies in the fact that there is a gap between modern and pre-modern societies, once called civilised and uncivilised. Denying its existence and the considerable efforts required on the part of individuals to bridge it has been very harmful. The dominant and enduring story of Aboriginal Australia has been the integration of Aborigines into modern Australian society. In the last forty years a lesser story has emerged. It is one of Aboriginal self-determination whereby Aborigines have sought to retain their collective identity. Aboriginal self-determination has interrupted the journey into the modern Australian society. The interruption has left many stranded.

This is not to argue that integration cannot occur on Aboriginal terms. But the terms of the implied contract between Aborigines and non-Aborigines have to be understood. Although full of fine words about 'closing the gap', government policies cannot possibly achieve their aim while accommodating Aborigines' hunter-gatherer lifestyle minus the hunting and gathering. The costs, as have become apparent, are measured in violent and degraded lives and, most disastrously, child sexual abuse. Questions need to be asked about the supposed cultural revival occurring among Aboriginal people and the devastation of Aboriginal children and women, mostly by men and boys in remote Australia.

Despite major increases for the rest of the labour force, Aboriginal labour force participation has increased only marginally in the last thirty years, mostly among educated Aborigines; there has been little change in remote areas. The labour force participation rate for Aboriginal people (59 per cent) is about three quarters of that for non-Aboriginal people (78 per cent); the unemployment rate for Aboriginal people (13 per cent) is about three times the rate for non-Aboriginal people (four per cent).[9] Community Development Employment Project (Aboriginal work-for-the-dole) participants are a major part of the labour force in some remote and very remote areas. Were CDEP participants otherwise unemployed, their numbers added to the unemployed indicate very high levels of unemployment in remote and very remote areas (Figure 1). In the Northern Territory, for example, there were 11,661 Indigenous people 'employed' (2006 census) of whom 8,646 were on CDEP (as at June 2006). In many areas there is a sufficiently close match between the ABS Census employment figures and the CDEP figures[10] to indicate that, when CDEP figures are removed from the Census employment figures, there is near total unemployment in these communities. By contrast, non-Aboriginal unemployment declines with remoteness.

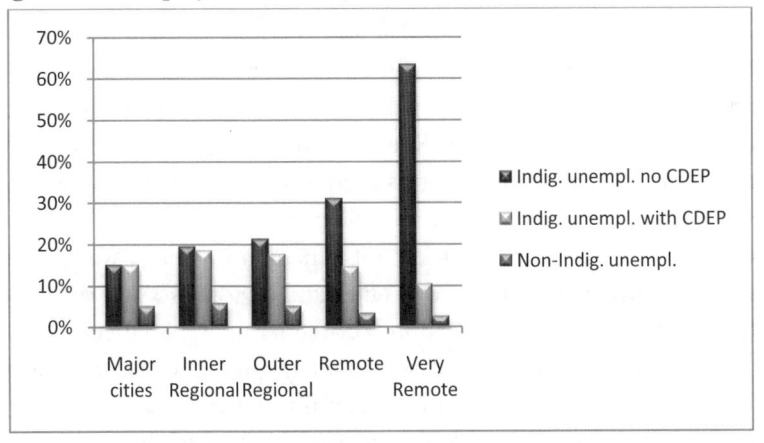

Figure 1: Unemployment rates by remoteness area, 15-64 year olds

Remoteness	Indig. unempl. no CDEP	Indig. unempl. with CDEP	Non-Indig. unempl.
Major cities	~15%	~17%	~5%
Inner Regional	~20%	~22%	~6%
Outer Regional	~20%	~22%	~5%
Remote	~30%	~32%	~4%
Very Remote	~63%	~13%	~2%

Data source: *Australian Bureau of Statistics, 2008a*. Population Characteristics 2006, Aboriginal and Torres Strait Islander Australians. 4713.0 table 7.1 91, table 7.7 98.

---

9 Productivity Commission, 2007a. *Overcoming Indigenous Disadvantage*, 3.46.
10 Department of Finance and Deregulation, 2009. *Evaluation of the Community Development Employment Projects Program*, p. 14.

The aspiration for strong mainstream job and business growth in remote areas may be great but the opportunities and the abilities of Aborigines living there are pathetic. Aboriginal people in remote areas are far less likely to speak English as a first language. For example, of those Indigenous people who speak an Indigenous language at home, 74 per cent live in very remote Australia, and 14 per cent live in remote Australia. Fifty six per cent of all Indigenous language speakers live in the Northern Territory where 59 per cent of the Indigenous population speak an Australian Indigenous language.[11] Aborigines are often in very difficult personal circumstances suffering low levels of self-esteem, high levels of drug and alcohol abuse and, in some instances, live in violent communities.[12] Work motivation is a real concern; as reported by officers of the Department of Families, Housing, Community Services and Indigenous Affairs, 'the men do not want to work.'[13]

In 2006, 31 per cent of Indigenous people in Australia lived in Major Cities. The remaining Indigenous population was evenly distributed across Inner Regional (22 per cent), Outer Regional (23 per cent) and Remote/Very Remote Australia (24 per cent). Nine out of the 37 Indigenous Regions accounted for half the Indigenous population of Australia. These were Sydney, Brisbane, Coffs Harbour, Perth, Townsville, Cairns, Adelaide, Tasmania and Wagga Wagga. The bulk of Aboriginal people live in cities and regions, so that the lesser gap between Aboriginal and non-Aboriginal unemployment rates is somewhat misleading in as much as programs to close the gap in the cities may well be far more powerful in terms of addressing the numbers of Aboriginal unemployed. Nevertheless, while city rates are a concern, the plight of the remote area Aborigines is extreme.

Faced by a strong ideological push to re-create an 'Aboriginal

---

11 Australian Bureau of Statistics, 2008a. *Population Characteristics 2006, ATSI Australians*, 4713.0, p. 43.
12 DFD, 2009, p. 16.
13 DFD, 2009, p. 16.

society', governments have condemned 100,000 or so Aborigines living mainly in remote areas to a living hell.

The elaborate inquiries in the 1990s into *Aboriginal Deaths in Custody* and *The Stolen Generations* and in the 2000s into Aboriginal child sexual abuse came up with the same answers, that 'aboriginal culture' must be respected and that 'aboriginal communities' must take charge of their destiny. But what if this 'solution' is the problem? What if the culture is no more than people behaving badly, a result of blighted environments, poor incentives, awful history, and an historic culture best relegated to museums and occasional ceremonies? What if these communities are hopeless, in economic terms and every other respect, and that their only rationale is that an ancient band of people once inhabited them or, more brazenly, where some remain in the hope that through land rights they may gain a windfall from a resources company? These are the uncomfortable questions that governments avoid asking lest they be labelled racist. Yet it is in avoiding them they are being racist and intellectually dishonest.

The poor behaviour exhibited by Aborigines trapped in remote communities can be mostly explained by long term unemployment and vestiges of the earlier culture. The overlay of history may add to the despair but not to the solutions. Those who want to solve the problems of Aborigines by having them remain on their land and retain or restore 'culture' invite scrutiny of their remedies. Unfortunately, Aboriginal culture and the technology upon which Aboriginal society depended and around which culture was built is not a story that invites respect in a modern world. Geoffrey Blainey's admirable history of Australian Aborigines, *Triumph of the Nomads*, despite the optimistic title and his acknowledgement of their hunter-gatherer skills, pulled no punches in the story of their survival.

> One of the sharpest observers of tribal life thought that the women of Bangerang, a group on the plains of northern Victoria, gave birth to six or perhaps even eight children

during the course of their life. Nearly half of those babies, he estimated, were killed at birth. He realised that nomadic people had no alternative but to kill superfluous babies.[14]

Aborigines did not prosper in Australia. They simply survived. They were small bands of hunter-gatherers who did not develop metal tools or writing and no political structures in as much as they had nothing to administer, no taxes, no surplus to distribute or hold, no means to hold prisoners, no public works to administer. As Jared Diamond explains: 'those developments arose elsewhere only in populous and economically specialized societies of food producers ... Australia's climate limited the population to only a few hundred thousand' which meant that Australia had 'far fewer potential inventors ... to experiment with adopting innovations.' Such were the barriers to innovation that there were 'regressions in technology.' The boomerang, for example, was abandoned in Cape York Peninsula; the Aborigines of south-western Australia ... 'may have abandoned arrows 5,000 years ago' and, when discovered by Europeans in 1642, Tasmanian Aborigines 'had the simplest material culture of any people in the modern world.'[15] They lacked even the rudimentary technologies of the mainland Aborigines because they were cut off from all centres of innovation.

> The documented instances of technological regression on the Australian mainland, and the example of Tasmania, suggest that the limited repertoire of Native Australians compared with that of peoples of other continents may stem in part from the effects of isolation and population size on the development and maintenance of technology.[16]

As Diamond succinctly sums up, Europeans colonised Australia, Native Australians did not colonise Europe. The Europeans had 10,000

---

14 Blainey, G. 1983. *Triumph of the Nomads.* Macmillan, p. 97.
15 Diamond, J. 1998. *Guns, Germs and Steel.* Vintage, pp. 311-12.
16 Diamond, 1998, p. 313.

years of innovation in closely settled, climatically suitable conditions to prepare. It was never going to be any other way than that Europeans (or Chinese or Japanese or Indonesians) colonised Australia. So what are Aborigines fighting for, what is there to preserve? Each step to preserve culture is a step away from the innovation that commenced 200 years ago. What survives of Aboriginal Australia is nothing like 200 years ago, so what culture is it, and whose is it?

The 'it' is a dream, a fantasy that something special remains, or has evolved, worthy of reclaiming. But what has actually evolved is ruin and despair. The 'it' belongs only to those who could not adapt to change. Do those who lay the blame for the ruin and despair of Aborigines at the feet of the whiteman seriously suggest that Aborigines would otherwise have survived in a form worth fighting for? Is this seriously what it is all about? And yet, in report, after inquiry, after policy statement, after program, after the whole paraphernalia of Aboriginal policy and politics, the long patient Australian taxpayer and citizen is asked to believe that there is some point to the exercise.

In 1972 Charles Rowley mused on the 'recovery'[17] of Aboriginal society. In the years since, and shortly prior, the lives of a class of Aborigines have deteriorated in pursuit of this recovery. The Aborigines in the scattered settlements of the Anangu Pitjantjatjara Yankunytjatjara (APY) lands in remote north-west South Australia, for example, have turned their noses up at the work provided for them through CDEP.[18] In the main, the scheme consists of each of ten communities having their men assigned to collect the rubbish and tidy up. The same thing occurs in many other Aboriginal communities. This work earns the disdain of Aborigines and they are reluctant to do it. The trouble is there is little else for which they are fit.

Moreover, in the real economy, the work would be done by one man and a truck and the residents would pay for the service. Where this has been tried, and the business run by Aborigines, the truck is

---

17 Rowley, C. 1972. *The Destruction of Aboriginal Society*. Pelican, p. 67.
18 See discussion of CDEP below.

used to go fishing and abandoned or bogged. Simply handing over the tools does not work. In Aboriginal Australia the taxpayers pay men to collect rubbish inefficiently, costing money and keeping people from doing anything useful. What a mess! For three generations this game has been played, and it shows. Reluctant workers and expensive and poor services are the norm, and still the whiteman takes the blame. And so he should for being so ignorant of the basic laws of economics and so disingenuous in support of Aboriginal culture.

Then there is the horrible violence of Aboriginal communities, the extraordinarily high incidence of murder, bashings and child abuse. Commissions of inquiry turned society's minds to the whiteman again, arguing that it must have been the fault of the colonists, without a thought that, when the conscious policy of integration ceased, a prehistoric and violent society simply returned to earlier ways, this time without some of the constraints of the old ways. A select group of Aborigines was encouraged to remain apart by educated black men and women and white academics. These people kept their own in thrall of a myth about a purer, simpler society. Indeed, there were elements of nobility, and there were elements of savagery, but there was also trade in women, as well as violence and crude and rough justice for men and women. Aborigines were not alone in these behaviours; they shared these traits with many pre-modern societies. But the current penchant for Aboriginal culture is used to shield corruption and abuse of power in Aboriginal communities. It is also used to slow the necessary steps to adjustment of Aboriginal people to the modern economy and society. All of those who have played the culture game, who have striven to create a life from Aboriginal misery, are to be condemned in the most severe terms.

Guilty are universities that compete for the prize of being the most 'Indigenous friendly'. These privileged institutions devise ever more elaborate schemes to recognise Aboriginal culture. They do so in direct contradiction to their primary obligations, which are to truth and merit. The standard fare is to establish an Indigenous Reconciliation Working Group formed by staff and students to promote, among other things, the 'Apology', to encourage course coordinators, lecturers and tutors to 'acknowledge the traditional custodians of the land on which the university operates' at the beginning of the first lecture for each course, 'invite Course Coordinators & Lecturers to explore opportunities to incorporate Indigenous content into their courses' ... 'Develop career services that enhance the employment outcomes of Indigenous graduands',[19] including work experience and internship opportunities, and so on and so forth.

Aborigines who make it to university on merit are in no need of special recognition and assistance. Something else is happening. On the one hand, there is a very strong suspicion that some Aboriginal students are pushed into university beyond their capability; others attend for the student payment that is their entitlement alone. On the other hand, universities want to be seen to be assisting the less fortunate. They do this in a way that undermines their integrity and adds fuel to the myths that prejudice is at the root cause of Aboriginal disadvantage. Aboriginal students are no doubt embarrassed to be treated in a way that suggests they need special assistance and that their culture is a commodity to be bartered for advantage among university vice-chancellors. Using Rudyard Kipling's famous phrase, the game of the whiteman's burden played out at university is symptomatic of a much larger and longer game played out in the last 40 years across the political realm.

The real story of Aboriginal society in the last 200 years is the accommodation that Aborigines have made to the modern world and the manner in which they have made their way into the broader society. The mechanisms are as bland as schooling, marriage, migration, and

---

19 University of Southern Queensland Reconciliation Action Plan 2008 is but one example.

work, hardly the stuff of heroic academic treatises or leaders' speeches calling for reconciliation and a treaty. Not a human rights lawyer, an Aboriginal professor, a left wing academic, nor a protestor's banner in support of land rights is to be seen in the integration agenda. But there are a host of stories recounting personal struggles to come to terms with a different world. A particularly illustrative account is that of Daryl Tonkin, a white timber cutter, and his Aboriginal wife at Drouin in Gippsland in the years from 1937 until 1975. Tonkin describes an idyllic bushie life at Jackson's Track for the Aboriginal mob and his family, a time when there was an accommodation of timber cutting and farm work, and satisfaction in keeping a large community together. In time, however, as the bounds of the settled area crept closer to Jackson's track, the most visible parts of the community became apparent. The Shire and 'church folk' insisted the families become more settled.

> They [the families] had been told that life at Jackson's Track just wasn't good enough to bring up children, that living in bark huts and eating bush tucker was unhealthy, that living on dirt floors and cooking over fires was unhygienic. They were told that the only right way was to live in houses, with fridges and bathrooms. They were frightened into believing that if they didn't improve their lives, the whitefellas would be forced to take the children away and protect them from such rough living.
>
> The main trouble for these [black]fellas was there was no work for them ... they were bored ... now they were living so close to town it was easy to go in and get some grog.[20]

There is inevitably, in this scene, the destruction of an apparently ideal way of life to make way for another. This scene has been played out thousands of times in thousands of places around Australia throughout two centuries. Some of it relates to Aborigines, but

---

20 Tonkin, D. and Landon, C. 1999. *Jackson's Track: Memoir of a Dreamtime Place*, Penguin, p. 265.

some of it to other communities, in particular but not exclusively to rural communities that have had to adjust to changed economic circumstances. Only in the last forty years, and in an earlier 'protectionist' period where it applied to full bloods only, has there been a significant public and intellectual support for keeping one group of people beyond the reach of the modern world. This desire to protect culture contains a major flaw; it assumes a stagnant society whose needs are unchanging. As the great Australian anthropologist, W.E.H. Stanner, commented:

> The blacks have grasped eagerly at any possibility of a regular and dependable food supply for a lesser effort than is involved in nomadic hunting and foraging. There is a sound calculus of cost and gain in preferring a belly regularly if only partly filled for an output of work which can be steadily scaled down. Hence the two most common characteristics of aboriginal adaptation to settlement by Europeans; a persistent and positive effort to make themselves dependent, and a squeeze-play to obtain a constant or increasing supply of food for a dwindling physical effort.[21]

The world changed for Aborigines the moment the whiteman arrived and bequeathed stored food. Much of the *raison d'etre* for their 'way of life' or 'culture' evaporated. That day, Aborigines wanted more because they could have more. The fact that they would have to change in order to continue to receive it is cast as a tragedy. It is only a tragedy if what is given up is more valuable than what is gained. Part of the tragedy of the last forty years is that the intelligentsia believe that what was given up was more valuable. The essential misconception of separatists and protectionists is that they want both to be left alone and to have all the rewards that others work to achieve.

Integration has delivered more Aborigines more happiness than

---

21 Stanner, W.E.H. 1960. 'Durmugam: A Nangiomeri' in Casagrande, J. B. (ed), *In the Company of Man*, Harper, p. 69.

the separatist and human rights agenda has ever dreamed. But the separatists deny the 'counter factual', that things would not have remained for Aborigines as they always had, living short, brutish lives, lives that none would now choose. At Daly River, Northern Territory, in 1932, Stanner observed 'two intertribal coalitions existed which were acute in conflict. The surface of life was, for the most part, peaceable enough but under the surface something like a state of terror existed.'[22] People may choose elements of their old life but in so choosing there are trade-offs. An insufficient investment in the self leaves Aborigines vulnerable and dependent on the whiteman. The whiteman's welfare keeps Aborigines dependent by removing the incentives to do better. And above all, the clarion call to culture focuses the mind on group solidarity, even though solidarity may be nothing more than a like-minded group of people behaving badly. None of this should have to be argued in the 21st century. Unfortunately, large swathes of the Aboriginal industry, those who are paid to deliver the policy and service paraphernalia that keeps Aborigines dependent, appear to need the sustenance of their morality play.

That morality play was best in evidence among the professional moralists, the churches. As the post-colonial ideologies swept the churches and universities in the 1960s the missionaries knew it was time to leave. Leaving was not an easy matter. The desire to prepare Aborigines for the modern world conflicted with the need to get out of the way and let Aborigines run their own lives, but, when the missionaries left, the training and discipline necessary to prepare Aborigines for the modern world was lost. As policy swung towards preserving culture, those Aborigines whose lives were seriously interrupted by the new regime were condemned by it. Their culture was both indefensible in modern terms and insufficient as a guide to life in the modern world. A powerful propaganda tool was an image of the idyll, an imagined beneficent ancient culture reconstructed

---

22 Stanner, 1960, pp. 82-4.

by intellectuals. The facts, well-recorded by early observers, of the Aboriginal culture in its brutal and basic insularity were lost, replaced by the ideals that white advisers preferred to see both in their own society and in the now defunct Aboriginal society and culture. The misconceived inquiries into Aboriginal Deaths in Custody and the Stolen Generations, and the Hindmarsh Island affair, further entrenched the romantic view by confusing culture with poor behaviour. The 'Apology' to the 'Stolen Generations' was an insult to the intelligence of those toiling to overcome the false pride in group solidarity, a false pride which ignored the dignity of work, the immense complexity of modern society and the efforts required to master it.

In the 1960s, the legal and social restraints on Aboriginal freedom were removed. For the first time Aborigines were able to complain at the injustice that had befallen them. And, in complaining, they created a story about their society. The story became so strong that some came to believe that it would be a good idea if they could be prosperous in modern terms and be 'cultural' as well. But complaining and picking the right path to happiness are very different things. Those who have chosen a path where their obligations are different to others have not been rewarded, and, in failing in the full glare of public attention and largesse, those who have failed have retreated further into their own world and further from the solutions they need.

> [T]he Aboriginal, once he had sat down, quickly lost the power to do more than supplementary hunting, if only because the processes of hard socialisation in which the Aboriginal personality was formed were so rapidly lost in circumstances where autonomy for the process was lost. It was not lost because of some special tyranny in the white 'boss'. As the history of the best-intentioned of the missions suggests, human kindness which stabilised the nomads in a dependent imitation or a dependent mendicancy had the same effect in the

end. Perhaps the answer lay in opportunities for stabilisation in situations where leadership and decision-making for change rested within the aboriginal society, the whites at the point of contact offering assistance and advice on request.[23]

But stabilisation and leadership are not enough. Self-determination, separatism, racial identity and land rights need to be placed into the context of the much longer trajectory of the accommodation of Aboriginal people of Australia to the modern world. Only in the Anglo new world – Australia, the USA, Canada and New Zealand – was the fate of Indigenous people given much consideration, and that consideration was afforded because of the extraordinary wealth and liberality of those nations and the sometimes ignored but nevertheless public intention of the British Empire at settlement 'to restrain the generally far more ruthless impulses of the colonists.'[24] When the United Nations Declaration on the Rights of Indigenous Peoples was adopted by the General Assembly on 13 September 2007, Australia, the USA, Canada and New Zealand voted against. Unfortunately, in April 2009, for the most puerile of reasons, the Rudd Government decided to adopt the Declaration. In September 2007 the four governments voted against the Declaration because the instrument was a bridge too far. It is ironic that these countries have come to the realisation that self-determination is a harmful ideology – after much experiment and serial failure they have decided that the game is up. The Aborigines who articulate the grievances are the result of an earlier regime of benign integration that gave them the skills to make their way. They did not live in a 'self-determining collective'; they lived in a family, which if it was functional sent them to school. If the family was not functional, the family lost the right to make that decision and they were sent to school anyway. More recently, the state has lost its way and declined to enforce minimum standards of obligation among

---

23 Rowley, 1972, p. 318.
24 Ferguson, N. 2003. *Empire: How Britain Made the Modern World*. Penguin, p. 109.

Aboriginal citizens, preferring instead that they remain Aboriginal. Australian Aborigines won their freedom decades ago, but they lost the keys to the door to the modern economy; indeed, they suffered serial programs that consciously denied them the keys. They were to become a kept people, frozen in time and place.

Too many researchers regard Aboriginal decisions as free expressions of their political will. Instead, they are too often a reflection of some base incentive, to be paid to not work, to receive a benefit while they remain in the community, to extract rent from the use of their land by a group who can add value to it. The desire to be left alone, free from the whiteman's ways is understandable; it represents a desire to not be bothered with the enormous investment the individual has to make in order to prosper in the modern society. The desire to escape the burdens of citizenship is ever present as is the desire to reap the benefits citizenship bestows. Culture and indigeneity are blind to remedies. As *a priori* goals they can reinforce bad behaviour as much as provide some sort of sanctuary. Escape to tribal lands is not escape from the evil whiteman, but escape from the whiteman who imposes the discipline required to live in the modern world, including the discipline to obey the law. Besides which, as a school principal from Punmu in remote Western Australia observed, '[p]eople are not land or culture oriented, they are self-focussed. It's about money and cars.'[25]

The most recent inquiry into Aboriginal child abuses in Australia, the 2008 Commission of Inquiry Report[26] covering the APY lands in South Australia, and replicating the earlier work of those in the Northern Territory, NSW and Queensland, reveals appalling behaviour. When a witness, described as a senior Aboriginal woman,

---

25 As told to the author at a conference of remote area school principals, 31 October 2005, Canberra.
26 Mullighan, E. P. 2008. *Children on Anangu Pitjantjatjara Yankunytjatjara Lands Commission of Inquiry: a Report into Sexual Abuse.*

stated, 'I think I am witnessing the demise of a proud people',[27] one can only wonder at what point she realised the obvious. Once proud is a nice piece of sentimentalism. Even supposing it is true, the demise has been obvious for decades. Why have governments not acted on the demise rather than pretend either that help is at hand or that there is something to 'recover' in Aboriginal societies? A key part of the separatist story is the vehemence with which the proponents attack their society. For example, after six weeks the Royal Commission into Aboriginal Deaths in Custody found that Aborigines died in custody at the same rate as whites. The fact was concealed.[28] The Inquiry continued at great expense for three years, determined to fulfil its mission to demonise the white society. It succeeded, but the cost was horrendous not only in money terms and in setting back the cause of integrating Aborigines into the modern world, but possibly by causing a rise in deaths in custody during the course of the Inquiry by reason of the extraordinary publicity the Inquiry attracted.

The 'Progressive' approach to Aboriginal policy is profoundly conservative. It seeks to preserve culture – indeed, to preserve a dysfunctional culture. How is this different from the accusation thrown at A.O. Neville, Chief Protector of Aborigines in Western Australia, who sought to protect full bloods from change as well as integrate half castes? He faced a far more difficult environment than the 1960s policy-makers, in particular the insecurity of early 20th century Australians in the face of real distrust arising from vastly different cultures, and the bleak prospects of changing a recently contacted tribal people.

> In many instances they struggle to improve themselves economically and socially, but they often give up the struggle very soon. Prejudice is an almost impossible barrier to break

---

27 Mullighan, 2008, preface.
28 Royal Commission into Aboriginal Deaths in Custody. 1991. Vol.3, p. 60, (see page 133).

down.[29]

Yet prejudice has broken down. In the many inquiries into child sexual abuse in Aboriginal communities held in the last decade prejudice is not noted as a factor, because the abuse is mostly Aboriginal on Aboriginal or, when white men are involved, it is adult against child, an altogether different dimension of vulnerability. Contrast this environment with the benign environment of the post-colonial era faced by H. C. Coombs, an architect of separatism. He chose a profoundly foolish path which is still causing harm. Living apart is precisely the mode of Aboriginal policy of the last 40 years and it is a disaster. Coombs lamented:

> No Aboriginal Nyerere [first President of Tanzania] has emerged to translate the Aboriginal way as the African leader did the social and moral principle of the African village life into a coherent political and social code relevant and applicable in the contemporary world. I wish that some Aboriginal leaders could evolve something equivalent to the Nyerere's Ujamaa Socialism as a guide and rallying point for their political action.[30]

For the record, Nyerere implemented a socialist economic program, established close ties with Maoist China, and introduced a policy of collectivisation in the agricultural system. Nyerere was what is often called an African socialist. He had tremendous faith in rural African people and their traditional values and ways of life. He believed that life should be structured around the ujamaa, or extended family, found in traditional Africa. He believed that in these traditional villages, the state of ujamaa had existed before the arrival of 'imperialists'. He believed that all that Africans needed to do was return to their traditional mode of life and they would recapture it. This ujamaa

---

29 Elkin, A.P. introduction to Neville, A.O. 1947. *Australia's Coloured Minority: Its Place in the Community*. Currawong, p. 12.
30 Coombs, H.C. 1976. *Aboriginal Australia 1967-1976: A Decade of Progress?* Murdoch University, p. 15.

system failed to boost agricultural output. By 1976, the end of the forced collectivization program, and the time when Coombs was waxing lyrical, Tanzania went from the largest exporter of agricultural products in Africa to the largest importer of agricultural products in Africa. It was a failure. It plunged Tanzania into further debt, a crisis in its balance of payments deficits and deteriorating relations with international donors. Commenting on his economic policies in his retirement speech in 1985, Nyerere declared, 'I failed. Let's admit it.'[31]

It is as unfair to castigate Neville as it is Coombs for their views analysed at another time when the circumstances in which they operated are so changed. But the Coombs legacy is that a separatist mindset remains. Too many working in Aboriginal policy believe in a dream that cannot be revived. No Aborigine wants to live the traditional life which the white romantic has designated for them, nor do they have the skills to so do. Perversely, those sitting on welfare and on work for the dole programs are cranky that modest jobs such as garbage collection are all they are offered. Although some of the most famous artists of the Pintupi at Papunya 'were trained as garbage men'[32] in the 1970s, not all Aborigines are artists. Most, in fact, expect more, but few administrators or Aboriginal leaders have the strength to tell them that the whiteman does not have the power to hand out money and jobs, at least not forever. The 'whiteman' is not defined by race or an unbending culture; rather, he and she is a skilled person able to use the world to best advantage. In this dimension of their lives, Aborigines have to become the same as the whiteman. The question is, how? Fortunately, some leaders and thinkers have emerged to lead the remainder of Aborigines, several generations late, into the only world that exists, the modern world.

---

31 Maier, K. 1998. 'Into the House of the Ancestors' *New York Times*. 1 February.
32 Bardon, G. and J. 2004. *Papunya: A Place Made After the Story, the Beginnings of the Western Desert Painting Movement*. The Miegunyah Press, p. 9.

Fortunately, there is a clear exit strategy, some of which is slowly being assembled by governments during the last five years. But, for every sensible government incentive, there are a dozen programs that create a disincentive to move, or work, or study or behave well. The exit strategy that unintegrated Aborigines need is here outlined alongside those that cause harm, including the destructive rallying cry for culture over economy. The readers may make up their own minds which is better for Aborigines.

1
Competing strategies in Aboriginal advancement

The widely supported goal of Aboriginal policy is to close the gap in living standards and life expectancy between Aboriginal and non-Aboriginal Australians.[33] How this should be achieved is problematic. For at least thirty years policy has been sympathetic to the idea that Aborigines would remain in another economy. There were two mutually reinforcing sources for this, from very different sides of politics. The first was the mainly southern intellectuals' romance with the 'culture cult' (a cult that holds that primitive culture is not inferior to modern civilization).[34] The second was the mainly northern settlers' practice of 'not-in-my-backyard' (Aborigines are best kept away from town). Each was ignorant and prejudicial to the interests of Aborigines,

---

33 Australian Government, 2009. *Closing the Gap on Indigenous Disadvantage: The Challenge for Australia.*
34 Sandall, R. 2001. *The Culture Cult: Designer Tribalism and Other Essays.* Westview, p. viii.

although the excuse in the latter case is the northerners had to face the painful adjustment of those who failed to integrate into town life. In hindsight, the period circa 1970 to 2006 will be viewed as an interruption to the long-run process of absorption and integration of the Aboriginal people, which commenced at European settlement. In hindsight it will be clear that no policy of separation could hold back the forces of change, but they could foul the process of adjustment and leave vulnerable people with false hope and no skills. Self-determination interrupted integration by preventing Aborigines from adapting to opportunities. The consequences have been tragic.

Closing the gap requires overcoming previous policy settings and establishing new ones. The contention here is that the best strategy is to encourage individuals to make sufficient investment in their capacity to enable them to conduct their lives without government support. The difficulty is that government support is the *sine qua non* of Aboriginal politics. The support is for individuals and for organisations. In common with other Australians, all eligible Aborigines receive government benefits. Unlike other Australians, eligible Aborigines have few obligations to fulfil in order to receive benefits. Only very recently have Aborigines, especially those in remote communities, had to, for example, demonstrate that they were searching for employment in order to qualify for unemployment benefits. A second element of government support is that Aboriginal organisations are funded to deliver programs to Aborigines. Only very recently have governments sought to have Aboriginal programs delivered by 'mainstream' providers. The change signals a significant emphasis on the consumer as opposed to the producer of services. The change also signals a shift away from Aboriginal self-determination and towards integration.

The competing strategies in Aboriginal policy revolve around the role and prominence given to culture and to the economy. The classic distinctions may be labelled integration strategies and self-determination strategies. Integration is here defined as a government and personal goal to ensure that an individual has skills sufficient to get a job and support a family. Moreover, the (regulated) market economy is the principal determinant of opportunities. How people live – that is, their culture – is by and large a private matter. Culture only becomes a matter for public policy when behaviour sanctioned by 'the culture' offends public decency and/or the law.

By contrast, self-determination is defined as a government and personal goal whereby collective political means are used as the principal determinant of opportunities. The prime value is equity; where equity means sharing the spoils of others' labour. The self-determination strategies give weight to cultural and group rights and denies that these may inhibit individual initiative. Self-determination has a second more modest stream than collective rights, and that stream gives weight to better government 'service co-ordination' and 'engagement' strategies. Although innocent in their apparent attention to a failing among governments to deliver better services to Aborigines, these strategies critically do not distinguish between capital creating services and capital destroying services. In the former case, government can intervene to encourage and promote good behaviour such as compulsory school attendance; in the latter case, better services simply result in meeting people to talk about 'gifted' services. They reinforce Aboriginal dependence.

Integration

The suggested and much travelled alternative path, integration, is not the same as assimilation. Assimilation is a physical, indeed genetic, process whereby people of different colour through procreation between races, in a sense, leave behind the supposedly 'weaker colour' and its attributes. The notion of assimilation was sometimes accompanied by strong objections to miscegenation, breeding between races. Such notions are misplaced; there is no weaker colour, and there are no weaker attributes *per se*. Moreover, the degree to which Aborigines marry non-Aborigines in Australia is extraordinarily high. The objection to miscegenation has been left in the wake of free choice. The level of intermarriage also makes a nonsense of the notion that racial prejudice is at the heart of Aboriginal despair. Where prejudice exists it is likely to be based on observations of bad behaviour – drunkenness and violence, not race.

Integration, by contrast, is a social and economic process. If entered into freely (albeit under vastly changed conditions from pre-European settlement) it is a measure that people are coping in the new conditions. The new Leftist fashion called 'social inclusion' does not seem to be applied to Aborigines who are deemed not to need to make the sacrifices that others must make in order to be included, for example, to learn English and attend school. This is at the heart of the matter. Aboriginal children in remote communities often have fewer skills than their grandparents, who thanks to missionaries and government officers were trained and able to cope with modernity. In doing so, they had choices to stay or go to work and earn, or spend more time at leisure. Their grandchildren are left to 'play' Aborigine without the need to hunt and gather, or indulge the ancient belief in tribal ritual. Instead, they converse in a pidgin language, attend sports days and funerals, and watch pornography and take drugs. This is not an exaggeration; these are the findings of the many recent inquiries into the Aboriginal condition in remote communities, the details of which are considered in chapter five.

The starting point for those who wish to have Aborigines functioning inside the mainstream economy is not Aboriginal organisational control, but the capacity of Aborigines. If governments want to close the gap in life opportunities they will have to intensify the shift away from self-determination (including collective land rights and separate administration of public programs) to the capacity of Aboriginal people to take advantage of opportunities in the economy.

The reason for the policy shift is that self-determination has failed too many Aboriginal people. It is also true that integration has been taking place throughout the entire self-determination period regardless of 'official' policy. After all, no Aborigines live a traditional lifestyle. Many Aborigines are fully engaged in the economy and live in cities and towns; many marry non-Aborigines (see Figure 4 on page 80).

The purpose of economic integration is not to demand that Aborigines leave their land but that they become economically independent. In becoming independent, Aborigines may remain on their land or they may move. The question is where and under what circumstances the prospects for becoming economically independent are greatest, and who should decide these matters. For example, Aborigines travel widely from homeland to town and regional centre for recreation, family reasons and living off others, but Aborigines rarely travel for work. If no suitable employment can be found locally, finding work elsewhere will lead to significant or permanent absence from home. To avoid this uncomfortable truth, governments develop 'make work' schemes like Community Development Employment Projects (CDEP) and economic development programs. These schemes do not solve unemployment; instead they intensify the problem by creating a disincentive for Aborigines to adjust to the market economy.

The transition to an integrated Aboriginal community will have its casualties, particularly among those who cannot adjust to the wider opportunities available in the economy. In this category are tens of thousands of Aboriginal men living in remote communities, in fringe town camps and, to a lesser extent, in urban ghettoes. They will find it difficult to cope, for example, with the removal of remote area exemptions that make receipt of welfare payments conditional on entering training or job search or CDEP. The winners will be women, if they can escape the violence of remote settlements and fringe dwellings, and children, if they can attend schools regularly, probably away from their communities. The front line troops in the transition will be Centrelink offices and officers, who will be under enormous pressure to let applicants move on to disability or other such pensions. The front line places will be regional centres in the far north and west, including the Alice Springs camps.

Self-determination

The idea of Aboriginal self-determination is a borrowed concept, taken from the aspirations of colonised peoples and their desire to run their own countries. In a colonial context this is a perfectly reasonable aspiration and it was largely fulfilled in the generation after the Second World War. The idea is problematic, however, for Aboriginal people who share their land with a dominant and modern people. Aboriginal people were always going to struggle to assert their identity where they could not place a boundary around a sovereign state. While Aboriginal peoples in sovereign states could choose to enter the modern world at their own pace and make their own mistakes, witness the terrible record of African states to make the leap from tribe to nation. Aborigines had no such opportunity. For that they can be grateful their fate was not far worse, but sad that perhaps in a theoretical sense they, too, may have become a nation of Aboriginal people. But a nation of Aboriginal people would have faced the pressures of modernisation. These as much as the whiteman's invasion are the source of the 'problem'. The whiteman was the vehicle for innovation, innovation from which Aborigines have benefited mightily. The strangeness of the last 40 or more years is that as Aborigines became more involved in the modern world, and intermarried with whites, identity became a social and not a purely racial construct. Consequently, claims to difference became weaker and the need to work up a sense of grievance against the whiteman became stronger. During the 1990s separatists worked very hard to create a sense of grievance. Unfortunately, the separatist agenda has compounded the plight of some Aborigines by holding them outside of the modern economy.

Pat Dodson, as a commissioner of the Royal Commission into Aboriginal Deaths in Custody, whose Commission 'required that he look only at underlying issues',[35] outlined his vision of Aboriginal self-determination in the Deaths in Custody Report. His brother, Mick Dodson, was counsel assisting the Commission from August 1988 to October 1990 and, as such, was not an author of the report, although his many views on the record prior, during and following the report are entirely consistent with Pat's views. There are many other elements of self-determination, such as a treaty between Aborigines and other Australians that the Dodsons and their supporters have raised elsewhere,[36] but the key assumptions of the Dodson agenda suggest that disadvantage is caused by Aboriginal subordination to non-Aboriginal society and that the solution lies in collective responses.

The Dodsons are worthy candidates to represent the self-determination view. Pat Dodson is often cited as the 'father of reconciliation'. Mick has had a long career in Aboriginal politics. He served as the director of the Northern Land Council in the early 1990s in addition to his work on the Deaths in Custody Commission. He later worked on the Bringing Them Home inquiry.

The self-determination agenda outlined in Box 1 was given life in the recommendations of the 1991 Royal Commission into Aboriginal Deaths in Custody. The essence of the self-determination agenda as proposed by the Dodsons and others was that Aboriginal disadvantage was the fault of the whiteman and that the remedy (short of removing the whiteman) was to have the whiteman grant Aborigines income to

---

35 Johnston, E. 1991. *Royal Commission into Aboriginal Deaths in Custody, National Report* Volume 1, preface.
36 See, for example, the Treaty Project completed in partnership with the Gilbert + Tobin Centre for Public Law and the Myer Foundation.

be distributed among Aborigines by Aboriginal organisations. The Commission found, for example, that 43 of 99 prisoners whose deaths in custody were the subject of the Inquiry (discussed below) were separated from their family as children. Separation was consequently held to be the key cause of strife later in life. There was little attempt to search for other explanations when the fate of those not separated was also known. While it was noted that all who died had little or no education, which is a known cause of strife later in life, that factor was not preferred. While it was known that many came from violent and broken homes (the reason for separation), which is a known cause of strife later in life, neither was that factor preferred.

In a report that did not find any wrongdoing by authorities in the 99 deaths in custody, no direct link was made to the extraordinary propensity for violence in Aboriginal society. Violence was instead associated with assimilation historically. While domestic violence and family breakdown were noted as present in the lives of the Aborigines in custody, nowhere was a link made to welfare dependence as a cause of criminal activity. Nowhere was a link made to the fact that so few Aborigines had a job or sufficient English to get a job. These alternative plausible explanations (that would have been favoured if it were white deaths being investigated) were buried.

Most disturbing is the notion suggested by some advocates that a 'National Aboriginal Language Policy should be compulsory; English, arithmetic and science not so.' Without English, arithmetic and science, Aboriginal language would be useless; the child would not be able to cope in society. This is precisely what has occurred in remote communities; especially, it seems, where 'two-way' education has occurred. Here it is asserted that Aboriginal people have the right to retain culture and identity if that is their wish. The problem here is after ruling out the illegal parts of Aboriginal culture such as polygamy and child marriage, and those parts which have been abandoned in the face of evidence to the contrary, i.e. 'increase ceremonies' do not

> **Box 1 The model of Aboriginal self-determination**
>
> *Assumptions –*
> • disadvantage is the product of domination of Aborigines by non-Aboriginal society
> • elimination of disadvantage requires Aboriginal people to control their lives and their communities
> • salvation lies in groups – medical services, women's, language study, cell visitor, adult education providers, legal services, child care, land councils, housing associations, media, commercial enterprises, the CDEP.
>
> *Agenda -*
> • The broader society to supply assistance and Aboriginal society maintain its independent status
> • ATSIC as an employing authority independent of the Australian Public Service
> • Block grant funding of Aboriginal communities and organisations
> • Program delivery should be made by Aboriginal organisations
> • Aboriginal people have the right to retain culture and identity; support local community museums and culture centres (Brewarrina Museum)
> • National Aboriginal Language Policy should be compulsory; English, arithmetic and science not so
> • Truancy - provide support, in collaboration with appropriate Aboriginals, to the juvenile and to those responsible for the care of the juvenile
> • There should be legislative recognition of: Aboriginal Child Placement Principles and Aboriginal Child Care Agencies
> • Extension of CDEP to rural towns with large Aboriginal populations
> • Restoring unalienated Crown land to Aboriginal claimants on an inalienable freehold basis with the right of the Aboriginal owners to determine entry.
>
> Data source: Royal Commission into Aboriginal Deaths in Custody, 1991 Volumes 1 and 5.

work as well as the whiteman's ability to provide, there is little that remains. For example, while support for local community museums and culture centres seems harmless, the results are not promising. The museum at Brewarrina in NSW, a hideous moulded concrete structure designed for the visitor to explore Aboriginal hunting and fishing, lies vacant because of a lack of interest on the part of locals to work in it. The town awaits the brewer Lion Nathan to fund the museum, that is, to pay Aborigines to display their long-abandoned means of providing for their sustenance because they are unwilling to do this from pride alone.

Elements of the self-determination model of service delivery are contradictory. For example, 'the broader society to supply assistance and Aboriginal society maintain its independent status' is a contradiction in terms. Dodson requires that Aboriginal organisations be given 'block' funding, meaning funds with no questions asked so that they can deliver services required by Aboriginal people. Nowhere is there space for Aboriginal people to express their views by purchasing services from a provider they choose. They are simply to receive what an official hands to them. As for the Aboriginal Child Placement Principles, this has in all likelihood caused extreme hardship in some cases, for Aboriginal children who have been left in the hands of the people who were their assailants. Such thinking has pervaded the judiciary as well as social workers who are too scared to break from ideology despite the evidence in front of them. The decision by a Queensland District Court judge in 2007 not to gaol,[37] not even to record a conviction for, some of the nine men and boys who had raped a 10 year old girl at Aurukun in Cape York is an example of the impact of self-determination thinking leading to terrible outcomes for Aborigines. Social workers had moved the child who was in a safe house with white foster parents, because they feared the 'stolen generation' tag. Fortunately, the decision was overturned on appeal.[38]

On the issue of land rights, although these have been granted extensively in remote areas, they are generally not economically prospective and therefore have not proved to be of great benefit to traditional owners. Moreover, land could be held to be somewhat of a curse as it has kept traditional people from making the adjustment they need in order to make a decent life in the modern world. The

---

37 *The Australian* 10 December 2007.
38 R v. KU & Ors; ex parte A-G (Qld) [2008] QCA 154 (13 June 2008).

least well-off Aborigines are living on their hard won land and the fact that they are able to survive, in a fashion, on benefits, means that they are unlikely to move to where their prospects are better. The Dodson model is simply a reflection of the inability of Aboriginal people to live as traditional Aboriginal people and attain the broader benefits of modern society. The more the Dodson's and Galarrwuy Yunupingu and their cohorts argue that their people can have it all and not change their behaviour, the greater is the gap created between expectation and delivery. The entire agenda is centred on group solutions and public funding and the return of lands.

It has never been acknowledged that Aborigines have always been 'disadvantaged' in comparison to the white society because it was a modern society. It is never acknowledged that a modern society requires far different preparation for survival than a Stone Age society. What Dodson's calls disadvantage is more likely to arise from inadequate adjustment to and preparation for modern society than from a loss of ancient culture or means of living. Dodson's case implies that collective political means are the only way Aborigines can establish equality with non-Aborigines. It may be that the elimination of 'disadvantage' requires Aboriginal people in some senses to control their lives and their communities collectively, but such devices could only be incidental to their progress. Once children learn the skills to prosper in the open society and the modern economy it is inconceivable that they will sit in remote Australia and await their elders to hand out program money 'earned' by committee.

The strategies compared

Self-determination and integration are polar opposites, but there are strategies which profess to achieve both. For example, Noel Pearson's goal seems to be to integrate Aborigines into the modern economy, but to use and preserve culture where possible. His principal means to achieve the goal is to stabilise communities and families by re-missionising his people. In this regard, the Family Responsibility Commission[39] is like a mobile mission, dispensing justice and passing judgment on behaviour and imposing penalties on incomes. By contrast, the Bennelong Society view is pessimistic about the efficacy of 'culture', which it regards as often antipathetic to the open society, or illegal, or simply an excuse for bad behaviour.

An alternative view is that of Fred Chaney, the former senator, Aboriginal Affairs Minister and National Native Title Tribunal member, who, when asked why successive governments had failed to solve Aboriginal deprivation, replied:

> [O]ne of the things ... we should have learned ... is that you can't solve these things by centralised bureaucratic direction. You can only educate children in a school at the place where they live. You can only give people jobs or get people into employment person by person. And ... you need locally based action, local resourcing, local control to really make changes.[40]

---

39 *Family Responsibilities Commission Act 2008* (Qld).
40 Interviewed on the ABC's *7.30 Report* on 19 April 2007, quoted in Wild, R. and P. Anderson, 2007. *Inquiry into the Protection of Aboriginal Children from Sexual Abuse*. Northern Territory Government, p. 21.

The Whiteman's Dream

Table 1: Competing strategies in Aboriginal advancement

Proponent	Economy	Culture	Policies		
			- land rights	- incentives	- politico-legal frame
Bennelong	Real economy No job, No house	Culture as a problem- Culture a private matter	Saleable rights Leasing ineffectual	Self belief as key motivation Rational incentives	No race power Reject UN Declaration on the Rights of Indigenous Peoples
LNP Opposition	No job, No house	Instrumental	Leasing 99 years WA LNP secured LNG deal in Kimberley	Incentives and obligations	Reject UN Declaration on the Rights of Indigenous Peoples
Pearson	Transitional	Culture as a solution- Culture a public matter	Leasing- Fighting 'Wild Rivers'	Income management	Collective self-determination and individual responsibility
Labor Government	Buy jobs	Culture as a solution Culture a public matter	Leasing 40 years WA ALP failed to secure LNG deal in Kimberley	Incentives and obligations Centrelink -weakened obligations	Accept UN Declaration on the Rights of Indigenous Peoples
CAEPR Reconciliation Australia Dodsons Churches	Mock economy	Culture as a solution Culture a public matter Culture as an end in itself	Collective and inalienable	Collective power as key motivation- Money as of right	Revive ATSIC Treaty Recognise Aboriginal law

Data source: Author.

Chaney wants to preserve Aboriginal culture, especially in places where people inhabit traditional lands, but, in so doing, he underestimates the adjustments that Aborigines in these places must make in order to survive. None of the necessary solutions to Aboriginal despair is in Chaney's kit bag. Each element of the Chaney statement reveals a lack of insight into human behaviour and motivation. The view is overly focussed on government programs when, at least as an ideal, Aborigines should be free from government programs. The sentiment does not comprehend that, whether centralised or decentralised (and whether black or white), bureaucracy is bureaucracy. The sentiment that children should be educated 'where they live' ignores the poisonous environments many remote Aboriginal children inhabit. The sentiment prevents Aboriginal children from being protected in circumstances where a non-Aboriginal child would be. The sentiment promotes the idea that people should be 'given' jobs. This is precisely the opposite of the ideal. People must earn them. In one respect only has Fred Chaney learned anything in his long experience in this field – only an individual, not a community, gains employment.

The strategy as represented by Chaney and, most disturbingly, quoted by the Wild and Anderson report into child sexual abuse in the Northern Territory, fails to grasp the danger in collective action. Collective action is harmful where it inhibits an individual's ability to invest in their future or where it excuses bad behaviour. It is not that integrationists cannot conceive of collective action based on identity. After all, the citizens of modern society operate as collectives all of the time, but the membership is voluntary and so it varies from worker, to consumer, to neighbour, to club member, to citizen. The integrationist recognises that membership is instrumental, not a destiny or birthright. One's life should not depend totally on the collective. Such dependence, whether it be on white bureaucrats or Aboriginal elders, is risky, limiting and, at times, stifling. Those who want Aboriginal self-determination must realize by now that they are locking people out of the market economy and, therefore, any chance of narrowing the gap in living standards. Those who want Aboriginal self-determination place a higher value on Aboriginal identity than on the factors that cause disadvantage. Those who want integration place a higher value on processes such as education and entering the labour market. Furthermore, they regard pursuit of identity to the exclusion of education and employment as inimical to closing the gap.

It is rare to find a guide to competing strategies in Aboriginal policy. Table 1 attempts to fill the gap by describing in five dimensions the attitudes of key proponents in Aboriginal policy, including the Australian Labor Government and the Coalition Opposition. The five dimensions are the characterisation of the overall position of the proponent, followed by particular examples of the proponent's position on land, economy, incentives, culture, and a politico-legal framework. Using the data from Table 1, it is feasible to place various advocates within the space of possible strategies, as shown in Figure 2.

In broad terms, competing strategies can be arrayed on two dimensions, culture and economy. Those who place a high value on Aboriginal culture (usually not defined by separatists, but in this schema meaning how people behave) will be positioned high on the vertical axis and those who regard adherence to Aboriginal culture as an impediment to progress would be placed low on the vertical axis. Those who advocate building an economy for Aboriginal people rather than allowing them to adjust to the market economy, for example, through special employment programs and *in situ* development (without economic justification), would be placed at the left on the horizontal axis. Those who advocate that Aborigines adjust to the economic opportunities presented as others have to would be placed at the right side of the horizontal axis.

The Bennelong Society position, for example, may be described as rational integrationist, seeing adherence to culture, where it conflicts with adjustment to the market economy, as a problem. Bennelong would be placed in the bottom right quadrant. A collection of advocates for self-determination (Mick and Pat Dodson, the Centre for Aboriginal Economic and Policy Research, Reconciliation Australia, the churches) believe in preserving and promoting Aboriginal culture through government programs and are prepared to excuse the avoidance of the market economy where its requirements conflict with culture. Dodson *et al* would be placed in the top left hand quadrant.

Figure 2: Typology of competing strategies in Aboriginal policy

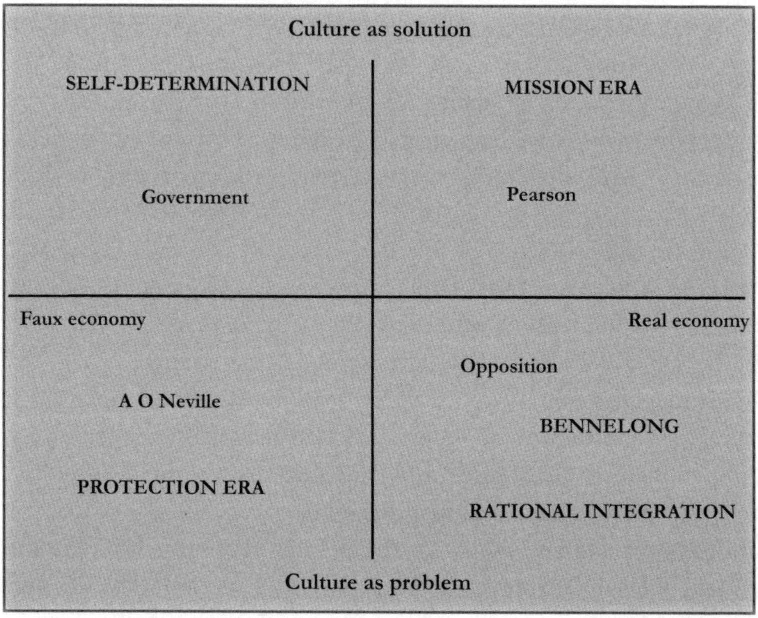

	Culture as solution	
SELF-DETERMINATION		MISSION ERA
Government		Pearson
Faux economy		Real economy
A O Neville	Opposition	BENNELONG
PROTECTION ERA		RATIONAL INTEGRATION
	Culture as problem	

Data source: Author.

The other two quadrants are less clear-cut. Noel Pearson advocates that Aborigines preserve their culture, or at least regard culture as a strength, and that Aborigines enter the market economy. In a sense, this is reminiscent of the later mission period when missionaries worked closely with Aborigines in remote areas and, to some extent, left culture to Aborigines as a private matter. At the same time, they educated Aborigines and prepared them for work. The bottom left hand quadrant may be represented by A. O. Neville, the protector of Aborigines in Western Australia early in the 20th century. This experience has a good deal more in common with the progressives than they would care to admit. Neville sought an integrationist path for half castes, but pursued a separatist path for full blood Aborigines, because he was pessimistic about their prospects for integration. Progressives pursue a separatist path for Aborigines because they believe that Aboriginal culture can survive even though the conditions in which it grew have been destroyed.

Allowing possible overlapping tendencies in such a simple schema, it is nevertheless apparent that the paths to closing the gap are very diverse. At present it is clear that the self-determination groups have been the dominant force in policy settings. As a consequence, the Australian Government (Rudd/Gillard 2010), like all governments seeking to secure the support of all groups, sits mildly in the top left hand quadrant. The Opposition (Abbott 2010 and judging its performance as the previous government) sits mildly within the bottom right hand quadrant.

It needs to be appreciated that Aboriginal people do not necessarily follow the script laid down by government, much less by lobbies. Moreover, public servants do not necessarily follow the script laid down for them by governments either. Failure by administrators to apply the law is a major cause of the failure to integrate Aboriginal people thus leading to their demise. Judges fail to gaol offenders, teachers fail to enforce school attendance, social workers fail to protect children – each 'respects the culture' and fails the client. Other policies are a work in progress and yet to be assessed. For example, was the 2007 Northern Territory Emergency Response (Intervention) by the LNP Government and continued by the Labor Government the last chance for remote communities or the first step in their eventual demise? These matters will be explored later. For the present the task is to outline the competing strategies in Aboriginal policy as these affect the expenditure of public funds and life chances.

1. The Churches

The self-determination agenda is shared by a number of groups. Perhaps the most surprising and disappointing are the various churches whose role was that of both protecting Aborigines from the onslaught of modernity and preparing Aborigines for such a world. The missions were not of a piece. At least seven churches were involved in mission work among Aborigines in Australia – Lutheran, Catholic, Anglican (Church Missionary Society), Seventh Day Adventist, Presbyterian (Australian Inland Mission), Methodist, and Congregational (the latter three now Uniting Church). The considerable history of missions will not be canvassed in this volume.[41]

Missionaries undoubtedly undermined the authority of Aboriginal elders. Those, for example, who were baptised and became members of a church were, by and large, forbidden to take part in the ancient ceremonies. When the elders brought pressure to bear on the converts to conform to the traditional ways, the missionaries encouraged them to resist and conform to the new ways they had introduced. But as Paul Albrecht of Hermannsburg mission points out:

> It is fashionable to blame Christian missions for destroying Aboriginal culture by destroying the Aboriginal religious belief system – the very foundation undergirding the culture. [T]his accusation cannot withstand rigorous analysis. The most serious blow to the religious belief system was not delivered by Christian missions but by Aborigines eating non-Indigenous

---

41 Readers interested in this aspect will find much of interest in an excellent series of papers edited by Swain, T. and D. B. Rose, 1988. *Aboriginal Australians and Christian Missions: Ethnographic and Historical Studies*, Australian Association for the Study of Religions.

foods – damper and beef – and drinking tea. Put another way, it was the inability of the belief system to validate itself in the face of the different adaptive system introduced by the European settlers that "white-anted" the Aboriginal culture. The Aborigines believed they had food and water because of the primary creative activity of the supernatural beings, and because they also were able to enter into, and continue, this creative activity. In their increase rituals they created the rain, they created the seeds from which the various plant foods grew, they were able to create and increase the number of kangaroos and other game they needed to survive. And if the kangaroos became thin, they could fatten them up![42]

McKnight likewise observes:

> I am well aware that in the past some missionaries employed corporal punishment ... however, the missionaries that I met ... were never guilty of such reprehensible acts. I believe that had it not been for the missionaries there would have been far fewer Aborigines in Queensland and elsewhere in Australia.[43]

The Berndts write:

> Particularly during the early periods of Aboriginal-European contact, mission stations were virtually the only refuge-places for Aborigines trying to escape from the depredations of the new settlers and their expanding townships ... without the protective authority of missionaries, the Aboriginal population would have been reduced even more savagely than it was ... Moreover, the Arnhem Land missions, along with Hermannsburg (in the 1940s), made possible the emergence of the outstation movement, which is generally believed to have

---

42 Albrecht, P. 2008. *Relhiperra: Aboriginal Issues*. The Bennelong Society, p. 48.
43 McKnight, D. 2002. *From Hunting to Drinking: The Devastating Effects of Alcohol on an Australian Aboriginal Community*. Routledge, p. 48.

begun much later.[44]

Children were removed, but which children survived? Those taken into care or those left to wallow in remote communities? A case study of the United Aborigines' Mission, Colebrook Home (1924-1973) at Quorn north of Adelaide and later in Adelaide, concluded that '[p]robably one of the most convincing endorsements of the operations of Colebrook Home were those wards who, on leaving the Home, did take up respectable positions within white society.'[45] Perhaps the most sensible comment of the reams written on the church missions to Aborigines in Australia is 'grudgingly or otherwise, one can say this of the missionaries: they tried.'[46] Sadly, the considerable efforts of the churches have not been recognised and a new generation of 'missionaries', mainly teachers and administrators, often lacking the language skills and insights of the original has come to the field late and underestimates the task at hand or is ignorant of the adverse impact of good deeds. The churches have been most vulnerable to attack for their role in protecting children, especially half-caste children at risk of death by the hand of their respective communities, in particular Aboriginal communities who refused to care for half-caste children.

There was a telling discussion[47] in 2000 at the Australian Citizenship Council chaired by Sir Ninian Stephen, between then Associate Professor Robert Manne and former Senator for the Northern Territory Bernie Kilgariff. Manne was boldly making the case for the wrongs of the 'stolen generations'. Kilgariff gently recalled that as a young man he had regularly walked the Todd River out from Alice Springs to pick up the babies left for dead, thereby saving their lives.

---

44 Berndt, R. M. and C. H. 1988. 'Body and Soul.' In Swain and Rose, p. 46.
45 Jacobs, J. et al 1988. 'Pearls from the Deep: Re-evaluating the Early History of Colebrook Home for Aboriginal Children.' In Swain and Rose, p. 154.
46 Burridge, K. 1988. 'Aborigines and Christianity.' In Swain and Rose, p. 28.
47 Personal recollection.

Manne fell silent. Indeed, Clifford Possum, one of the most famous Australian Aboriginal artists who was born around 1932 in a dry creek bed on Napperby Station, 195 kilometres northwest of Alice Springs, 'was saved from death from malnutrition as a child by a pastor at a local mission.'[48]

Despite the perfectly defensible role that they played in Aboriginal policy for a century, the churches have now lost confidence in their abilities and in their experience. The foundation document of Judith Wright's Aboriginal Treaty Committee,[49] for example, featured a photograph of Rev. Father Percy Smith with old boys Charles Perkins and John Moriarty of his Anglican boarding house of St Francis in Adelaide as if to disprove the very thesis at the heart of the treatise and its separatist leanings. These two successful advocates for Aborigines were successful in their own right; they were able to earn a living outside the beggared and dependent existence of their kin. This is self-determination in a way that collective self-determination, which mistakes the political form of self-determination for the needs of the individuals, could never achieve.

In a further withdrawal from a proud mission heritage, 'reconciliation' was introduced in 1988 when 14 heads of Australian Christian Churches issued a statement, *Towards Reconciliation in Australian Society*.[50] The necessity for reconciliation largely arose from the failure of Judith Wright's Aboriginal Treaty Committee.[51] A grateful Hawke Government ran with it as a means of keeping the constituency occupied, knowing that it could not deliver national land rights or accept the breach of sovereignty that a treaty implies. There are still

---

48 Gennochio, B. 2008. *Dollar Dreaming: Inside the Aboriginal Art World*. Hardie Grant Books, p. 16.
49 Harris, S. 1979. 'It's Coming Yet ... :An Aboriginal Treaty Within Australia Between Australians.' *Aboriginal Treaty Committee*, p. 54.
50 Quoted in Gardiner-Garden, J. 1998a. 'From Dispossession to Reconciliation.' *Research Paper* No. 27. Department of the Parliamentary Library, p. 16.
51 Wright, J. 1985. *We Call for a Treaty*, Collins/Fontana, p. 284.

people who support the notion of a treaty. Patrick Dodson, former chair of the Council for Aboriginal Reconciliation, in commenting on the Preamble to the Constitution, stated, 'The Aboriginal people are owners of this country. If they want to put anything in there, put the fact down that we own Australia and that ought to be reflected in any preamble or any constitutional reality'.[52]

Nevertheless, the rout of previously orthodox views is pretty well complete. Anglicans in Melbourne have shown their propensity to belief in symbolism rather than analysis in their swoon for the Apology, which they characterised as an 'unequivocal statement about historical injustices, the appalling consequences to which those injustices gave rise, and the commitment of generations now living to repair the damage of the past, face realistically the challenges of the present, and secure a decent life for all Australians in the future'.[53] This, notwithstanding the fact that Anglican missionaries saved numerous Aborigines from death at the hands of their own. Anglicare Australia has declared that it is 'deeply concerned at the severity and widespread nature of the problems of child sexual abuse and community breakdown in Indigenous communities in the Northern Territory, catalogued in the *Little Children are Sacred* Report'. But all it could suggest in response was 'to work collaboratively with Governments and the communities affected to ensure that children are protected [and] develop ... a long term plan to address and resolve the causes of child abuse including joblessness, education, parenting and life skills, poor housing, and commit the ongoing necessary resources to this.'[54] The Anglicans had a plan; they abandoned it. After one hundred years in the field speaking the languages of Aboriginal Australia, marshalling their meagre resources to educate Aborigines – indeed, a generation of Aboriginal leaders – all they can come up with is a

---

52 *ABC Radio National*, Thursday 12 August 1999.
53 Anglicare Australia, *Press release* 23 February 2008.
54 Anglicare Australia, *Press release* 29 June 2007.

retreat into symbolism, further government reliance for Aborigines and a pathetic and anti-intellectual acceptance of misplaced guilt for past actions as a guide to future strategies.

In a similar vein, the prize for the most extraordinary foolishness in the Anglican Church must be awarded to Dr Peter Adam, principal of Ridley College, the main Anglican theological college in Victoria. In 2009, he said that all non-Aboriginal Australians should be prepared to leave the country if the Aboriginal people want that, 'making restitution for the vile sin of genocide'.

> It would in fact be possible, even if very difficult and complicated, for Europeans and others to leave Australia. I am not sure where we would go, but that would be our problem.
>
> No recompense could ever be satisfactory because what was done was so vile, so immense, so universal, so pervasive, so destructive, so devastating and so irreparable.
>
> The prosperity of our churches has come from the proceeds of crime. Our houses, our churches, our colleges, our shops, our sport grounds, our parks, our courts, our parliaments, our prisons, our hospitals, our roads, our reservoirs are stolen property.[55]

The Brisbane Catholic Justice and Peace Commission has similarly retreated. In response to 'The *Bringing Them Home* report it recommended the Federal Government become a signatory to the *Declaration on the Rights of Indigenous Peoples* ... and ... on International Human Rights Day ... to express its solidarity with Indigenous people who are still waiting for justice.'[56] The National Council of Churches in Australia urges its flock to support the United Nations' Millennium Development Goals and Indigenous Peoples and Make Indigenous Poverty history. The analysis underlying the urgings is as shallow as that applied by Mick Dodson, that 'Indigenous poverty' is caused

---
55 Anglican Church, Diocese of Melbourne.
56 Catholic Justice and Peace Commission, *Press release* 10 December 2008.

by 'colonisation, loss of traditional lands, loss of languages, loss of traditional law and loss of cultural practices.'[57] It is, however, the churches that are lost – there is not a single intelligible idea presented in their many outpourings. They have no concept of what motivates people and they have forgotten every lesson that their parents taught them about raising children, particularly the necessity for thrift and hard work.

Fortunately, while sections of the churches' intelligentsia have decidedly immature ideas about Aboriginal policy, their schools are boarding children from remote centres, thus integrating them and saving them from a short and awful existence in remote communities. The students do not graduate as 'Aborigines'. They graduate as educated citizens. These successes are far greater than any who remain in communities.

Costs and benefits of self-determination

To understand the impact of the self-determination era on Aborigines, it is essential to understand what would have happened to Aboriginal people regardless of self-determination, that is, to understand what other factors were shaping their lives. To achieve this, underlying trends in Aboriginal society prior to self-determination have to be identified. In the broadest sense, these were changes to language, custom and lifestyle and the absorption of Aborigines by intermarriage into the broader society. Without the active intervention of self-determination 'policy', the following would probably have happened. It is important to understand why:

1. Closed Aboriginal culture was vulnerable to the open society

The hunter-gatherer society was a closed culture. It had little capacity to understand externally-caused events; most events were

---

[57] National Council of Churches in Australia.

interpreted through ritual. Science did not exist and innovation was slow and insufficiently widespread to take hold. The culture was rigid and vulnerable to outside forces. Although it had great capacity to survive in the wild against natural forces or people of similar levels of development, it had almost no capacity to understand or adapt to an innovative and open society. The rigidity and vulnerability of Aboriginal culture was bound to crack in the face of a far greater force. While some Aborigines argue that they live their culture, the lifestyle of the most 'traditional' Aborigines bears little relationship to how they earn an income. The most commonly cited aspect of Aboriginal culture, loyalty to kin, may well be a major impediment in adjusting to new circumstances. Family can hold back individuals. This is a cruel irony. The key support becomes, in some circumstances, the chief instrument of doom. Even crueller is that so many Aboriginal families are in such strife that they break up anyway, leaving only little support and a residual of loyalty through practices such as humbugging (threatening people, usually family and friends, for cash).

2. *Innovation destroyed local languages*

Aborigines have all but lost their languages. Had their world been receptive to the innovations that the rest of the world was experiencing at the time of European settlement of Australia, one or two Aboriginal languages may have dominated, at least in the sense that these would have been widespread and used as the basis for broader intercourse among a large proportion of Aborigines. In these circumstances it may have been possible for these one or two languages to have survived post-European settlement. Nevertheless, to those who spoke the displaced languages, the fact that they were displaced by English rather than a dominant Aboriginal language may be neither here nor there. Indeed, the reason for the large number of languages was because of the crude nature of the economy and the lack of wider contact. Although there are instances of items traded between Aborigines across very large areas of Australia and multilingualism among many groups, the very low density of contact points did not lend itself to a widespread shared language. Large numbers of languages, as for example in Papua New Guinea, are a certain sign of insularity. Destroying insularity destroys languages, but one could not, in good conscience, or in fact, return to the insularity of a previous time. Undermining a dominant language would undermine the ease with which Aborigines now communicate. It readily follows that there is no obligation on the part of the dominant language group to preserve Aboriginal language, especially where few speakers exist and where the common language, English, is essential for livelihood.

3. *Living standards could never have risen in the old economy*

While it is generally true that the whiteman took Aboriginal land without compensation, the value of that land in modern terms was near worthless. Aborigines earned a subsistence living. Given that Aborigines argue for equal access to the benefits of modern society, and that only the whiteman or integrated Aborigines can hope to create sufficient value from the land to generate the benefits of the modern society, it is arguable that Aborigines have been more than well compensated. After all, no Aborigine will accept the return of land *sans* the benefits of the modern economy. Yet, the arguments mounted for Aboriginal compensation are facile.

> The fact that I wake up each morning in a warm, safe, comfortable home, secure in the knowledge that the schools I send my children off to are organised to enhance their life chances and choices, and that good health, employment opportunities and respect are the norm, not the goal in our lives, has been made possible through the 208-year exploitation of land that belonged to Indigenous Australians since the beginning of time.[58]

---

58 Quoted in Sowell, T. 2005. *Black Rednecks and White Liberals*, Encounter, p. 264.

The comment completely ignores the contribution of the new people to the standard of living that could never have been generated in the Aboriginal economy. As the African American, Thomas Sowell argues, differences in life chances are attributed to the seizure of land by Europeans.

> If this were meant seriously as an empirical proposition, rather than as an ideological indictment, then the most obvious question would be: were there no differences in life chances between the Europeans and the aborigines before they met, when they were each living in their own respective homelands? Are differences today greater than they were then? Would this woman be any more deserving of her windfall gain in England than in Australia?[59]

The conclusion drawn in the above example is that Aborigines should not have to change in order to achieve equality. Those who use this critique of settler society want both groups to have the same outcomes without having the same causes when both are living in the same country. Comparing like with like, the present owners of Aboriginal land have not fared well, but they are vastly better off than in their previous incumbency. More important is that they are much worse off than others not on Aboriginal land. Aboriginal income is immensely higher than any the old economy could generate but the income of a class of Aborigines, those sitting on their land, is lower than other Aborigines (see Figure 16-19 on pages 275-280).

On basic elements, culture, language and economy, Aboriginal society was vulnerable. Moreover, the less it changed culturally the more it suffered economically. This does not mean that culture should not be 'respected' or a means of inducing adaptation to new circumstances. But it is critical to understand that a fundamentally closed society is unlikely to lend itself to promoting positive change.

---

59 Sowell, 2005, p. 264.

On this rare occasion it is helpful to 'blame it on society'. In each of these three elements – culture, language and economy – the result suggests that, in the face of the global advance of modernisation, the default case is that Australian Aborigines would have had to integrate in ways that considerably changed their behaviour. Using the default case as a basis from which to measure the impact of self-determination, the costs and benefits appear as follows:

- The most obvious gains from self-determination are the growth of an identifiable political class prominent in public life and debate which acts as a voice; a large number of Aboriginal associations, which act as a vehicle for group solidarity and a cipher for public funds; and a considerable but largely unproductive Aboriginal estate.
- In terms of costs it is probable that self-determination produced a poorly prepared Aboriginal land owning and occupying class. This class's attempts to recover culture, including language, are doomed by forces much greater than public policy. It is ironic that the things that Aborigines are not short of – land, welfare income, spokesmen and consultation – are what are holding them back.
- An absence of self-determination would have enhanced the following: movement off the land, intermarriage, general economic and cultural adjustment, and better education. These adaptations would have created more options and choices. There would have been failures and tragedies, of whom Bennelong was the first but, in time, adjustment would have reduced the destructive behaviour that now pervades Aboriginal communities.
- The local environment of the Aboriginal estate has been degraded in some respects, first by Aborigines in their hunting and burning and, more recently, by Europeans, with the introduction of hard-hoofed animals and crops. Most

important, however, is that the capacity for restoration rests outside Aboriginal knowledge.
- Aborigines were marginalised by prejudice in an earlier period until the 1970s; since that time they have been shown the door to modern and open society, but some have been prevented from grasping the opportunities because of inability to adapt, an inability reinforced by clinging to land and culture.

Exit strategy

At the close of the period of the experiment in self-determination the broad conclusion is that self-determination was a big price to pay for publicly-funded Aboriginal organisations, Aboriginal leaders, Aboriginal art and dance, all of which survive in other cultures without self-determination. These changes wrought by self-determination to the larger forces of integration mean that the changes required in policy are perhaps more difficult than was the position faced by policy makers in the pre self-determination era. The policy issue is how to move from the current position to the path of integration. Integration until 1965 took place in a very different environment, with lower expectations on both sides, low incomes, and greater authority invested in institutions such as missions and teachers. In 2010, while there are almost unlimited funds, both in the hands of Aborigines and governments, the place is also awash with grog and drugs, and disrespect for authority. In this venture, cultural practice that is not harmful may be harnessed in order to allow Aborigines to find a place in the modern economy. Whether culture survives after entry into the modern world is a matter for Aborigines. By contrast, cultural practice that is simply bad behaviour should be changed.

The policy task is to map a pathway that will lead to the greatest number of Aborigines entering the modern economy. The deficit approach, which assumes that a 'gap' in income and services can be filled by gifts rather than behavioural change, is a dead end. No Australian government has dared outline a pathway to the future. The reams of policy documents issued by governments are a dance in which Aboriginal leaders are paid off in programs. The programs have few objectives; in some cases, where they exist, they are confused. 'Closing the Gap', for example, is a funding strategy; it is not a direction because it does not address the causes of the gap. The causes are not lack of funds and programs; they are learned anger, ideology, poor incentives, bad behaviour and ignorance.

The pathway to integration can accept land rights as a legal fact, but it must also recognise that land can be an impediment to adjustment. Similarly, royalties need to be put beyond reach of those who want to live off them. They must only be used to fund education. In the choice to develop Aboriginal settlements or abandon them, settlements without an economic base should be abandoned. A most important transition mechanism is that temporary housing only should be made available to those who cannot buy their own. All children must attend school up to 15 years, and to do so will almost certainly require them to live in a larger centre.

Whether culture can be preserved or even utilised for integration is problematic. Albrecht argues[60] that Aboriginal culture should be taken seriously, not to preserve it, but to use it to assist Aborigines to adjust to current social and economic situations. The approach is ideal, but there are considerable difficulties in doing so. For example, it is evident in the elaborate funerals of the Yolngu people of East Arnhem Land that the whiteman is funding a lifestyle, which is damaging for the people concerned and increasingly more expensive and irrational.

> Beginning in the mid 1970s, Yolngu funerals have become exponentially longer and more elaborate affairs [a result of the

---

60 Albrecht, 2008, p. 90.

portable morgue] ... The funeral of an important and senior person can attract up to 400 people from a wide region, and take several months. Although the 400 will not be present all of that time, funerals are a major cause of continual intra-regional mobility on a massive scale. In some years ... funerals are a continual presence.[61]

In education, cultural considerations have policy-makers in a quandary:

> If the children are given a European education then the Aborigines complain that their culture is being neglected and they accuse the White Australians of cultural genocide. If, however, the children are not given a European education then the Aborigines complain that they are being given a second rate education and are prevented from competing with the Whites on their own terms.[62]

In economics, culture prevents insight:

> The more traditional Aborigines have always overlaid their economic concepts on the Australian economy. The automatic provision of welfare benefits has merely reinforced their traditional concepts. As they see it, the new ritual demanded by the Australian economy is the filling in of forms (applications). If this ritual is performed correctly then the money will be there to be collected.[63]

Culture can also be used to excuse bad behaviour:

> A mother is embarrassed and angry because a school's Home Liaison Officer had been pressing her to send her young

---

[61] Morphy, F. (ed) 2007. 'Agency, Contingency and Census Process: Observations of the 2006 Indigenous Enumeration Strategy in Remote Aboriginal Australia.' *Research Monograph* No. 28. ANU E Press, p. 34.
[62] McKnight, 2002, p. 142.
[63] Albrecht, 2008, p. 90.

daughter to school. The mother accuses the school of lacking cultural understanding of Aboriginal people. The school's alleged mishandling of her child had led to the child being too fearful to attend school for the whole year. This child was seen on many occasions during that year caring for a group of up to ten younger members of her extended family while the parents involved played cards. She would beg money to buy food for these children and try to keep them amused.[64]

Culture suggests hiding behind the group to avoid individual obligations. As the President of the United States, Barack Obama; remarked to African Americans:

> Parents, we can't tell our kids to do well in school and then fail to support them when they get home. For our kids to excel, we have to accept our responsibility to help them learn. That means putting away the *Xbox*, putting our kids to bed at a reasonable hour. It means attending those parent-teacher conferences and reading to our children and helping them with their homework.[65]

The essential message was the same as that delivered by George W. Bush in 2000 to challenge the 'soft bigotry of low expectations' among blacks and Hispanics in the USA.[66] These sentiments are applicable to Australian Aborigines. They bring into focus a central challenge for policy-makers. Is there any good in group solidarity, also known as 'culture', especially solidarity based on those aspects of culture that promote or excuse poor behaviour?

This is the fundamental challenge of Aboriginal politics and one that echoes Thomas Sowell when he discusses 'Breast beating versus cultural cringe.'[67] By breast beating Sowell refers to the tendency to

---

64 As told to the author by Dr Steve Etherington.
65 Address to the 100th convention of the National Association for the Advancement of Colored People on 16 July 2009.
66 Interview with *Time Magazine*, 1 August, 2000.
67 Sowell, 2005, p. 257.

group breast beating that accompanies demands for compensation or special rights. The cultural cringe is the individual feeling that a culture exhibits poor behaviour from which a member should shy away. The issue is, which acts as a spur to improvement? Obama, Bush and Sowell agree that the cultural cringe is the more likely. Rejecting a culture of bad behaviour is essential. If Aboriginal culture consists of so much that is bad behaviour, the bellicose defence of the culture, so evident in report after report, is an impediment to solutions. So much of Aboriginal policy has been based on asserting cultural difference (even as the difference declines and despite some instances of cultural revival), on claiming rights which belittle obligations, mute incentives pouring scorn on the whiteman's ways.

The challenge in Aboriginal policy is to change behaviour, to have Aboriginal children attend school, find a job and make a life independent of government. To the extent these are difficult to achieve has little to do with a lack of government assistance, as that assistance has been massive. The assistance, indeed, has displaced effort and reinforced breast beating. The culture has become the goal and has thus become an impediment to individual responsibility. The path to integration will need to be mapped out explicitly. It is the only hope for closing the gap. At present governments simply move from one funding program to another. Aware of bad behaviour, aware of perverse incentives that hold people into present arrangements but too afraid to offend, governments demonstrate no convincing argument for any position.

> In the present situation men and women know that there will be enough money to keep them alive and that they will have accommodation and some sort of employment. Any time they wish they can demonstrate their independence by doing what they please even if this means being fired from work, expelled from school or for serious offences being sent to prison. Whatever they do they can be certain of being looked after. But

in the past it would be inconceivable that they never learned to hunt or refused to hunt and yet expected to be fed and cared for.[68]

Prejudice exhibited by some citizens against Aborigines is most likely against bad behaviour such as 'pride and violence as a way of life',[69] not against race. Often prejudice within Aboriginal communities is directed at the well-off or the hard workers, who rise above the pack, the middleman minorities,[70] not those who simply have no clue about how to engage the economy. The pack mentality is evident in remote communities where it is difficult for an individual to rise above the pack. Group think can lead to copying bad rather than good behaviour.[71]

By contrast, those who exult the culture are those whose own children sleep safely in their bed at night. Only these people would assert that 'Only when a group shares this sense of ethnic honour can it achieve community closure and compete successfully for a fair share in economic and political opportunities."[72] As another astutely observed, '"Doing culture" [welcome to country, dances] can reinforce one's indigeneity ... or it can make one appear unreal.'[73] The whole business of proving one's identity to gain a reward is fraught:

> [E]very time Aboriginal people vote or make an application to the housing commission, they are reminded of identity issues. Although eligibility criteria for social benefits provided by the government, such as pensions or rent subsidies, applies

---

68 McKnight, 2002, p. 141.
69 Sowell, 2005, p. 7.
70 Sowell, 2005, p. 65.
71 Sowell, 2005, pp. 285-6.
72 Dagmar, H. 1990. 'Development and Politics in an Interethnic Field.' In Tonkinson, R. and M. Howard Going it Alone?: *Prospects for Aboriginal Autonomy*. Aboriginal Studies Press, p. 102.
73 Lambert-Pennington, A.K. 2005. 'Being in Australia, Belonging to the Land: The Cultural Politics of Urban Aboriginal Identity.' Doctoral thesis, Department of Cultural Anthropology Duke University, p. 186.

to all Australians, proof of Aboriginality relies in part on a biologically essentialist condition. While these experiences may be inevitable, given that Aboriginal people want recognition, the consequences are not. The policing of Aboriginality seems to affect fairer-skinned Kooris disproportionately, and demands for proof are sometimes read as challenges to their identity. There is a painful indignity in having to prove one's identity in order to participate in a sporting event or to run for elected office. However, without proof there is no recognition. Here we glimpse the double edge of Aboriginality and its impact on Aboriginal people's daily lives.[74]

The political strategy to idealise Aboriginal culture and use it as the glue to rekindle a sense of worth among Aborigines is the reason many Aborigines fail to embrace modern society and feel resentful of its gifts. The halfway house strategy wherein Aborigines run their own organisations but are sustained by others is a recipe for dependence. The strategy relies on an amoral view of progress, that by simply occupying land a group of people should be entitled to the benefits of the intelligence and ingenuity that is produced from it by others. This is rent-seeking at its worst. It is rarely appreciated that rent-seeking does not contribute to the producers; it destroys the rent-seekers by denying the ability to learn how to produce. It denies them a purpose for living.

The culture cult so accurately described and analysed by Roger Sandall[75] has been revealed as a conceit of the intellectuals. Intellectuals impervious to economics and having no understanding of the productive aspects of life, condemned Aborigines to an existence that emulated a dead culture and left them vulnerable to the worst aspects of modern society. Aboriginal culture was the product of a rudimentary economic system and created a very illiberal society.

---

74 Lambert-Pennington, 2005, p. 29.
75 Sandall, 2001.

It should have been the last place that intelligent people sought refuge against a liberal democratic market society. The political strategy devised by the political Left has resulted in many blighted lives and many deaths. Those who wrote ceaselessly in defence of the indefensible, killed Aborigines just as surely as any redneck grazier of the 19th century. The Leftist Ralph Folds summed it up; you cannot have culture and money.[76]

---

[76] Folds, R. 2001. *Crossed Purposes: the Pintupi and Australia's Indigenous Policy.* UNSW.

2

Identity at any price

Despite Folds' caution, that you cannot have culture and money, culture is used as the Trojan Horse precisely for the reason of gaining money, most of which is funnelled through Aboriginal organisations. As a policy goal, restoring Aboriginal culture has a plausible defence. Some argue that increasingly the focus of attention is on Aboriginal law and cultures as the problem – 'if only Aboriginal people would stop being Aboriginal then we could help them'; and 'our solution to Aboriginal people's "problems" is still that Aboriginal people cease to be Aboriginal.'[77] We shall come to the problem of Aboriginal culture soon, but the cultural 'apologists' proceed to argue that

> we (meaning the government) need instead to invest in Aboriginal *community owned* not just in Aboriginal *community based* services. There is already a strong nucleus of initiatives: Night Patrols, Safe Houses, Community Justice Groups, Sober-up

---

[77] Blagg, H. 2007. 'Zero Tolerance or Community Justice? The Role of the Aboriginal Domain in Reducing Family Violence.' *Indigenous Family Violence Prevention Forum*, Queensland Centre for Domestic Family Violence and Research.

facilities. They are currently under-resourced and under-valued but they are excellent vehicles for expanding new initiatives. These arrangements have been loosely mapped out in the reports such as the Cape York Justice Study.[78]

Culture and identity as expressed through organisation has exploded in recent decades as the numbers identifying as Aboriginal climb but, in terms of race, Aborigines have never been less aboriginal. Two types of Aborigine are readily distinguished: those whose appearance is unlikely to have caused them to suffer prejudice (the late identifiers who live in the open society), and those who are by looks and behaviour sufficiently different to have caused them grief (those in remote communities and some regions). These two, not exclusive categories by any means, suggest that an Australian Aboriginal identity has to be created as it is no longer obvious and no longer very different. Aborigines of remote Australia have little in common with those in other parts of Australia who claim an Aboriginal heritage. As racial identity has faded, Aboriginal leaders have had to appeal to other elements of identity, faux culture, faux corporations, Potemkin villages and a pretend economy.

From race to identity

The special regard in which Aborigines are to be held depends in part on a changing definition of what it is to be an Aborigine. The Australian Government has a three-part administrative definition of an Aboriginal person. It involves ancestry, self-identification and acceptance by an Aboriginal community. This is not the same as the definition in legislation which refers to 'a person of the Aboriginal race of Australia'.[79] The Federal Court has interpreted this

---

78 Blagg, 2007.
79 Gardiner-Garden, J. 1998b. 'Identifiable Commonwealth Expenditure on Aboriginal and Torres Strait Islander Affairs.', *Current Issues Brief*, No. 18. Department of the Parliamentary Library, p. 7.

sometimes relying on ancestry alone, at other times abandoning it altogether.[80] Some Aborigines in the 1996 ATSIC Regional Council elections in Tasmania challenged the Commonwealth's all-embracing administrative definition, although, when it has suited their interests, other Aborigines have pushed for a more broad ranging definition which does not include ancestry. During the Royal Commission into Aboriginal Deaths in Custody, for example, Aboriginal groups argued that Tony Majurey, 'a Maori who had no Aboriginal descent but had become a member of an Aboriginal community, should be regarded as an Aboriginal within the terms of reference' of the Commission.[81]

Box 2: Census questions on race and origins Data

1966 Census	•'State person's race … If of more than one race give particulars, for example, ½ European-½Aboriginal, ¾ Aboriginal-¼Chinese, ½ European-½Chinese.'
1971 Census	•'What is this person's racial origin?'
1981 Census	•'Is the person of Aboriginal or Torres Strait Islander origin?'

Data source: Australian Bureau of Statistics, 1999. 'Population Issues, Indigenous Australians 1996.' *Occasional Paper*, 4708.0, p. 9.

The change from a racial definition to an associational definition is reflected in the changing questions in the Census in recent years allowing more people to identify as Aboriginal. As shown in Box 2, the term, 'race', was used as an identifier for the last time in the 1966

---

80 Gardiner-Garden, 1998a, pp. 5-9.
81 Wootten, J.H. 1989. *Report of the Inquiry into the Death of Thomas William Murray*, Royal Commission into Aboriginal Deaths in Custody, June. See also O'Dea, D.J. 1991. *Regional Report of Inquiry into Individual Deaths in Custody in Western Australia*, volume 1, March.

Census. It was thereafter softened to racial origin in the 1971 Census, then dropped altogether in favour of the term 'origins' in the 1981 Census. It does not come as any great surprise that, as shown in Figure 3, the count of Aboriginal and Torres Strait Islander people started to rise after the 1966 Census and even more so after the 1981 Census. Indeed, the Indigenous count increased 340 per cent in the 30 years to the 1996 Census compared with a 53 per cent increase for the total population.[82] In terms of the contribution to the rise in numbers since 1966, the main movers were the southern states, 13 per cent rise in the NSW share of Australia's Indigenous population (20-33), four per cent in Victoria (3-7) and Tasmania (0-4, a huge leap in the number identifying), Queensland steady (28), and a decline in other states, SA (7-6) and WA (21-13), and the Northern Territory (2-1).[83]

An observation from Australia and other Anglo-settler countries with similar patterns of identification as a source of growth is that the changes in census count probably 'chart the movement of ethnicity from the biological to the social realm.'[84] Aboriginal numbers are about where they were at the time of settlement,[85] but nothing like who they were. The current stock is a different people. The cause of the rise probably stems from more liberal attitudes toward racial origins and, therefore, preparedness among people to identify their origins whether or not these are apparent. This preparedness to 'self-identify' is wholly welcome but it does invite debate about the purpose of identification and what consequence it carries for public policy. In broad terms, and more than 200 years after Europeans settled in Australia, those whom we regard as Aborigines are little like the original inhabitants to whom the label native Aborigine once applied. A possible cause of the rise

---

82 Australian Bureau of Statistics, 1999. 'Population Issues, Indigenous Australians 1996.' *Occasional Paper* 4708.0, p. 1.
83 Author calculations based on Australian Bureau of Statistics, 2008b. *Australian Historical Population Statistics*, Table 2.2, Cat. 3105.0.65.001.
84 ABS, 1999, p. 55.
85 Flood, J. 2006. *The Original Australians: Story of the Aboriginal People*, Allen and Unwin, p. 27.

of self-identifiers is the significant increase in the rate of Aboriginal intermarriage which occurred a generation or two earlier.

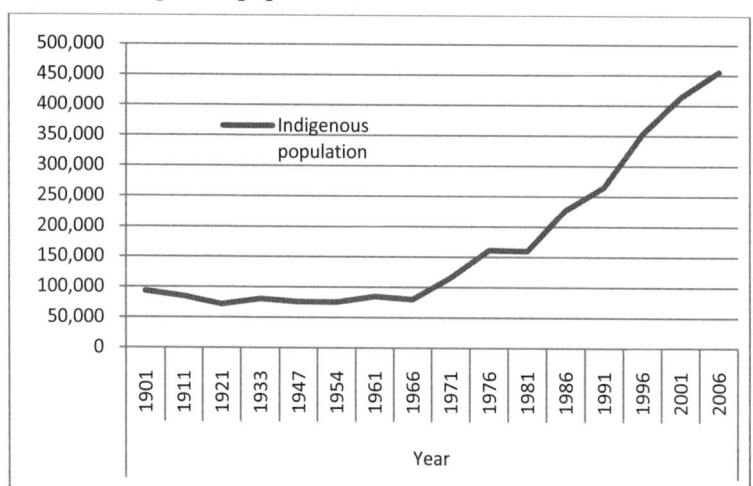

Figure 3: Indigenous population, 1901-2006

[Chart showing Indigenous population from 1901 to 2006, rising from approximately 100,000 in 1901 to approximately 450,000 in 2006]

Data source: Australian Bureau of Statistics, 1999. 'Population Issues, Indigenous Australians 1996.' *Occasional Paper* 4708.0 and Population Characteristics, Aboriginal and Torres Strait Islander Australians, 2006 4713.0.

The Australian Bureau of Statistics has recorded the ratio of Indigenous people of mixed descent to those of solely Indigenous descent from 1901 to 1966, as shown in Figure 4. As noted above, after the 1966 Census the ABS ceased asking for race in terms of fractions or 'half-caste'. Whilst all these data have associated data quality concerns, the Bureau considered the distinction between more than 50 per cent Indigenous and less than 50 per cent Indigenous unreliable for the 1961 and 1966 censuses.[86] Nevertheless, in general these data suggest that an increasing number of Indigenous people were of mixed descent, with the ratio of mixed to sole descent approaching one in 1961 and 1966. These data have been converted to

---

86 ABS, 1999, p. 45.

percentage of Indigenous marriages of whom one is Indigenous. For censuses after 1966, it is possible to measure, at least approximately, some aspects of intermarriage by analysing the number of two-parent families where one partner is Indigenous and the other is not. Figure 4 also shows the proportion of mixed couples (that is, with one Indigenous and one non-Indigenous partner) as a proportion of all Indigenous couples (that is, where at least one partner is Indigenous) from 1986-2006.

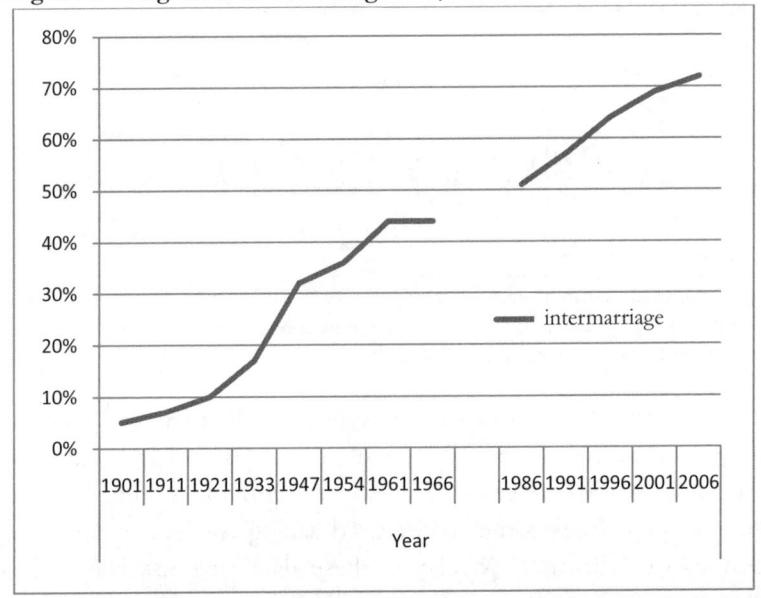

Figure 4: Indigenous intermarriage rate, 1901-2006

Note: The ratio of Indigenous people of mixed descent to those of solely Indigenous descent from 1901 to 1966 expressed as a percentage. For 1986-2006 the proportion of mixed couples (that is, with one Indigenous and one non-Indigenous partner) as a proportion of all Indigenous couples (that is, where at least one partner is Indigenous).

Data source: Australian Bureau of Statistics, 1999. 'Population Issues, Indigenous Australians 1996.' Occasional Paper 4708.0, page 45 and Centre for Population and Urban Research, Monash – customised data from the 2006 Census.

The level of intermarriage in Australia is not uniform and reflects the historical geography of European settlement, highest in the southern states where significant contact was early and lowest in the north where significant contact was more recent. For example, in 2006 the percentage of partnered Indigenous persons whose partner is non-Indigenous in Sydney was around 83 per cent; in the Northern Territory, outside Darwin, it is less than 10 per cent (and as low as four per cent for males), figures that have not changed a great deal since 1986.[87]

Language is a strong identity marker. In round terms, of the 431,000 Indigenous people who were counted in the 2006 Census, 372,000 spoke English only. Some 41,000 spoke an Indigenous language together with English, well or very well. Only 11,000 or 2.6 per cent speak an Indigenous language and do not speak English well or at all (or not stated).[88] In other words, the number of Indigenous people who cannot communicate in English is very small. Moreover, of those Indigenous people who speak an Indigenous language at home, 74 per cent live in Very Remote Australia, and 14 per cent live in Remote Australia. Around 56 per cent of all Indigenous language speakers live in the Northern Territory where 59 per cent of the Indigenous population speak an Australian Indigenous language.[89]

The highest regional increases in the Indigenous population between 2001 and 2006 occurred in the Indigenous Regions of Coffs Harbour (25 per cent), Non-Metropolitan Victoria (25 per cent), Wagga Wagga (21 per cent) and Melbourne (20 per cent). As in previous censuses, high Indigenous population growth occurred in more urbanised locations. A decline in Indigenous census counts was observed in some Indigenous remote regions between 2001 and

---

87 Centre for Population and Urban Research, Monash University – customised data from the 2006 Census.
88 ABS, 2008a, p. 43.
89 ABS, 2008a, p. 43.

2006 in remote Australia.[90] Indigenous people comprised 90 per cent or more of the total census count in more than 60 Indigenous Areas. All of these areas were in northern and central Australia and included Mowanjum and Tennant Creek – Towns Camps (both 100 per cent Indigenous people), Looma and Amoonguna (99 per cent), and Bayulu, Cherbourg, Mer, Yarrabah and Maningrida Outstation (97 per cent).

There is a great deal of difference between propinquity and integration. Aborigines living in the city may be, by choice or circumstance, in many essential ways unlike their neighbours. But this distinctly non-uniform Aboriginal geography and identity makes argument about special kinship with the land a reflection of a sub-set of Aborigines. A 1994 survey, for example, shows that 25 per cent of Aborigines did not recognise a particular area as their 'homeland'; that is, an area of land to which they had ancestral and/or cultural links. Furthermore, in 2002, 22 per cent of Indigenous people were living in their homelands/traditional country.[91] In broad terms, no more than 100,000 Indigenous people live in areas that may bear some broad relationship to their original land. In terms of land 'identity', an even smaller number will be able to claim native title or land rights successfully because of the need to prove an affiliation with lands by means of local ancestry and some continuity in acknowledgement of traditional laws and customs.

Aboriginal programs fuel identity

The period of expanded identity coincided with a period of greater funding. The Australian taxpayer has responded generously to Aboriginal despair. In real terms, identifiable Commonwealth

---

90 Australian Bureau of Statistics, 2007a. *Population Distribution, Aboriginal and Torres Strait Islander Australians, 2006* 4705.0.
91 Australian Bureau of Statistics, 2004. *National Aboriginal and Torres Strait Islander Social Survey, 2002* 4714.0.

expenditure in Aboriginal affairs saw a dramatic rise in the early to mid-1970s, then a fall from $947 million in 1975-76 to $596 million in 1978-79, not recovering the 1975-76 level until 1983-84 ($960 million). From the mid-1980s onwards there has been an almost uninterrupted rise in real expenditure, apart from small and quickly recovered declines in the mid-1990s and 2005-06.

When expressed as a percentage of total Commonwealth expenditure, identifiable Indigenous expenditure shows the same sharp increase and fall in the mid-1970s, followed by almost continuous growth to 1992-93. The mid-1990s saw fluctuations with the percentage rising and falling year to year but still trending upwards. Since 1997-98, however, it has remained relatively stable around 1.35 per cent, fluctuating between a high of 1.43 per cent in 1999-2000 and a low of 1.24 per cent in 2001-02. In 1968-69 identifiable Indigenous expenditure accounted for only 0.18 per cent of total Commonwealth expenditure while in 2007-08 it accounted for an estimated 1.37 per cent. When plotted as a percentage of GDP, Commonwealth Indigenous-specific expenditure shows a pattern broadly similar to when it is plotted as a percentage of total Commonwealth expenditure. Growth is fairly constant until the early 1990s with a very clear stabilisation at around one-third of one percentage point since then. Therefore, when measured against the economy as a whole, as measured by GDP, there has been no real growth in Indigenous-specific expenditure since the early 1990s.

Further complicating the task of estimating per capita expenditure is the fact that much of Indigenous-specific expenditure has not been simply 'on top of' that which Indigenous Australians might benefit from by being Australians. A large proportion has substituted for expenditure that would normally be provided under mainstream assistance programs (for example, Community Development Employment Projects for Newstart, Community Housing for housing under the Commonwealth-State Housing Agreement, Aboriginal Legal Aid for general legal aid, Aboriginal Medical Services for

Medicare supported services). A further amount has been for services which are generally the responsibility of state and/or local government. At the same time, Indigenous Australians have often utilised mainstream services and benefits at a lower rate than other Australians (for example, Pharmaceutical Benefits and Aged Care).

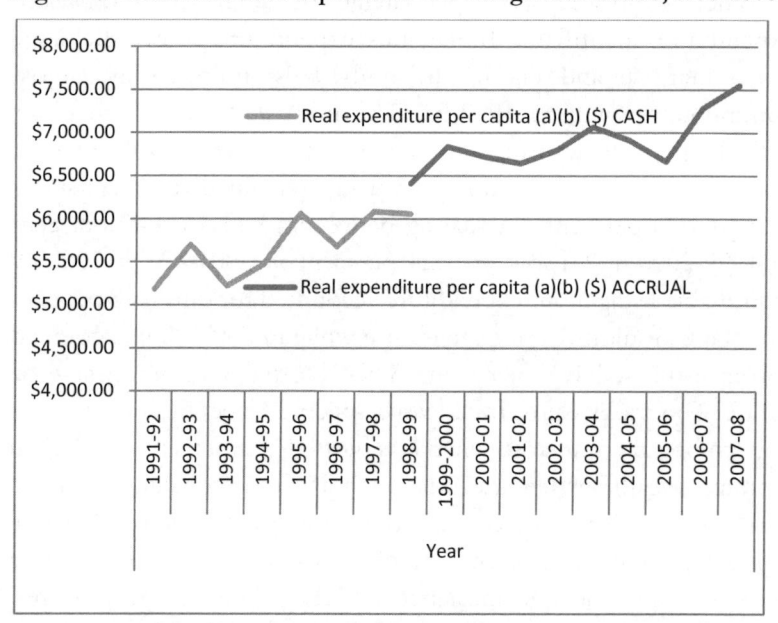

Figure 5: Commonwealth expenditure on Indigenous affairs, 1992-2008

Notes: The estimates and projections of the Indigenous population presented are experimental. Because of this volatility and the unknowns, two main projections of the Indigenous population have been generated (low and high series). The projection comes from the 2001 Census, however, as the low and high projections are higher than the actual 2006 Census measure and the low projection is closest to the actual at 2006, the low projection alone has been used in the expenditure per head calculation.

Expenditure data are presented on both a CASH and ACCRUAL accounting basis and the two sets of data are not comparable.

(a) The per capita figures have been calculated by dividing the financial year expenditure by the estimated/projected population at the beginning of each financial year.

(b) Real figures have been converted to 2007-08 dollars using the Implicit Price Deflator for Non-Farm GDP.

Data source: Adapted from John Gardiner-Garden, 2008. Commonwealth Indigenous-specific Expenditure 1968–2008. Parliamentary Library Research Paper no.10.

Detailed studies of single-portfolio areas need to be conducted to produce meaningful per capita expenditure figures. An example of such a study is the report on health expenditure which shows that, from 1995-96 until 2004-05, there has been little change in the per person health expenditure ratio for Indigenous compared to non-Indigenous Australians. In 2004-05, $1.17 per person was spent on Aboriginal and Torres Strait Islander health for every $1.00 spent on the health of non-Indigenous Australians. Average total health expenditure per Aboriginal and Torres Strait Islander was $4,718 compared with $4,019 per person estimated for non-Indigenous Australians. Total health expenditures for Aboriginal and Torres Strait Islander peoples were estimated at $2,304 million in 2004-05, or 2.8 per cent of national expenditures on health services, the same proportion as for 2001-02.[92]

Expenditure figures grossly understate levels of expenditure on those in need. More than 300,000 Aborigines are in the labour force, working and living in capital cities and country towns. They are unlikely to require assistance above and beyond that required by other Australians. About 200,000 Aborigines are dependent on welfare. The majority of these, 130,000, live in cities and country towns. Only about 70,000 live in remote areas. Of these, perhaps 10,000 live on small outstations.[93] The expenditure shown in Figure 5 should therefore be read as being spent on a far smaller population than the entire population of those who identify as having Aboriginal origins. The truth is the most rapidly growing part of Aboriginal society is that part which does not need help – those who live in cities but wish to identify with a long distant ancestry. Those who are soaking up the massive increases in taxpayer support are a small minority of a small minority. It is these remote areas in the main where some Aborigines live in ways not acceptable in a civilised society.

---

92 Deeble, J., Agar J. S. & Goss, J. 2008. 'Expenditures on Health for Aboriginal and Torres Strait Islander Peoples 2004-05.' *Australian Institute of Health and Welfare*, p. x.
93 ABS, 2008a.

Governance obsession

Money alone has not fuelled the resurgence in Aboriginal identity. A fundamental element of self-determination has been to funnel public moneys through Aboriginal organisations. There has been a large growth in 'community organisations', so much so that one observer noted, 'One might be forgiven for concluding that the main activity on Mornington is getting elected to committees, attending meetings, discovering what has occurred at meetings and how it affects oneself.'[94] The comment is common to many if not all Aboriginal communities; life is lived through politics because most incomes are transfers, not earned as part of a productive enterprise. Public servants and meetings is all Aboriginal people know. It is a false and unproductive world. When the organisations fail their people it is said to be a crisis of governance. Some have argued that 'Indigenous communities in Australia are in crisis and it is increasingly recognised that this is a crisis of governance'.[95] Fundamental issues of individual bad behaviour, not wanting to work and violent behaviour are transported into another realm; they are deemed to be problems of governance. The governance problem has spawned an entire industry[96] to solve the 'unique' aspects of Aboriginal governance, both at the level of the local association and corporation, and at a broad political level. Aboriginal governance is, indeed, a problem, but only because governments continue to play to two entirely contradictory tendencies, democratic accountability and traditional authority. Aboriginal organisations based on a broad

---

94 McKnight, 2002, p. 133.
95 Sullivan, P. 2007. 'Indigenous Governance: The Harvard Project, Australian Aboriginal Organisations and Cultural Subsidiarity.' *Desert Knowledge CRC Working Paper* No. 4, p. 1.
96 McCallum, D. 2005. 'Law and governance in Australian Aboriginal communities: liberal and neo-liberal political reason.' *The International Journal of Children's Rights* Vol 13. Sullivan, I., Hunt, J. and D. Smith, 2007. 'Indigenous community governance project: Year Two Research Findings.' *Centre for Aboriginal Economic Policy Research Working Paper* No. 36/2007.

representation of the community are bound to cross traditional lines of authority.

> Having neutered the traditional Aboriginal authority structure through its form of land rights, the government has further compounded the problem facing Aboriginal authorities by forcing Aboriginal 'communities' to incorporate themselves under Australian laws in order to qualify for government assistance. This has made it possible for people without legitimate authority – in Aboriginal eyes – to take on positions of authority in Aboriginal 'communities'. These people, because they are not encompassed in the traditional authority structure, do not consider themselves accountable to the Aboriginal leaders or the Aboriginal people, nor are the leaders or the people able to hold them accountable. Consequently they act very much as a law unto themselves, and the government for fear of being accused of acting paternalistically, and interfering in Aboriginal self-determination, don't hold them accountable either. The results can be seen in the breakdown of law and order – a situation bordering on anarchy in many Aboriginal 'communities', the misuse of funds, and the destruction of housing and other infrastructure on Aboriginal settlements.[97]

Governments have to make contact with legitimate Aboriginal leaders if they genuinely desire to hear what the more traditional Aborigines have to say. Traditional governance, however, is confined to very small family and clan groups. Because government programs dispense money on a larger scale, for example, for a community school, or as of right to individuals, traditional lines of authority are undermined. There is not much to be gained in upholding traditional authority when it offends the principles of equity in the entitlements of communities and individuals to public goods. New forms of governance, if devised, presumably must comply with democratic

---

97 Albrecht, 2008, p. 51.

principles, which also undermine traditional authority. This problem is unsolvable until the community has resolved the power struggle within.

> The councillors are all Aborigines but there is still [1999] deference to White people, at least to those who have authority. They shy away from making decisions ... This reluctance to make a decision is a traditional feature of the Mornington Islanders and indeed of many hunting-gathering peoples who ... prefer to leave matters in the hope that something will turn up and that problems will solve themselves ... Making decisions can cause controversy and fragment the group; consequently people prefer to talk about matters without coming to an irrevocable decision.[98]
> In Western forms of institutionalized democracy, individuals are expected to look after their own interests by voting, following the issues and openly criticizing wrong ... decisions. Aborigines, however, were used to looking out for others (their own kinsmen) and not openly criticizing people for this could lead to fights. They see nothing wrong with nepotism. To them it is a splendid concept which they vigorously and unashamedly practice. In brief, our forms of democracy depend on a kind of institutionalized individualism which was unknown among the Mornington Islanders.[99]

McKnight argues that the Mornington Island Shire was unable to work in this context. He regarded it as a sham democracy which had created much tension and conflict. He believed that the Shire was the ultimate cause of the Mornington Islanders despair. This is unlikely. There would, however, be less conflict if fewer people relied on collective decisions, that is, if people generated their own incomes. Once again the anthropologist has little idea of economy,

---

98 McKnight, 2002, p. 111.
99 McKnight, 2002, p. 184.

and a poorly conceived idea of democracy. The liberal democracy and the market economy rely on the individual but also the need to gather in groups for different purposes. Those groups are, however, fluid and responsive to myriad events, not the one small group for all purposes and for all time.

At the national political level, the experience has been bruising. Lowitja O'Donoghue, former chair of the Aboriginal and Torres Strait Islander Commission (ATSIC), has been reported as saying, 'it is male leaders were preoccupied with drinking, gambling and womanising.'[100] In 2009, having learned from the earlier ATSIC experience, the Human Rights and Equal Opportunity Commission, with Mick Dodson as a special adviser, suggested a model for an Indigenous congress.[101] Curiously, the congress is a chamber of peak associations. It is not a directly elected chamber as was the case with ATSIC. The puzzle of the model and the Rudd Government's entertainment of it is, why the retreat from democracy? Aborigines established their own representative bodies – William Cooper's Australian Aborigines League in 1936 and the Federal Council for Aboriginal Advancement in 1958 – a long time ago. They barely had a penny, but they had integrity which stemmed from membership. HREOC has now retreated from a membership-based democracy to a college of trusted service providers and lobbyists. This is a triumph for what is often called the 'industry' and a sure illustration that Aboriginal politics has always been about the 'industry' and its rewards, rather than some broader project to emancipate Aborigines.

HREOC has proposed a permanent National Representative Body established as a private company limited by guarantee, 'free from government influence/control'.[102] To achieve this, it asks for

---

100 *The Australian*, 12 March 2009.
101 Australian Human Rights Commission, 2009. *Our Future in Our Hands: Creating a Sustainable National Representative Body for Aboriginal and Torres Strait Islander Peoples.*
102 AHRC, 2009, p. 22.

$250 million of government funding. What would William Cooper, sitting at his kitchen table in Footscray, make of it? The National Representative Body would comprise a National Executive, a National Congress, an Ethics Council, and an Administrative/Executive Support Unit. National Congress would consist of 128 delegates with voting rights, drawn from 3 chambers, 40 from national peak bodies, 40 from sectoral bodies, researchers and experts, and 40 selected on merit and appointed by the National Executive.

This is an extraordinary collection. It is a self-appointed policy elite unconstrained by the common sense of the Aboriginal people who have no voting rights. It also incorporates a very cunning start-up phase. The HREOC Steering Committee, consisting of Aboriginal politicians Mick Dodson and Lowitja O'Donoghue and a handful of HREOC acolytes who advocate a treaty 'between Australia's First Peoples and the Australian Government',[103] will have their term extended to coincide with the commencement of the Co-Chairs of the Body. In other words, the Indigenous Congress will be an oligarchy, carefully vetted for their credentials. This is all about maintaining the old infrastructure of self-determination.

The model is a confirmation that, in HREOC eyes, Aboriginal society is no more than a collection of government-funded associations — land councils and service providers. Increasingly, however, the rationale of the service providers has shifted and they are under pressure to compete with mainstream providers. Many, having started as political associations, are now running a business, albeit in the welfare sector. The HREOC model is seriously flawed. Either this is a peak bodies' forum or it is a representative body. If it is a peak bodies' forum, it should fund itself; if it is a representative body, it must allow for direct election of delegates. Where is the vote for Aborigines, or members who want to join? The HREOC proposal is fundamentally pessimistic about giving Aboriginal people the freedom to determine

---

103 AHRC, 2009, p. 38.

their own voice. A people that does not trust itself to vote is a people doomed.

The Labor, Liberal and National parties are undeniably propped up by public financial support, and are governed by a professional cadre. They, by contrast, maintain the essence of association: election of office-bearers by the membership; and payment of joining and annual fees. In the HREOC consultation (does it ever stop?) Aborigines rejected the idea of paying a membership fee: 'the majority of participants did not see these options as important in funding the representative body.' Instead, they opted for 'a future fund financed through a percentage of mining tax.'[104] The point is simply not understood; integrity must be demonstrated by joining. Political parties present candidates for public office to the electors. HREOC wants public funding without the elections. A public fund for the machinery of the Aboriginal 'party' is not acceptable. Moreover, the Aboriginal elite lacks confidence not only in their people, but in themselves.

The Commonwealth minister has said that the Government is prepared to provide 'modest and appropriate recurrent funding for the body'[105] benchmarked against funds provided to similar autonomous, peak representative bodies. A small secretariat for a pan-Aboriginal advocacy organisation should be the absolute limit. Any pretence to be anything else must require election at large. The arrogance of the HREOC submission is breathtaking. William Cooper would be embarrassed.

Beyond political representation is the power of the disbursement of public funds through Aboriginal associations. The major bodies in Aboriginal politics register as Aboriginal corporations under the *Corporations (Aboriginal and Torres Strait Islander) Act 2006* (Cth) (CATSI

---

104 AHRC, 2009, p. 47.
105 Macklin, J. 2009. 'National Representative Body for Indigenous Australians.' Press release. 27 August 2009.

Act).[106] Although many Aboriginal associations are called corporations, they actually operate to collect and disburse public funds. Sometimes they operate in lieu of local government (but without a taxation base). As a result, much Aboriginal life is consumed by Aboriginal corporations and too many Aboriginal incomes are dependent on preferment from their leaders.

There was considerable growth in Aboriginal corporations in the 1990s. It reached a peak in 1997-1998 (see figure 6), overlapping the period of high morality which derived from the inquiries into *Deaths in Custody* and *The Stolen Generations*. Corporate functions range from providing services such as health care and power supply to holding land; many corporations have multiple functions. Fifty five per cent of Australia's 2,500 Aboriginal corporations[107] are located in remote and very remote areas although only one-third of Aborigines live in these regions. The major purpose of most corporations is to 'achieve and spend grants of money from the State and Commonwealth Governments and from any other sources.[108] Their purposes may be completely at odds with a commercial orientation; for example, their purpose may be to 'maintain and renew Aboriginal traditional culture,[109] or 'to help and encourage Aboriginal people ... to maintain, restore, revitalize and renew their traditional language and culture.'[110]

---

106 Aboriginal associations can register as associations and cooperatives or they can register under the Australian Securities and Investment Commission (ASIC).
107 Office of the Registrar of Indigenous Corporations (ORIC).
108 ORIC. *Yamatji Marlpa Aboriginal Corporation Rule Book 2009* and *Southern Aboriginal Corporation Rule Book 2009*.
109 ORIC. *Yamatji Marlpa Aboriginal Corporation Rule Book 2009*.
110 ORIC, *Southern Aboriginal Corporation, Rule Book 2009*.

Figure 6: Registered corporations by year, 1989-90 to 2007-08

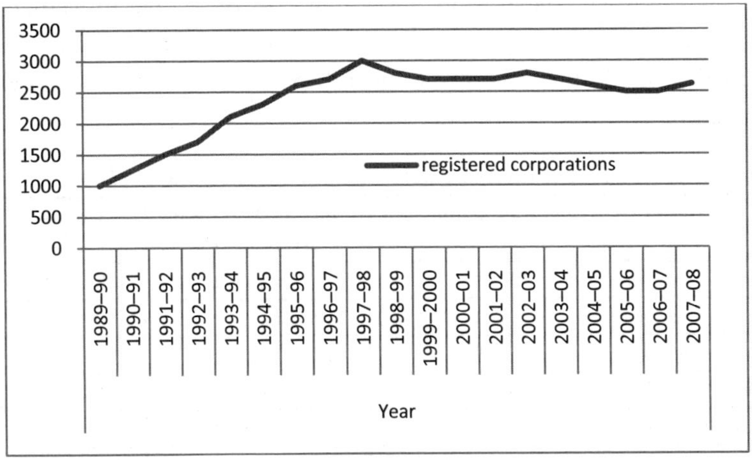

[Chart showing registered corporations rising from ~1000 in 1989-90 to ~3000 by 1997-98, then leveling off around 2700-2900 through 2007-08]

Data source: Office of the Registrar of Indigenous Corporations, FaHCSIA *Annual Report* 2007-2008, part 2.

Some groups registered under the CATSI Act generate substantial private income, corporations linked to mining compensation or to the Aboriginal arts industry. Many hold significant community assets that were funded publicly and are now held privately by the corporations. Much of the 'earned' income of the Aboriginal corporations is derived, however, from using Community Development Employment Projects (CDEP) labour. As shown in Table 2, Bawinanga is based in Maningrida in East Arnhem Land and runs CDEP together with many other functions. As of June 2008, it had an income of $30.5 million, of which $12.7 million were derived from grants. The number of employees at the end of the financial year was 625, mostly CDEP employees.[111] More concretely, CDEP labour is used in most of the activities; thus the corporation not only receives a third of its income through grants, it is subsidised by the use of CDEP labour. Julalikari Council (Tennant Creek, NT) incorporates CDEP and

111 ORIC, *General Report June 2008*.

various community and municipal functions. It has 69 vehicles, mainly four-wheel-drives, sedans and buses that are for people movement excluding tippers and graders of which there are less than 10. The council owns 26 properties.[112] Only 178 persons are on the register of members.[113]

Table 2: Top 10 corporations by income and assets during 2005–06

Aboriginal Corporation name	Income & assets	Rank	Grants
Bawinanga (Maningrida NT)	$40.3 million	1	$11.7 million
Julalikari Council (Tennant Creek NT)	$23 million	2	$11.0 million
Kaarta-Moorda (Cannington WA)	$20 million	3	$13.5 million
Marra Worra Worra (Fitzroy Crossing WA)	$20 million	4	$12.8 million
Bungala (APY Lands SA)	$20 million	5	$10.0 million*
Kurra (Kiwirrkurra via Alice Springs NT)	$19 million	6	Not available
Anangu Pitjantjatjara Services (APY Lands SA)	$16 million	7	$10.0 million*
Yamatji Marlpa (Pilbara WA)	$16 million	8	$15.3 million#
Southern (Albany WA)	$4.5 million^	9	$3.7 million^
Derby Aboriginal Health Service Council (Derby WA)	$16 million	10	$ 4.0 million*

Note: *2007. # includes native title services. ^2008, land and building assets worth $32 million.
Data source: Office of the Registrar of Indigenous Corporations.

Bungala, which operates on APY Lands South Australia, has a total income at June 2008 of $17.5 million; $15 million is from grants.[114] The main activities are listed as municipal services, construction, employment training and land management. In essence, CDEP pays and trains the labour which is used to collect rubbish in the communities. Elsewhere, ratepayers would pay rates; the service would be provided commercially. This basic service 'soaks

---
112 ORIC, *Audit Report 2006-07*.
113 ORIC, List *of Names and Addresses of Members 2005-06*.
114 ORIC, *General Report June 30 2008*.

up' most of the labour on the lands and has done so for more than 30 years. Bungala is separate from the Anangu Pitjantjatjara Services Aboriginal Corporation (AP Services), established in 1993, which is under special administration, appointed on 16 February 2009 to help AP Services 'with its money story and other problems.'[115] The corporation provides services and infrastructure on the lands which includes essential municipal services such as water and power supply, drilling and bore maintenance, collection of rubbish, construction and maintenance of sewerage systems, roads, aerodromes and other infrastructure. Notwithstanding great hopes for self-determination with the passing of the *Anangu Pitjantjatjara Yankunytjatjara Land Rights Act 1981* (SA),[116] things have not turned out well.

Land councils are perhaps the greatest part of the governance obsession in Aboriginal collective life. The role and functions of land councils are set out in Section 23(1) of the *Land Rights Act*. They include:

- To find out and express the wishes of Aboriginal people about the management of their land and legislation about their land.
- To negotiate on behalf of Traditional Owners with people interested in using Aboriginal land or land under claim.
- To assist Aboriginal people to carry out commercial activities.

Essentially land councils are paid to talk; for example, 'ascertaining the views of Aboriginal people is the core work of the Northern Land Council; [in 2007-08] 1,404 consultations were held, with 825 of these in remote locations ... not including 73 community forums.'[117] The NLC is a $24 million a year business, primarily funded through

---

115 ORIC, *Newsletter February 2009*, Issue 1.
116 Morley, R. 2005. 'The Pitjanjatjara Land Rights Amendment Act: Addressing Governance on APY Lands.' *Indigenous Law Bulletin* 6(15), p. 10.
117 Northern Land Council, 2008. *Annual Report 2007-2008*.

the Aboriginal Benefits Account[118] to undertake the above functions. In addition to its core ABA financing, the NLC receives a number of separate grants; the most important is its native title grant. $15 million came from Indigenous Land Use Agreements in 2007-2008 (distributed to traditional Aboriginal owners and related Aboriginal associations).

It also 'brokers' public funds in make-work activities such as Aboriginal ranger programs, which employ 400 locals. These funds are a variation of the CDEP program, under the Caring for Country program, for instance. Although it claims that 'commercial assistance is a key strategic focus of the NLC', it fails to attract any that would not otherwise occur, such as the Telstra Fibre Optic cable and the Bonaparte Gulf pipeline. It complains that 'government investment continues to be disappointing.' Under the lease agreement, 2500 people making up 19 land owning groups will share in around $10 million during the term of the lease between the traditional landowners and the owners of the Bonaparte Gas Pipeline.

The Australian Government has approached the Northern Land Council with a proposal that they establish an education trust fund. Elsewhere, in the past, such monies have been used for immediate and often wasteful consumption. The proposal is that, if the land-owners establish an education trust fund for children throughout the region and allocate at least 90 per cent of the projected benefits to the trust fund, the Australian Government will match them dollar for dollar up to a maximum of $10 million. There are precedents for this in the NT, with recent agreements between Newmont Asia-Pacific and Warlpiri traditional owners establishing a series of programs under an education trust.[119]

While the rise and consolidation of these corporations occurred prior to the Howard years, there was only a slow movement in the

---

118 Aboriginals Benefit Account, *Annual Reports*.
119 Hon Jenny Macklin, 2008. Press release 20 June 2008,

Howard Governments to address the risks inherent in a model of community that essentially had a single locally-beholden entity disbursing public monies. These monies were disbursed, sometimes on a grace and favour basis, and, as importantly, prevented communities from adjusting to economic opportunities beyond the confines of the corporation. Although the decision to mainstream service provision has placed these services under some competitive pressure, much of the architecture of the Aboriginal 'industry' has been left untouched.

Mainstreaming and contestability have been key themes in recent years.

> Although Indigenous specific services are necessary in some circumstances, their primary purpose is to complement rather than replace the mainstream.
>
> The Australian Government is keen to ensure the best services are available for all Indigenous Australians regardless of who is providing the service.[120]

A more sensible approach is to ensure that Aboriginal communities are governed in the same way as other communities, that is, on a wider constituency basis and only where matters are decided at arm's length. Local collective agreements are poison in any community. Community resources are best handled by public officials or by politicians literally and figuratively at a distance from the point of delivery.

The final guideline relates to race-based legislation. Because of the divisive nature of this legislation and its dubious benefits, all legislation based on race should be phased out. Aboriginal social disadvantage and needs should be addressed through legislation currently used to meet social disadvantage and needs in the Australian community generally. Apart from the government ceasing to collect a special royalty on minerals and gas extracted from Aboriginal land – much of which is then paid to the land councils in the Northern Territory

---

[120] Australian Government, 2007. *Secretaries' Group on Indigenous Affairs Annual Report 2005-06*, pp. 1,2.

and used by them to further their political agenda, and not to alleviate Aboriginal disadvantage – such a shift would have minimal impact on the welfare of the more traditional Aborigines. Aboriginal land in the Northern Territory, presently held by land trusts and administered by land councils, should, wherever traditional title and owners can be identified, be returned to the traditional owners, who should then be granted freehold title under the same conditions as other Australians. Similar arrangements should apply in the states that have granted land to Aborigines through land trusts.

3

Defensibility of Aboriginal culture

Writing in the early 1980s, Ken Maddock remarked that 'the persistent talk of human rights in connection with traditional Aboriginal societies shows that they are being judged and that the quality of life they provide for their members is seen as relevant to the making of policy. This raises the question of the defensibility, in modern times, of these societies.'[121] Aboriginal culture is a matter for public debate and scrutiny because some Aboriginal elders and, following their lead, recent government inquiries[122] into child sexual abuse, having found bad behaviour among Aborigines, make a leap to the refuge of 'culture' to solve the problem. Those who argue for a return to culture as a remedy for present strife must therefore defend the practices they seek to invoke. Unfortunately, the practices, which make up fundamental elements of Aboriginal culture, do not make a pretty picture.

---

121 Maddock, K. 1982. *The Australian Aborigines: A Portrait of Their Society*. Penguin. Second edition, p. 162.
122 These are discussed in the following chapter.

If one suspends reality for a short while, it is possible to understand the appeal that Aboriginal society, at a safe distance, has for egalitarians. There is a certain romance in each being equally poor.

> There were no materially rich and poor in Aboriginal society. This common economic standard, enforced and maintained by the clan, had the effect of 'playing down' the already minimum degree of stratification, and producing something of an egalitarian society.[123]

In a modern context, and in combination with alcohol, such egalitarianism is very destructive:

> the emphasis on egalitarianism fits well with an activity which in the end makes everyone broke and no one can hold his or her head up higher than other people ... There is always, but always, pressure to pull people down and nothing does that quicker than alcohol ... 'Well, he drinks too. He is no better than anybody else.'[124]

It is possible to understand the appeal of the Aborigine to the mystic in us. According to Wade Davis in 'Sacred Geography', in the Canadian Massey lecture series, 'the other cultures of the world are not failed attempts to be modern, failed attempts to be us. Each is a unique and profound answer to a fundamental question: What does it mean to be human and alive?'[125] When waxing lyrical about the 'genius' of Aboriginal society he readily admits that 'the Aboriginal people were never touched by the desire to improve the world' and that 'the purpose of humanity [in the Aboriginal world] is not to improve anything ... [but] to sustain the Garden of Eden'. This is a profoundly nihilistic approach to life. Aborigines were wiped out

---

123 Albrecht, 2008, p. 64.
124 McKnight, 2002, p. 199.
125 Davis, W. 2010. 'The Wayfinders: why ancient wisdom matters in the modern world.' *Massey lectures*. Canadian Broadcasting Corporation.

by nature at various times and places, the environment was not benign, and Aborigines did their best, as poor as it was, to alter the environment by hunting the macropods to death[126] and burning as much as a third of Australia's forests,[127] altering for all time the Garden of Eden. There is an honesty in Davis's mysticism, mysticism that he can well afford as he travels the world as a correspondent for *National Geographic*, filling the glossy magazine with pictures of a world imagined by wealthy modern people. Yet his mysticism and fascination with the Garden of Eden misunderstands the skills and tensions of traditional Aborigines and condemns contemporary Aborigines to poverty.

It is important to understand the true relationship between Aborigines and environment. Peter Latz has drawn attention to the use Aborigines made of fire in the 'care' of their land including how their use of fire may have turned the centre of Australia into a desert. Fire, too, was an important aid in hunting, even if it was rarely used to kill the animal directly.[128] Geoffrey Blainey has noted that fire dominated the life of the Aborigines to an even greater degree than the motor-engine dominates western nations today. Fire, too, had its unintended consequences. In Australia, every day for millions of days, countless fires had been lit or enlarged for countless purposes. Many of those fires had unintended effects: 'In the Warburton Ranges of Western Australia five aboriginal boys were seen using firesticks to hound wild cats from the grass and scrub, and during the course of the afternoon they caught three large cats. In the opinion of Richard

---

126 Roberts R. G. and B. W. Brook, 2010. 'Paleontology: And Then There Were None?' *Science* 22 Vol. 327. No. 5964, page 420. Flannery, T., Kendall, P. and K. Wynn-Moylan.1990. *Australia's Vanishing Mammals: Endangered and Extinct Native Species*. RD Press.
127 Jones, R. 1969. 'Fire-stick Farming.' *Australian Natural History*, (16)7, p. 224.
128 Latz, P. 1995. *Bushfires and Bushtucker: Aboriginal People and Plant use in Central Australia*. IAD Press, 29. See also Latz, P. 2007. *The Flaming Desert: Arid Australia: a Fire Shaped Landscape*. Alice Springs.

Gould, an anthropologist who watched, the cost of that catch was the burning of nine square miles of country ... There can have been few if any races who for so long were able to practise the delights of incendiarism.'[129]

The Commonwealth Government's Caring for Country program is based on a similar misconception of Aboriginal environmentalism. The Aboriginal concept of caring for country is not related to environmental concerns. Inasmuch as Aborigines cared for country, it could better be summarised as guarding the sites of significance and caring for sacred objects. For Aborigines, land care did not encompass care for the environment, as we understand the term. They had no concerns about denuding scrubland, polluting the environment or anything of the kind. The primitive state of their technology (such as stone axes), and the peripatetic nature of their existence, frequent moves from one site to another, meant they did not evolve any rules regarding appropriate land care as this is understood today. This has become glaringly obvious when Aborigines live in one location and have access to modern technology. 'They are often very destructive of the environment, denuding and fouling the immediate environs of their camping/township areas'.[130]

The wide appeal of Aboriginal culture displayed in Aboriginal art, the most famous being the dot paintings from the western desert, is also understandable. These works are very attractive. The genesis of western desert art, however, gives cause to think again. One of the leading lights in western desert art, Clifford Possum, studied with Albert Namatjira at Hermannsburg. He then moved to Papunya to take on construction work when the Aboriginal settlement was established in the late 1950s. For a time Possum taught at the school at Papunya and worked as a stockman. Less well known is that in 1971, a 30 year old white artist and elementary school teacher, Geoffrey Bardon, encouraged the local men to paint. Previously, Aboriginal

---

129 Blainey, 1983, p. 76.
130 Albrecht, 2008, p. 53.

art had consisted of body painting and drawing in the sand. The art inspired by Bardon was a departure from these origins. Most important is Bardon's observation at Papunya which suggests art was a good therapy as much as an expression of culture.

> There were vicious fights among the various tribal groups, and the enforced stay and the attendant idleness at the camps and the absence of game nearby were only the beginning of the terrible enemy of all the people: drunkenness ... Alcohol which could rage through the camps like a fire, day and night, and seemed to incite men and women to a particularly terrifying violence.[131]

The egalitarianism, the oneness with nature and spirituality and the art, much changed by the whiteman, are all desires that the whiteman has for Aborigines. These attributes are always idealised. They mask the real life of the Aborigine which was and remains mired in violence. Violence is central to and pervasive in Aboriginal life, and yet it is usually excused by those who desire to build a new life around culture. Those who care about the future of Aboriginal people need to revisit some unpleasant truths about Aboriginal culture. Those charged with assisting Aboriginal people too frequently want to hide from real debate, preferring to cover up, suggesting that media attention on violence in Aboriginal communities has 'damaged the cause of reconciliation'.[132] How the truth can harm the cause of reconciliation is a mystery. What will become clear in this chapter is that the policy path that praises Aboriginal culture without qualification is a bleak and morally bankrupt dead end.

---

131 Bardon, 2004, p. 8.
132 Reconciliation Australia, 2006. *Annual Report 2005-06*, 8.

Explanations of violence in Aboriginal society

Apart from a brief period under missionaries, Aboriginal society is and remains violent. Much of it centres on male control over women for sex, and which dispenses all too readily with babies and the aged in a constant and desperate struggle for survival against nature or, in better endowed areas, from usurpers. In traditional Aboriginal society women were 'given a proper good hiding'[133] when it suited men; abortion and infanticide were widespread. Indeed, nomadic people had no alternative but to kill surplus babies. At the other end of life, the elderly were simply abandoned when they became too old or sick to move camp.[134] The tragedy of current policy-makers is that historic violence is denied and recent violence excused by blaming the whiteman, as if that were a remedy. Regardless of how strong the link is between present violence and historic violence, a theme taken up explicitly by Stephanie Jarrett,[135] Aboriginal culture with its attendant violence is a significant barrier to Aboriginal success in the modern world. The policy path that advocates a return to Aboriginal culture not only points to the path of collective bad behaviour, it condones violent and abhorrent practices that block the path to adaptation.

Violence in contemporary Aboriginal society is well-recorded. 70 per cent of Aboriginal women in custody in NSW are victims of child sexual assault.[136] Aboriginal communities living in rural and remote areas are 45 times more likely to be victims of domestic violence than

---

[133] McKnight, 2002, p. 121.
[134] Blainey, 1983, p. 97.
[135] Jarrett, S. *Aboriginal Violence*. forthcoming 2011.
[136] This study surveyed 45 per cent of all Aboriginal women in prison in NSW over a period of a week, quoted in Aboriginal Child Sexual Assault Taskforce, 2006. *Breaking the Silence: Creating the Future. Addressing Child Sexual Assault in Aboriginal Communities in NSW*, New South Wales Government, p. 39.

non-Aboriginals.[137] Women from the NPY region in Central Australia are 67 times more likely than others to be victims of domestic violence related homicide.[138] Indigenous females and males are, 35 and 22 times respectively, as likely to be hospitalised due to family violence-related assaults as other Australian females and males.[139] The Australian Institute of Health and Welfare report, *Family Violence Among Aboriginal and Torres Strait Islander Peoples*, draws on data from the 2002 National Aboriginal and Torres Strait Islander Social Survey in which approximately 9,400 Indigenous Australians aged 15 years and older participated. A number of different questions were asked and, to some extent, the answers suggest some inconsistencies in the meaning attached to the questions.

Nevertheless, about one in four Aboriginal or Torres Strait Islander people aged 15 years or older reported being *a victim of physical or threatened violence in the twelve months* before the survey. Although the rates were similar among those living in major cities (25 per cent) and in remote areas (23 per cent), people in remote areas were much more likely to report that family violence was a *neighbourhood problem* (41 per cent compared with 14 per cent in non-remote areas).[140] Moreover, although approximately 16 per cent of Indigenous people reported that they, their family or friends had *witnessed violence in the past 12 months*, the proportion in remote areas who reported that they, their family or friends, had witnessed violence (30 per cent) was three times as high as for Indigenous people in non-remote areas (10 per

---

137 Gordon, S., Hallahan, K. and D. Henry, 2002. *Putting the Picture Together, Inquiry into Response by Government Agencies to Complaints of Family Violence and Child Abuse in Aboriginal Communities*, Department of Premier and Cabinet, Western Australia, p. 424.
138 Lloyd, J.2008. 'Domestic Violence Related Homicide Cases in Central Australia.' *International Conference on Homicide: Domestic Related Homicide*. Australian Institute of Criminology.
139 Australian Institute of Health and Welfare, 2006. *Family Violence among Aboriginal and Torres Strait Islander Peoples*, p. x.
140 AIHW, 2007. *Family Violence among Aboriginal and Torres Strait Islander Peoples*, p. 9.

cent). Further, in remote areas, 17 per cent of Indigenous people reported that abuse or violent crime was *a problem for them*, their family or close friends in the past 12 months, compared with nine per cent of Indigenous people in non-remote areas.[141] There is a real suspicion that the *victim* statistics belie the *neighborhood problem*, *witnessing* and *problem for them* formulations. The report indicated that there may still be considerable under-reporting of sexual violence and child abuse in surveys because of the associated shame,[142] which may help to explain the willingness to answer a disembodied question but a reluctance to answer a question concerning violence to the person.

The figures are extraordinarily bad, very well known and, unfortunately, enduring. The most disappointing aspect of Aboriginal violence is that its existence in traditional Aboriginal society is denied. One such example comes from Mick Dodson:

> We have no cultural traditions based on humiliation, degradation and violation ... Most of the violence, if not all, that Aboriginal communities are experiencing today are not part of Aboriginal tradition or culture.
>
> Physical punishment is not unknown in Aboriginal culture as it is in other cultures. However, in Aboriginal culture it was highly regulated and governed. Carried out by and witnessed by people with particular relationships with the perpetrator and the victim.
>
> The violence occurring in Aboriginal communities today is not part of Aboriginal tradition or culture. It is occurring principally because of the marginalisation of Aboriginal people, the economic and welfare dependency, continuing high levels of unemployment, the dissolution of our culture and tradition

---

141 AIHW, 2007, p. 43.
142 AIHW, 2007, p. 112.

and the breakdown of societal and community values.[143]

No anthropologist would agree with Dodson that traditional Aboriginal society was not violent, yet his remarks were allowed to pass without comment or demur. The usual accomplices at the Australian Broadcasting Corporation were happy to let Dodson promote the notion of Aboriginal benevolence. It may be that there has been deterioration since the coming of the whiteman but, on the evidence of many observers, the situation has always been bad. McKnight has written that:

> It was quite noticeable in the early years of my fieldwork that none of the older women had scars on their face or had been disfigured although they were active participants in the fights. True, in the pre-mission period women were occasionally killed, usually for adultery. A few women suffered permanent injury from broken limbs ... but the incidence and the degree of violence towards women were much less than nowadays.[144]

Dodson is not alone in seeking to lay blame for Aboriginal violence on factors beyond Aboriginal culture. Memmott's 2001 review of studies of Aboriginal violence repeats his earlier explanations of violence in the material submitted to the Deaths in Custody Inquiry,[145] with a heavy emphasis on colonial expansion and the later control period of mission stations. No mention is made of Aboriginal culture, other than to highlight the diminished authority of elders. The report uses violence statistics to reinforce the view that rates of violence are higher in discrete Aboriginal communities, especially mission settlements, where it is assumed that 'repression'

---

143 Dodson, M.2003. 'Violence, Dysfunction, Aboriginality.' *Address to the National Press Club*, 11 June.
144 McKnight, 2002, p. 121.
145 Memmott, P., Stacy, R., Chambers, C. and C. Keys, 2001. *Violence in Indigenous Communities*. Report to Crime Prevention Branch of the Attorney-General's Department, p. 12.

by the whiteman was greatest, in contrast to the south-east corner of Queensland. Nothing is said in explanation of the lower levels of violence in south-east Queensland. The data is consistent with the theory that the latter are integrated – they no longer live as traditional Aborigines, that the culture is broken and that violence is not tolerated in the broad society. On the basis of the data, Memmott suggests that 'culture' should be reestablished. The data suggests the opposite conclusion.

To reach his unsubstantiated conclusion, Memmott relies on a study of violence in five Cape York communities where three important factors were identified as immediate causes of violence: jealousy, payments of debts, and payback. Each of these factors is given a 'modern' interpretation, but each has explicit cultural origins. More important, nowhere is it acknowledged that jealousy and payback are frowned upon in all civilised societies.

The mindset that disables the modernist from passing judgment on the primitive may serve some bizarre egalitarian notion of rights, but the consequence of the disability is to condemn Aborigines to a violent existence. It also allows the researcher to remain above the fray and not condemn bad behaviour except by laying blame at the whiteman's feet. In the Cape York study, jealousy between males and females was the most common cause of violence. Memmott draws on the Robertson taskforce for an explanation of the violence. It states 'that relationships are one of the few commodities available to many Aboriginal people. The feared loss of a valued relationship is far more personally threatening in a context of ongoing poverty and deprivation than it is for an individual who has access to other opportunities for self-gratification and self-definition such as meaningful employment.'[146]

This confected excuse for bad behaviour is in grave error. Traditional Aboriginal society was shockingly poor and violent, with

---

146 Memmott et al, 2001, p. 22.

the apparent saving grace that violence was dealt with in traditional ways. An increase in material wealth and the collapse of the old rules removed controls on violence within the society. Poverty did not cause violence. More particularly, family violence and jealousy were intimate aspects of traditional Aboriginal society, in some ways controlled by the tradition of polygamy, in others fanned by polygamy, as when wives fought. Traditionally, the effect of polygamy was to lower the age at which women married for the first time (increasing the proportion of marriageable women) and to raise the age at which men married for the first time (reducing the proportion of marriageable men).[147] When these rules broke down, at the advent of the settler society and especially under the missionaries who forbade polygamy, jealousy knew no bounds. Advocates for return to Aboriginal culture surely cannot be advocating that Aborigines revert to polygamy to control violence between men and women? It is illegal, hardly desired by women and unlikely to lead to a breakout of peace.

Failure to repay a debt was also identified by Memmott as a cause of fighting and was portrayed as worse in Aboriginal communities where few people have any disposable income and most people are poor, needy and welfare-dependent. While debt and poverty may be bedfellows, violence does not always follow, and violence should never be condoned as a means of settling debts. Payback is a more likely explanation for debt-related violence. Payback is commonly associated with paying someone back for a grievous act. It is a deeply traditional aspect of Aboriginal society and can also apply to debts, as well as gambling itself.

> It may be that people gamble (and drink) with such abandonment because they have decided it is difficult to keep money for themselves when surrounded by importuning relatives ... Another motive for gambling is the opportunity to obtain money without being beholden to others, i.e. without the

---

[147] Maddock, 1982, p. 68.

obligation of a 'pay back'.[148]

Indeed, violent payback has been a feature of traditional societies and persists until a superior set of rules and procedures are established to prevent it. Unfortunately, 'culture' is an excuse to continue bad behaviour:

> There are now three kinds of violence in Aboriginal society – alcoholic violence, traditional violence, and bullshit traditional violence. Women are the victims of all three. By 'bullshit traditional violence' is meant the sort of assault on women which takes place today for illegitimate reasons, often by drunken men, which they then attempt to justify as a traditional right.[149]

Distinguishing causes of violence is important, but concentrating on recent apparent causes of violence and under-appreciating the wrongdoing is not the way to understand the problem or the path to solutions. Best to start at the beginning, then understand that appeals to tradition point in precisely the wrong direction. Failing to apply the law for whatever reason leaves Aboriginal men, in particular, in a position where they learn to get what they want through violence with impunity; failing to apply the law also condemns their victims.

Traditional violence

David McKnight, a British anthropologist who studied Mornington Island Aborigines with whom he had contact from 1966 to 1999, provides excellent guides to violence in Aboriginal society. He made eighteen field trips and lived with the islanders for more than five years in total. He knew them and the region around the Gulf of Carpentaria, Doomadgee and Burketown, and the literature on Australian Aborigines, well. McKnight divides the recent history into

---

148 McKnight, 2002, p. 75.
149 Bolger, A. 1991. *Aboriginal Women and Violence*. Australian National University, North Australian Research Unit, Darwin, NT, p. 50.

three periods: early contact; mission days; and canteen days. The first volume of relevance is *From Hunting to Drinking: the devastating effects of alcohol on an Australian Aboriginal community*.[150] The second, *Going the Whiteman's Way: kinship and marriage among Australian Aborigines*,[151] is concerned particularly with how the young people successfully defied the elders and married whom they pleased with the assistance of missionaries. The third volume, *Of Marriage, Violence and Sorcery: the quest for power in northern Queensland*,[152] explores the raw tools of political power in Aboriginal society, the power of men over women for sex. Three volumes of his work, supported by the observations of Pastor Albrecht of Hermannsburg and Tonkinson at Jigalong, serve as a factual base to understand the essential persistence of violence in Aboriginal society and the policy dead end that lies in invocation of culture.

McKnight makes clear that while the move from traditional society to the mission constituted a major disruption to Aboriginal society, as big a disruption was that between work in the cattle industry and the coming of welfare. The inability to adjust to new circumstances, not from ancient to new economy, but from one new economy to one non-economy, that is, welfare, is clearly a major factor in Aboriginal despair.

> Over the years the cattle industry became the most important industry in the Gulf area. The Aborigines were keen to work on the cattle stations where they could learn new skills, earn money and escape from missionary control. A gap developed between the generations. The older people on Mornington Island had once lived an independent hunting and gathering life. In contrast, most of the station working generation were raised

---

150 McKnight, 2002.
151 McKnight, D. 2004. *Going the Whiteman's Way: Kinship and Marriage among Australian Aborigines*. Aldershot.
152 McKnight, D. 2005. *Of Marriage, Violence and Sorcery: the Quest for Power in Northern Queensland*. Aldershot.

in the mission and spent much of their lives on the mainland employed as ringers.

In the early 1950s the dormitories were closed and the Mornington Islanders were once again responsible for raising their children, but by the mid-1960s this was causing some problems because they had never really learned to be effective parents while on the cattle stations.

In the mid-1960s Aborigines began to regain more control over their lives, at least in terms of European-Australian ideologically conditioned values (democracy, liberalism, individualism ...). It was no longer illegal for them to drink alcohol, but they were not allowed to bring alcohol into the missions and government settlements. Even this restriction was soon lifted, and in 1975-76 a beer canteen was built on Mornington. The heavy consumption of alcohol and the replacement of a mission by a Shire ... had devastating consequences. ... A considerable amount of government money was poured into the community and people soon discovered that it was no longer necessary to work in order to obtain money.

Since the advent of the canteen and Shire there has been much violence, rape, self-mutilation, homicide and suicide.[153]

McKnight's observations make plain that violence increased with the coming of alcohol and the breakdown of traditional constraints. He also makes it abundantly clear that violence at a level and of a type completely unacceptable in a modern, open and liberal society was condoned in traditional society. While grog is a problem, violence in Aboriginal ancient and modern society was and is present and acceptable. Remedies to Aboriginal violence are not about to be found in cutting out access to grog alone.

In 1966, fighting seemed to be the main social activity. There

---

153 McKnight, 2002, pp. 2-3.

were fights practically every day and on some days there were several.[154]

It seemed strange to me that there was so much fighting because the people were kind and compassionate with a rich sense of humour. Despite ... this, violence would suddenly occur and the very people who seemed kind and compassionate became dangerously aggressive and struck one another so harshly that they frequently had to receive treatment at the Mission hospital and sometimes the flying doctor had to take them to the Mount Isa hospital.[155]

In the early 1970s the Mornington Islanders became eligible for unemployment benefits and many people became disinclined to work (even if they could obtain employment) when they discovered they could obtain as much money for not working as they could for working. Some of this new money was used to purchase alcohol. By 1975 the situation had become so serious that the Mission board appointed a former army officer to stop the violence ...[156]

A striking change in 1977 was that in all the fights ... there was no talk about upholding the Law; indeed, there was no talk about upholding anything, for because of alcohol the fighting was irrational.[157]

During the period of extended [canteen] hours and unrestricted sales there was more drunken violence and a woman was brutally attacked, raped and murdered by a gang of youths.

Part of the problem is that the sexual mores had changed ... [T]here were cases of child abuse. It was no longer safe for a female child to be alone ... [A]nother indication of the

---

154 McKnight, 2005, p. 79.
155 McKnight, 2005, p. 79.
156 McKnight, 2005, p. 111.
157 McKnight, 2005, p. 126.

collapse of sexual mores are cases of incest which in the old days would, I am sure, have been punished by spearing one or both offenders.[158]

McKnight's and Tonkinson's most telling observations were on the treatment of Aboriginal women in Aboriginal society.

> In brief, this is a power struggle centring on marriage. (Was it ever otherwise among Australian Aborigines?) The struggle was between the Mission and the Mornington Islanders (particularly the elders), among the elders themselves, between the elders and young people, and among young people (particularly between classificatory brothers) in their competition for spouses. In the pre-Mission days men struggled not only to get married but to get as many wives as they could ... The struggle for wives was intense and resulted in killings not only by spearing but by sorcery.[159]
>
> There is no doubt ... that men traditionally claimed strong rights to the appropriation of female sexuality. These rights were sometimes exercised in cementing ties with, discharging debts to, or atoning for crimes against, other men.[160]
>
> In the end, the basis of all decisions is the relative lack or possession of naked power: in general, under the old rules men imposed controls on women's sexuality, and some men were able to control other men's sexuality. In the give and take of compromises, various rhetorics and justifications were used; these are the kinship and marriage 'systems.' However, behind them were the spear, the club, and sorcery ...[161]

The missionaries were successful not just because they

---

158 McKnight, 2002, p. 97.
159 McKnight, 2004, p. 222.
160 Tonkinson. R. 1990. 'The Changing Status of Aboriginal Women: Free Agents at Jigalong.' In Tonkinson, R. and M. Howard (eds)1990. *Going It Alone: Prospects for Aboriginal Autonomy*. Aboriginal Studies Press, p. 129.
161 McKnight, 2004, p. 226.

had power but because young men and women favoured the advantages of the new order and they found it expedient to shun the traditional rhetorical discourse and to manoeuvre the mission superintendent to speak on their behalf. The new order gave people an opportunity to avoid control by the elders and to marry who they pleased.[162]

Aboriginal housegirls [were] in a very different, and in some respects more favourable, position than in desert society. Being young they did not enjoy senior ritual status in their own society and if they were junior wives in a polygynous marriage, they were under the authority of both their older co-wives and their husbands. Traditionally, if wives aroused their husband's ire, no-one outside the family interposed in domestic contexts unless a woman was being seriously wounded ... In their new situation as valued workers and sexual partners of the European boss, housegirls could flee to the sanctuary of the homestead.[163]

Women frequently seek sexual liaisons with Whitemen and when they are successful they are able to live better than Aboriginal men, which surely must be galling to Aboriginal men even though they often get money and beer from their quasi-White brother-in-law or son-in-law.[164]

Despite his obvious regard for the Aborigines of Mornington Island, McKnight did not resile from matter-of-fact description of the shocking behaviour of Aboriginal men and boys.

It was decided that the older men would take delinquents to Forsyth Island for a couple of weeks and teach them to hunt and make handcrafts. It was a solution that had often been tried before but without success. The older men were concerned about how they would get their grog if they were in the bush

---

162 McKnight, 2002, p. 214.
163 Tonkinson, 1990, p. 129.
164 McKnight, 2002, p. 202.

with the delinquents.[165]

With some noticeable exceptions there seems to be very little genuine concern for anybody who is ill, because in their present state they are of little value. Drinking mates who have fallen on bad times are quickly forgotten. I have witnessed scenes of men weeping for the recent loss of a spouse and crying all the way up to the canteen to drown their sorrows.[166]

The topic of parental neglect is of particular importance. Older children may be ignored for years with their parents suddenly taking an interest in them when they are legally allowed to buy beer. Many children have had to be taken away from habitually drunken parents and given to the mother's sister ... or some other close relative.[167]

I mentioned that in 1977 many children were neglected. By 1985 the situation had become worse and many children were forced to fend for themselves. Children from the ages of 3 to 10 suffered in the competition for food with older siblings and were noticeably thin. But by the time they were about 10 they began to fill out more because they could fight back.[168]

[Men's] social role has been undermined and consequently they turn to drink and violence. The unsettling matter of land rights increases their uncertainty and insecurity and diminishes their authority and prestige. The women in turn are caught up in the money-getting world where traditional skills are not enough. They turn against their men who no longer have cultural authority over them but who often resort to physical force in an attempt to control or belittle them.[169]

---

165 McKnight, 2002, p. 101.
166 McKnight, 2002, p. 110.
167 McKnight, 2002, p. 131.
168 McKnight, 2002, p. 136.
169 McKnight, 2002, p. 202.

The essence of Aboriginal violence in the present is the loss of male control over women leaving the brittle male ego shattered.[170] Earlier attempts to integrate Aborigines into the wider economy met with some success particularly in the cattle industry, where Aboriginal men were employed as stockmen. As McKnight points out, Aborigines were hired because of the whiteman's stereotype that Aborigines were closer to nature, but at least the cattle industry and missions created a bridge from the hunter-gatherer economy to the market economy. Unfortunately, there are now few jobs available in the cattle industry and while, among current government programs, there are attempts to recreate the stockman era, these have met only with very modest success.[171] Too few Aborigines want to work as a result of three generations being paid to not work.

When employment in the cattle industry collapsed and the missionaries left, Aborigines fell back on the dole and on their old ways, this time without the constraints of old laws or the missionaries, and fuelled with alcohol. According to Albrecht, there are two major reasons why alcohol has such a detrimental effect on Aboriginal society. Firstly, since there are no traditional rules regarding its use – only rules instituted by the ancestral spirit beings have binding force – it has so far proved difficult, if not impossible, for Aboriginal societies to establish rules which its members consider binding. The second is that, as yet, there are no traditional or learned mechanisms for different land owning clans to work together on social issues. And, as most Aboriginal 'communities' are made up of different land owning clans or remnants of clans, they have no mechanisms for arriving at an acceptable consensus for dealing with their alcohol problem.[172] The fact that policy-makers fall back on culture explanation speaks of the policy-makers' wishes rather than the victims' needs. Return

---

170 An observation made to the author by the husband of an Aboriginal woman from Yuendemu Northern Territory.
171 Indigenous Land Corporation, 2009. *Annual Report 2008-09*, p. 49.
172 Albrecht, 2008, p. 20.

to traditional culture will not save Aborigines from alcohol and violence.

After 30 years of post-missionary adjustment, Aborigines living on their own lands have been locked out of the modern economy; yet it would be foolish to recreate Aboriginal culture. Turning to Aboriginal culture as a means of stopping the violence in Aboriginal society is a cruel hoax played by those who no longer live a traditional way, no matter how strongly they may identify with their Aboriginal origins.

Culture inhibits adjustment

As McKnight argues, people have been affected by alcohol, drugs and by being beaten. There is a deep-seated social reason for people's complete misunderstanding of what is happening: 'they no longer have a meaningful cultural framework in which to operate their lives and to evaluate what is being said and done.'[173] That framework can hardly be restored when it no longer works in modern society but, more importantly, it prevents people from adapting to new circumstances. The reason for maladaption lies in the culture itself. Numerous aspects of the culture work against the strongest elements of the modern and dominant culture. Paul Albrecht explains the weak merit principles that operate in traditional Aboriginal society but which, despite the earnest wishes of egalitarians, are very important in modern society.

Generally, Aboriginal culture exhibits weak savings and merit principles, the humbug or 'try-ask' and 'knock-back' system, and loyalty, which inhibits mobility to different employers. These aspects of Aboriginal culture make adjustment to the modern economy and workforce very difficult.

> There was in the past little reason for saving and little opportunity to do so. People ate whatever food was available and naturally

---

173 McKnight, 2002, p. 144.

had no hesitation in drinking as much water as they wanted. So there were few or no constraints about consumption and from what I observed there was (and is) little or no concern about leaving food or water for other people. Each person is primarily concerned with looking after himself or herself ... But people could afford to be apparently selfish because there were rules that ensured that everyone was looked after despite individual feelings.[174]

At various times in the past, the organisation for which I worked employed Aborigines in the position of shop 'manager'. All the men so employed were competent to carry out the functions required of them – selling articles at set prices, making correct change, buying other articles at set prices. The experience, repeated in each instance, was that after a period of quite satisfactory operation, a stock take would reveal substantial discrepancies between sales (as represented by cash on hand) and remaining stock. What had happened was that kin had brought such pressure to bear on their relative, that he simply had to part with stock to fulfil his obligations as a kinsman, or lose his standing. We were convinced that there was never any intentional dishonesty involved. Similar problems arise today with the employment of checkout operators. The demands of kin often force them not to charge for goods taken from the shop. ... In a nutshell it can be said that the values and attitudes stressed by the Aboriginal wider kin group are the exact opposite of those needed by individuals and the group as a whole to function in the Australian society.[175]

As McKnight has observed of the Mornington Islanders, traditional ways of sharing, asking and demanding have not been totally discarded but they have been much affected by money, alcohol

---

174 McKnight, 2002, p. 200.
175 Albrecht, 2008, p. 66.

and by the political changes that have been imposed.

> Nowadays the Mornington Islanders never (or rarely) offer to give. White people often criticize them for this. They grumble that they give freely but their generosity is unacknowledged or never reciprocated. However, for the Mornington Islanders, if a person wants or needs something, then he should ask. The person who asks is in the weak position and the person who is asked is in the strong position. From what I observed, those in the strong position frequently take advantage of the situation and introduce all sorts of obstacles, and if in the end they do give, it is often with great reluctance. Outside the golden circle of close kin the Mornington Islanders are not generous people, at least not nowadays. They boast that they are generous but their generosity is quite circumscribed.[176]
>
> In their relationships with White people they want White people to be as generous to them as they themselves are, or should be, with their close kin. Failure to live up to that close expectation results in a view that White people are stingy. They fail to appreciate that White people on Mornington Island do not have an inner circle of close kin that they can turn to when they are in need. It is sadly amusing to watch White people in their initial encounters with the Mornington Islanders being generous to a degree that they have been led to believe that Aborigines are, but gradually becoming disillusioned and sometimes hostile, when their generosity is deprecated and unreciprocated.[177]
>
> Gambling accords with the optimism of the hunter-gatherers. Just as people expect to be successful hunters so they expect to be successful gamblers … Instead of hunting food, as in the past, people now mainly hunt money and beer. Just

---

[176] McKnight, 2002, p. 74.
[177] McKnight, 2002, p. 74.

as people 'hunt' for a part of his kill so they now hunt the successful gambler.[178]

Paul Albrecht observes that traditional Aborigines have a problem with the employer-employee relationship as normally expressed in a modern contractual relationship.

> Contact with the Australian society and involvement in its economy, does not appear to have appreciably altered the Aborigines' traditional patterns of interaction and co-operation. They remain substantially the same as they have for centuries. When and where they have entered the modern economic system, the basis on which they interact and co–operate (work), is still largely a personal one. The idea of a contractual relationship appears to be only vaguely sensed if at all.
>
> Many Aborigines, especially in the early years of contact, took the surnames of the Europeans for whom they worked. Although there were various reasons for this phenomenon, one important one was that it expressed, at least as far as the Aborigine was concerned, a personal relationship between him and his employer. And it was largely on the basis of this relationship that he worked for him. The personal nature of this work relationship is further borne out by the fact that some Aborigines, even today, will only work for 'their boss', and no-one else. If for some reason he cannot provide them with work for a period of time, they will just 'sit down' until such time as he again has work for them. (Admittedly this is a situation which pertains more in the pastoral industry than in the urban employment context, but pertain it does.)
>
> Often in the course of conversations with Aborigines, I have asked one or the other what he has been doing. Invariably the answer has been 'helping' so-and-so, rarely do they say 'working'

---

[178] McKnight, 2002, p. 76.

for so-and-so. This choice of verbs (both are equally well-known) also reflects the personalistic approach of Aborigines to work. Another thought which quite often finds expression in the course of conversations, is that of 'doing a favour'. That is by working, he is first and foremost doing the employer a favour. The thought of earning his living by this means often runs a poor second.

Aborigines' approach to work is still very largely coloured by his traditional outlook [and] ... this affects employer-employee relations. The Australian employer looks on work as a contractual relationship, while for the Aborigine it is more of a personal relationship. This being the case, the Aborigine cannot understand why the 'boss' wants to be so exact about wages, or why he is displeased if he wants some extra time off. This fact that both look at the work relationship from a different point of view, often leads to friction. Australian employers who have 'sensed' and taken into consideration the Aboriginal attitude, have had far better work relations with Aborigines than those who have stuck to the more contractual type approach.[179]

... when the outstation movement began at Hermannsburg, all the groups who moved out established and worked their gardens until they found out that various forms of government assistance were in no way tied to them doing something like establishing and tending a garden.'[180]

Key aspects of Aboriginal culture inhibit Aboriginal adjustment to life in a modern society. The choice arises then, does the Aborigine who wants happiness choose an ancient, indeed long abandoned culture to satisfy the desires of some black leaders and some white intellectuals, or does he and she decide to ignore the group think, and go mainstream, risking some loss of group solidarity but gaining the prize of a far richer life – even one that contemplates what it means

---

179 Albrecht, 2008, p. 97.
180 Albrecht, 2008, p. 92.

to be human and alive in the open society.

Self-management demands that Aborigines formulate public goals and set up structures to control and manage activities necessary to achieve these goals. However, if they are to hold their own against an overpowering European-Australian majority, they will have to choose goals and organisational procedures that go beyond a desire to retreat into their own world.[181]

The task ahead for Aboriginal people is not to hide in collective bad behaviour, but to resist it. Recourse to collective and institutional fixes to the Aboriginal problem, without consideration of the central character, the individual person, are doomed to failure. When much of the behaviour of 'failing' Aborigines is bad, then the behaviour has to change. Waiting for a change to society is forlorn. By illustration, Stephen Hagan is a well-known Queensland Aboriginal academic and activist. He changed his behaviour some years ago. He stopped drinking, denied his in-laws a place to stay, and stopped lending them money. In other words, he stopped playing cultural games. Is it as simple as this?

> I reprioritised my personal and family goals … I discerned the critical proactive role I needed to play in support of my immediate family. I took those decisions knowing they were directly opposed to the desire to always attempt to satisfy the shallow expectations of my extended family and friends.
>
> In its infancy, this process was quite painful as I stopped lending money to my family and friends most of which anyway was never returned in full, or sometimes at all, and I declined requests from them to bunk down for the night at my residence when visiting from out of town.
>
> While initially my actions put me offside with disgruntled relatives and longstanding acquaintances, it nevertheless gave me complete confidence to provide uncompromising safety and financial security for my family and an increase in quality

---

[181] Dagmar, 1990, p. 113.

time with them.[182]

As Stephanie Jarrett has eloquently stated, 'violence has less to do with Aboriginal men's loss or brokenness due to white colonisation … [I]t has more to do with traditional expectations, mores, and "permissions" to be violent. No matter how unfair they, their family, or their community have been treated or continue to be treated by mainstream Australia, it is … the mainstream context where Aboriginal violence is more effectively suppressed and less tolerated by Aboriginal people themselves.'[183] In short, old men's rights have been lost and women's and children's rights have been gained in recent decades. Men's power over women, especially initiated men's power, was the only genuine cultural and collective right in Aboriginal society. Do any human rights advocates want to argue the case that this right should be restored?

Folly recognising law and custom

There has been a persistent desire among some Aboriginal leaders and advocates to have customary law accepted under Australian law. The Preamble written by the Aboriginal Treaty Committee in 1989 sought the protection of Aboriginal identity, languages, law and culture as part of a treaty between the Commonwealth government and Aboriginal people,[184] and the Reconciliation Council has expressed its support to have Indigenous customary law recognised,[185] as has the Australian Law Reform Commission in its 1977 consideration of Aboriginal customary law. Despite concluding that, as a general principle, codification or direct enforcement were

---

182 Hagan, S. *The Australian* 18 May 2009.
183 Jarrett, S. 2009. 'Violence: An Inseparable Part of Traditional Aboriginal Culture.' *The Bennelong Society Occasional Papers,* p. 34.
184 Harris, 1979, p. 85.
185 Council for Aboriginal Reconciliation, 1994. 'Agreeing on a Document: Will the Process of Reconciliation be Advanced by a Document or Documents of Reconciliation?' *Key Issues* Paper 7, Australian Government Publishing Service.

not appropriate forms of recognition, the Commission nevertheless continued to argue the recognition case, arguing that the extremely serious reservations against the recognition of traditional law such as the problem of unacceptable rules and punishments needed to be brushed aside in the name of recognising the fundamental human rights of Aborigines.

The Law Council of Australia's new policy on Indigenous Australians describes customary law as 'sophisticated and complex',[186] while the Western Australian Law Reform Commission has recommended that the *Constitution Act 1889* (WA) be amended to recognise the unique status of Aboriginal people as the descendants of the original inhabitants of the State. The Law Society of South Australia has urged the Recognition of Aboriginal Customary Law[187] and the special status of Aboriginal people is already recognised in the Victorian and ACT Charters of Rights and Responsibilities.[188] The Rudd Government acceded to the Declaration on the Rights of Indigenous Peoples even though the Howard government, together with the governments of New Zealand, the USA and Canada, had for very sound reasons rejected it.[189]

Understandably, Aboriginal elders see the possibility of the restoration of law and order coinciding with the restoration of their authority.

> Community Elders want to sit down with the Australian lawmakers and find a way that they can reassert their traditional laws with the backing of the Australian Law. Attitudes would

---

186 *The Australian*, 18 February 2010.
187 The Law Society of South Australia.
188 Charter of Human Rights and Responsibilities Act 2006 (Vic) Part 2 section 20. *Human Rights Act* 2004 (ACT), Preamble.
189 Explanation of vote by the Hon. Robert Hill, Ambassador and Permanent Representative of Australia, Declaration on the Rights of Indigenous Peoples, the United Nations General Assembly, 13 September 2007. Explanation of vote by Robert Hagen, U.S. Advisor, the Declaration on the Rights of Indigenous Peoples, the United Nations General Assembly, 13 September 2007.

change to abuse and violence. At present everyone just accepts it because they feel powerless to do anything about it. If this power is restored then there will be a snowball effect and soon attitudes will change.[190]

But the authority of elders lapsed generations ago, and for a host of reasons. As McKnight, Tonkinson and Albrecht have illustrated, the moment Aboriginal women and young men gained access to a stronger power in the protection of the missionaries, they quickly escaped the cruel powers of old men. The Warlpiri elders are dreaming if they think that they can re-establish their authority, especially when that authority would only be enforced by the whiteman. Their only hope of restoring authority is by winning respect through leadership and good behaviour. The fact that some policy-makers continue to pander to the delusions of elders to return to something which not only preceded their experience, but is wrong in principle, says a great deal about those people. As Paul Albrecht explains:

> Aboriginal customary law has an entirely different base to Australian law. Aboriginal customary law was instituted by the supernatural beings who were active at the beginning of time, creating the flora and fauna, shaping the landscape, and giving men the laws by which to live and regulate their lives and interpersonal and inter-group relationships. Since these norms were given by the supernatural beings and not instituted by men, men cannot change them, or add to them; they can only choose not to obey them. Generally, consensus in more traditional Aboriginal societies can only be achieved around these supernaturally given norms, because they are the only absolutes in Aboriginal societies. Everything else is personal, subject only to what one's kin will allow. More traditional Aboriginal societies find it difficult to formulate new laws, binding on members of their society, because there is no provision in Aboriginal law to create new laws.[191]

---

190 Quoting a Warlpiri elder in Wild and Anderson, 2007, p. 176.
191 Albrecht, 2008, p. 90.

Second, customary law was frequently harsh and applied in an arbitrary manner.

> Strehlow once related to me the remarks one of his informants had made to him on the punishment he and some of his fellow initiates received for disobedience. I recount this because it illustrates the quite ruthless approach of the elders to gaining obedience, and thus laying the foundation for the authority they wielded. It is a strictly enforced rule that actors in a ceremony are required to continue acting their parts as long as the singers continue chanting. On this occasion, the elders gathered the young disobedient men for the performance of an emu ceremony. As this ceremony requires the actors to dance on their knees, it is usually performed on soft ground, in the cool of the day or evening. On this occasion, the elders scheduled it to take place in the heat of the day and on rough stony ground. While they themselves sat in the shade of a tree chanting, the young men performed on their knees on the hot stony stage. As their knees became more and more lacerated, the old men merely smiled and continued chanting. ... It was this blatant exercise of power, as much as anything, which reinforced in no unmistakable manner the ultimate authority of the old men. [192]

Would any lawmaker, judge or politician, condone such practices?

Third, Aboriginal law condones abhorrent and illegal practices. The debate about the recognition of customary law has been restimulated by the legislation accompanying the Northern Territory intervention. A number of judges have objected to the restrictions placed on their sentencing options, a not unreasonable stand for them to take. One such critic, Brian Martin, Chief Justice of the NT Supreme Court, has only himself to blame. He argues that there have been few occasions in which customary law has been taken into account in the NT courts either in sentencing or culpability.[193] There is one occasion, however, when it was. It is one judgment he would like to forget.

---

192 Albrecht, 2008, p. 73.
193 Martin, B. 2007. 'Customary Law.' *Judicial Conference of Australia Colloquium 2007*, p. 30.

> **Box 3   Chief Justice Martin in Queen v GJ**
>
> I do not have before me proof that the objections by the child made you realise that she was not consenting. At the least, it is a reasonable possibility that your fundamental beliefs, based on your traditional laws, prevailed in your thinking and prevented you from realising that the child was not consenting…
>
> The young child who was promised to you and all other young girls in the Northern Territory and throughout Australia are entitled to the protection of the Northern Territory law. So, too, are older girls and women entitled to the protection of the Northern Territory Law.
>
> I appreciate that it is a very difficult thing for men who have been brought up in traditional ways which permit physical violence and sexual intercourse with promised wives, even if they are not consenting, to adjust their ways.
>
> It must be said, however, that there was nothing in your Aboriginal law which required you to strike the child or to have intercourse with her. Within your law it was your choice whether you struck her. It was also your choice whether you had intercourse with her and whether you took her as your wife.
>
> I accept that these offences occurred because the young child had been promised to you. This is not a case where you simply sought out a young child for sexual gratification …
>
> I must also remind you about how the child felt. She was upset and distressed and I have no doubt that your act of intercourse with her has had a significant effect upon her. The child has provided only a very brief Victim Impact Statement in which she does not speak of any emotional and psychological impact upon her. That is not surprising. This is a child who has been shamed within a community that obviously has very strong male members and strong traditional beliefs …
>
> Mr GJ, I have a great deal of sympathy for you and the difficulties attached to transition from traditional Aboriginal culture and laws as you understood them to be, to obeying the Northern Territory Law.
>
> Mr GJ, that means that you must go to gaol for one month and I hope that you will be able to come out of gaol after one month and return to your community and to your family.
>
> Source: Transcript of proceedings at Yarralin on Thursday, 11 August, 2005: The Supreme Court of The Northern Territory, SCC 20418849, The Queen v GJ (Sentence), Martin CJ.

The infamous sentencing remarks at Yarralin, Northern Territory, on Thursday, 11 August 2005, in *The Queen and GJ*, are apparently regretted but, nevertheless, stand in the record. The case concerned the deprivation of liberty, unlawful sexual intercourse and beating of a 14 year-old girl by a male. The result was a conviction of 24 months, which following his imprisonment leading to the trial, in effect had him released after one month, for assault and unlawful sexual intercourse. The sentence was imposed in *GJ* in the remote community of Yarralin on 11 August 2005. On 3 November 2005 the Court of Criminal Appeal of the Northern Territory heard the Crown appeal against the sentence in *GJ* and, on 22 December 2005, allowed the appeal, and marginally increased the sentence.[194] Martin argued that: 'The reasons for the present level of child sexual abuse in Aboriginal communities are many and varied. They include the effects of colonisation and "learnt behaviour". ... [Martin] does not take the view that this absolves Aboriginal people from responsibility in dealing with this issue, but it goes some way to explaining why it exists and provides an insight into how to deal with it more effectively.'[195]

Undeterred, Martin notes that the Wild and Anderson Inquiry gained the impression that Aboriginal custom is 'extremely important to Aboriginal people' and that the Northern Territory Law Reform Committee's *Report on Aboriginal Customary Law* reached the same conclusion. It recommended in 2004 that the government establish an inquiry with a view to recognising certain traditional sanctions formally.[196] Martin's judgment, and the decision of the Court of Appeal, in my opinion, did not deal with the matter effectively; it reflected, instead, a political response by a judiciary at the expense of the future security of Aboriginal women in the NT.

There can be no doubt that the coming of the Europeans had

---

194 Martin, 2007, p. 32.
195 Martin, 2007, p. 33.
196 Quoted in Martin, 2007, p. 37.

a massive impact on Aboriginal societies and Aboriginal law, and helped to create a situation of lawlessness in Aboriginal societies. However, while it is inviting to think of Aboriginal customary law having played a similar role in keeping the peace and settling disputes in Aboriginal societies that the modern law plays in Australian society, it is a fallacy to think that recognition of Aboriginal customary law, in itself, would ameliorate law and order problems among Aborigines. In any Aboriginal group, whether defined on the basis of land or kin, there is no central authority to deal with infringement of laws. Law enforcement is the responsibility of the individual and his kin. Only in matters like land and sacrilege is the whole group involved, with the lead being taken by individual(s) who have primary responsibility for dealing with the offence. Hence, sending people who have broken the law back to their 'communities' to be dealt with by their 'elders' is simply another instance where we have not understood Aboriginal societies, and the way in which breaking of the law is dealt with.

4

Inquiries into white morality

Added to the overwhelming evidence of the damage done by the self-determination policies of the last forty years, and to the intellectual apologies for denials of the damage, is the damage done by some major propaganda exercises of the last decade, the legacy of which has been to slow and, in many cases, prevent the economic integration of Aborigines. Between 1991 and 2000 three major inquiries in the assertion of cultural rights added weight to the separatist agenda. These were *The Royal Commission into Aboriginal Deaths in Custody Report* (1991), The Human Rights and Equal Opportunity Commission Report, *Bringing Them Home* (1997) (and its court sequel, *Cubillo v Commonwealth*), and *The Hindmarsh Island Royal Commission* (1997) (and its court sequel, *Chapman v Tickner*). The first two are especially important because they may well constrain the hands of policy-makers and public servants from making essential changes to the rules by which Aborigines live.

Royal Commission into Aboriginal Deaths in Custody (1991)

The Royal Commission into Aboriginal Deaths in Custody was established in 1987 by the Commonwealth and joined by all States and the Northern Territory. An initiative of Gerry Hand, Commonwealth Minister for Aboriginal Affairs, it was a response to growing public concern that Aboriginal deaths in custody were too common, and that public explanations were too evasive to discount the possibility that foul play was a factor in many. Between 1980 and 1989, 99 Aborigines and Torres Strait Islanders died in the custody of prison, police, or juvenile detention institutions. Many members of the Aboriginal community assumed that many of the deaths would have been murder committed by prison or police officers.

The Commission reported in 1991. It produced 110 volumes of evidence and recommendations, totalling over 12,000 pages at a cost of almost $30 million. At the time, it was the most expensive inquiry in Commonwealth history.[197] For all this, the Commission stated:

> The conclusions reached in this report will not accord with the expectations of those who anticipated that findings of foul play would be inevitable. ... Commissioners did not find that the deaths were the product of deliberate violence or brutality by police or prison officers.[198]

The Commission also found that although Aboriginal people were in custody overwhelmingly more frequently than the general community, 'Aboriginal people in custody do not die at a greater rate than non-Aboriginal people in custody.'[199] Indeed, the Commission noted that, at least for those Aborigines who had encountered the law, 'the death rate of those Aboriginal people on non-custodial orders is

---

197 Brunton, R. 1993. *Black Suffering, White Guilt: Aboriginal Disadvantage and the Royal Commission into Deaths in Custody*, Institute of Public Affairs.
198 RCADC, 1991. *National Report*, Volume 1.2.2.
199 RCADC, 1991, Volume 1.3.1.

approximately twice that of Aboriginal prisoners.'[200] In other words, the risk of death might actually be greater outside custody. Further analysis of the Commission data published later indicated that:

> Young adult Aboriginal males have almost exactly the same probability of dying when they are in the community as when they are in prison. The risks of death in custody experienced by Aboriginal people and non-Aboriginal people are similar. ... The finding that both Aboriginal and non-Aboriginal people have risks of death in police custody that are far higher than they have in the community would not be surprising to many, but the finding that, in both groups, the risk of prison death is similar to that in the community is perhaps more novel.[201]

There are at least three disturbing aspects of the Commission and its findings. First, just six weeks into the Inquiry the Commissioner and the Commonwealth Government were made aware of the primary conclusion that Aboriginal people in custody do not die at a greater rate than non-Aboriginal people in custody. My former parliamentary colleague, the late Senator Bob Collins of the Northern Territory, conveyed this to me some short time after the Commission knew. The fact was confirmed in 1992 by the author of the research, who wrote:

> The hostility towards the work of the Criminology Unit reached a climax only a few months after the work started, when it became clear that the research showed that Aboriginal persons in either police or prison custody were no more likely to die than were non-Aboriginal people. This general finding was interpreted by some significant elements of the staff as undermining the very foundations of the Royal Commission.

---

200 RCADC, 1991, Volume 3, p. 60.
201 Biles, D. and D. McDonald, 1992. 'Overview of the Research Program and Abstracts of Research Papers.' *Australian Institute of Criminology Research Paper* No. 22, p. 631.

> To even hint that such a conclusion was possible was seen as disloyal, misguided and obviously wrong. At one stage the very existence of the Criminology Unit within the Royal Commission was threatened. It was able to continue its work, however, albeit with a smaller staff.[202]

The response by the Government was to not reveal this fact, and to set the Commission another, altogether different task. The initial task was to inquire into the deaths and into 'the conduct of coronial, police and other inquiries.' The new task declared, 'you are authorised to take account of social and cultural and legal factors which, in your judgment, appear to have a bearing on those deaths.' The Commission turned from a 'super' coronial inquiry into a 'super' social science exercise into the causes of Aboriginal disadvantage. Much of this exercise was not at all new to the policy community:

> Of the ninety-nine [deceased], eighty-three were unemployed at the date of last detention; they were uneducated ... only two had completed secondary level; forty-three of them experienced childhood separation from their natural families through intervention by the State authorities, missions or other institutions; forty-three had been charged with an offence at or before aged fifteen and seventy-four at or before aged nineteen; forty-three had been taken into last custody directly for reasons related to alcohol, and it can safely be said that overwhelmingly in the remaining cases the reason for last custody was directly alcohol related.[203]

The Commission started on a narrow inquiry for which it was well qualified. When its terms of reference expanded, it embarked on a study for which it was not well qualified. It simply jumped from

---

202 Biles, D. and D. McDonald, (eds) 1992. *Deaths in Custody Australia, 1980-1989: The Research Papers of the Criminology Unit of the Royal Commission into Aboriginal Deaths in Custody*, Australian Institute of Criminology, Foreword.
203 RCADC, 1991, Volume 1.2.17.

questions of evidence to questions of social policy. In so doing, it took up the policy fashion of self-determination in the hope that this would stem the flow of incarceration and deaths in custody. Moreover, it made great claims about the impact of children's removal from their parents; this stimulated a second grand inquiry, *Bringing Them Home*, of which more below.

Figure 7: Prison custody deaths by Indigenous status, 1982-2006 (rate)

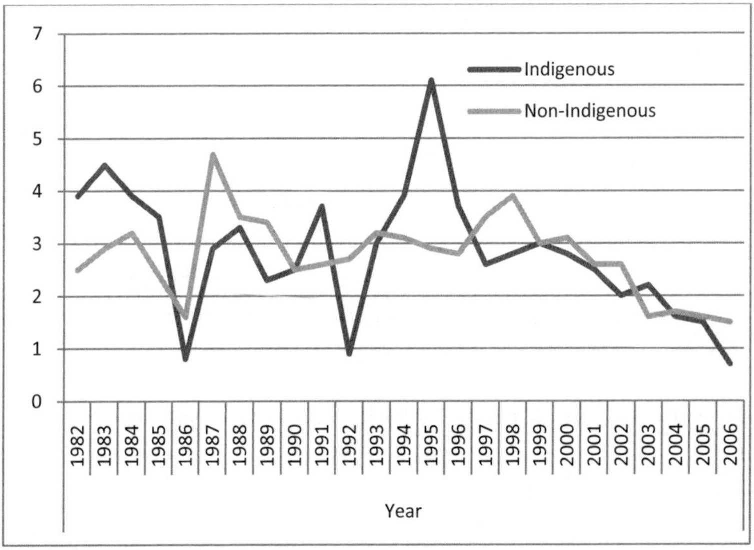

Data source: Joudo, J. and J. Curnow, 2006. 'Deaths in Custody in Australia: National Deaths in Custody Program Annual Report 2006.' Research and Public Policy Series No. 85, p. 38.

The second disturbing aspect was the interpretation of the evidence that led to the Inquiry. The evidence from Figure 7 and Figure 8, *Prison custody deaths by Indigenous status* (by rate and by number), shows two trends. The first is a spike in the rate of deaths in custody for Indigenous and non-Indigenous in 1987; the second is that the rate spike and the actual deaths were far more pronounced for non-Aborigines than Aborigines. Despite these results there was no inquiry into non-Aboriginal deaths in custody following the rise in those deaths. Clearly, the Government was discriminating on grounds of race. Deaths in custody are a matter of great concern but, on the evidence, there was no basis for an inquiry into Aboriginal deaths in custody alone.

The third disturbing aspect of the Inquiry was its impact on deaths in custody, not in terms of its recommendations, but in terms of the possibility that the massive publicity associated with the Inquiry could have caused deaths in custody. The evidence shows a major rise in the rate and number of Aboriginal prison deaths in custody for Aborigines in 1992 to 1995. Indeed, apart from a drop in 1992, the trend was increasing for the number of Aboriginal and non-Aboriginal deaths for the period 1989 to 1999-2000. The period, 1992 to 1995, was largely filled with public discussion of the Inquiry, its recommendations and the political battles over their implementation. In that period, and that climate, the rate and number of Aboriginal prison deaths alone rose substantially.

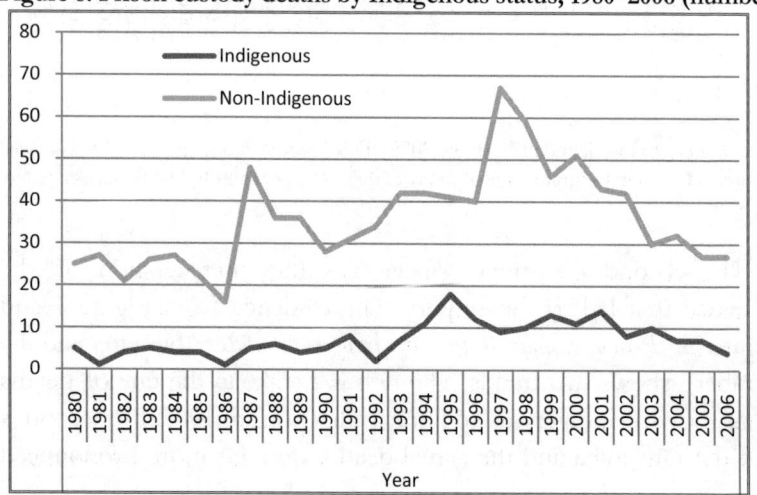

Figure 8: Prison custody deaths by Indigenous status, 1980–2006 (number)

Data source: Joudo, J. & J. Curnow, 2006. 'Deaths in Custody in Australia: National Deaths in Custody Program Annual Report 2006.' Research and Public Policy Series No.85, p. 38.

What caused the jump in Aboriginal prison deaths in the period 1992-1995? The research indicates that 'self-inflicted deaths and deaths due to natural causes have consistently been the two most common manners of death since 1980.'[204] These causes were apparent in the spike of 1992-1995. No explanation for the spike has been provided. In the various reports following the Inquiry there is no accounting for the significant lift in the rate of Aboriginal deaths in prison custody, many of which are suicide. Is it possible that the enormous media coverage given to the Commission and the reports of the implementation of its findings could have had a social contagion effect labelled the Werther effect?[205] David Phillips, a sociologist, coined the term, the 'Werther effect'. It describes imitative suicidal behaviour operating as contagion transmitted via the mass media. The copycat explanation never rated a mention in reports by the Australian Institute of Criminology but it is entirely plausible that the Royal Commission into Aboriginal Deaths in Custody which commenced on false grounds (a rise in non-Aboriginal deaths), and continued, knowing that the rate of Aboriginal deaths was no different in the relevant period to non-Aborigines, may have caused some deaths in custody by shouting from the rooftops about Aboriginal deaths in custody.

---

204 Joudo, J. and M. Veld, 2005. 'Deaths in Custody in Australia: National Deaths in Custody Program Annual Report 2004.' *Australian Institute of Criminology Technical and Background Paper Series*, No.19.
205 In the mid-1770s a peculiar clothing fashion swept across Europe. For no immediately apparent reason, young men started dressing in yellow trousers, blue jackets and open-necked shirts. This mildly eccentric fashion spread from region to region in a manner strangely similar to the epidemics that were continuing to plague the Old Continent. It turned out that these 18th Century fashion victims all had one thing in common; they had all been exposed to the first novel of Johann Wolfgang von Goethe, *The Sorrows of Young Werther*. Goethe's novel recounted the desperate plight of Werther, a young man hopelessly in love with a happily married woman called Charlotte. In this intense and romantic tale, Goethe describes Werther's rather peculiar penchant for wearing a colourful mélange of blue jackets, yellow trousers and open-necked shirts, and for having shot himself.

Fortunately, since that time, there has been a shift in the number and nature of deaths occurring in prison and police custody. Where most deaths in police custody used to be due to hangings, they are now primarily due to external/multiple trauma, most often the result of a motor vehicle pursuit, and to gunshots. This change in cause of death reflects two things. Firstly, the number of deaths occurring in police cells has decreased. When hanging points in police cells and lock-ups were identified as an issue by the Royal Commission into Aboriginal Deaths in Custody, efforts were made to reduce those, which may explain in part the drop in hanging deaths. Secondly, the expansion of the term 'police custody' to include custody-related operations since 1990 (this does not affect the figures on prison deaths) has meant that the opportunity for deaths to be recorded that occur as a result of vehicle pursuits, shootings and sieges has increased greatly.[206]

Unfortunately, there are still those who believe that the best way to reduce deaths in custody is to reduce the prison population despite the evidence of the Commission that deaths in communities are as frequent as deaths in custody. For example, in the Pilbara, 'virtually half of all Indigenous males aged between 15 and 34 years of age are arrested at least once each year; and around 313 Indigenous adults are subject to some form of detention or supervisory order at any one time. These represent quite substantial impacts on regional participation. However, if just three categories of offence were eliminated (traffic, public order, and offences against justice procedures, all of which are regulatory in some way), then cases brought before the criminal justice system would be halved.'[207]

There are two problems with this sentiment and that which lies

---

[206] Joudo, J. and Curnow, J. 2006. 'Deaths in Custody in Australia: National Deaths in Custody Program Annual Report 2006.' *Australian Institute of Criminology Research and Public Policy Series* No. 85, p. 35.

[207] Taylor, J. and B. Scambary, 2005. 'Indigenous People and the Pilbara Mining Boom: A Baseline for Regional Participation.' *Research Monograph* No. 25, Australian National University E Press, p. 151.

behind the Deaths in Custody Inquiry. First, prison is not such a punishment for some Aborigines. For example,

> Men seem unconcerned about being sent to prison. I did not record any complaints about ill treatment. ... There is no social stigma about having been in prison. I was often told that men regard prison like home. There are cases of youths purposely getting into trouble so that they will be sent back to prison. That may seem hard to believe but from what I was told young Mornington Islanders rather enjoy prison where they were fed, have a place of their own, can watch TV, play games, and meet fellow Mornington Islanders and other Aborigines from all over Queensland.[208]

A similar observation was made to me in 2006 by a Queensland magistrate. The magistrate would travel by plane with the prisoners to Cairns from the remote community where the hearing and sentencing had taken place. On the morning after the hearing magistrate and prisoners would gather at the airport. The atmosphere was one of sending someone on holiday rather than to gaol.

Second, the solution to Aboriginal deaths in custody or, indeed, over-representation in custody, is not letting people escape punishment. Such a policy is more likely to compound than solve their problems. While it is clear that 'the probability of getting caught has a more deterrent effect on criminality than the term of the punishment',[209] the notion of simply turning a blind eye is too prevalent in discussions about justice to Aborigines. The reason too many Aborigines are gaoled is that too many commit crimes. If the solution to the problem is not to gaol so many Aborigines for the crimes they commit, Aborigines would rightly conclude that breaking

---

208 McKnight, 2002, p. 146.
209 Gary Becker on crime and punishment. http://home.uchicago.edu/~gbecker/Nobel/nobel.html#Household.

the law is not wrong, thus causing real confusion, which in cultural terms is unfortunate because Aboriginal culture was quite exacting on crime and punishment.

The direct and practical responses[210] to the long list of recommendations arising from the Deaths in Custody Inquiry were useful to the extent that authorities became acutely aware of the risk to prisoners. The evidence above suggests solid improvement in lowering the deaths in custody for both Indigenous and non-Indigenous prisoners. In addition, and despite the Commission's focus on separated families as the source of imprisonment and, by implication, deaths in custody, deaths in custody have declined despite the fact that in the relevant timeframe the cohort of prisoners from 'separated' families continues its march through the penal institutions.

More recently, however, the news is not very positive. The Queensland Crime and Misconduct Commission report, *Restoring Order: Crime Prevention, Policing and Local Justice in Queensland's Indigenous Communities*, in effect has given up.

> Since the time of the Royal Commission into Aboriginal Deaths in Custody there has been a great deal of focus within governments on reducing the overrepresentation of Indigenous people in the criminal justice system, particularly in custody. A long period of criminal justice policy, and Indigenous affairs policy more generally, has failed spectacularly in achieving this fundamental goal.
>
> With the exception of the introduction of alcohol reforms and the Welfare Reform Trial and its Family Responsibilities Commission, there has been little or no sustained effort to reduce the level of crime and violence in these communities through the implementation of an appropriate range of

---

[210] Australian Government, 1992. *Aboriginal Deaths in Custody: Response by Governments to the Royal Commission.* Australian Government Publishing Service.

strategies with this focus. Instead, too much faith has been put in the notion that tinkering with the criminal justice system will produce positive results. Such faith must be abandoned.[211]

The Queensland Crime and Misconduct Commission also recommended abandoning overreliance on strategies unlikely to lead to substantial crime prevention. The recently-established Murri Court, for example, which consists of Aboriginal elders sitting with the convicted during sentencing was, according to the CMC, 'unlikely to greatly reduce crime or violence'. The Commission also suggested that 'increasing police diversion from the criminal justice system in these communities is also unlikely to have a substantial impact on crime.'[212] Clearly, the difficulties of Aborigines and crime and punishment are not close to being solved, but at least one substantial body, the Queensland CMC, is sufficiently confident in its understanding to walk away from a string of recommendations and thinking from the Royal Commission into Aboriginal Deaths in Custody.

Hindmarsh Island Royal Commission (1995)

In the early 1990s, Tom and Wendy Chapman wanted to develop a marina on Hindmarsh Island, South Australia. Planning authorities insisted that a bridge should be part of the proposal. They received the requisite approvals after completing the necessary consultations and conditions, including consultations about Aboriginal issues. Opposition to the bridge arose from non-Aboriginal residents who did not want their view of the river impeded by a bridge. These and environmental and aesthetic arguments were tested and failed. As recorded by Chris Kenny, a journalist who reported the subsequent controversy, one objector said to another, 'Let's see if we can get

---

211 Crime and Misconduct Commission Queensland, 2009. *Restoring Order Crime Prevention, Policing and Local Justice in Queensland's Indigenous Communities*, p. 327.
212 CMC, 2009, p. 328.

some Aboriginals down from Murray Bridge to help us with our cause'.[213] Another phase in the protests commenced. This time Aboriginal middens and graves were the focus. Much later, after the Aboriginal heritage objections had failed, a female anthropologist said to an Aboriginal activist, 'it would be nice if there was some women's business'.[214]

Subsequently, in 1994, Ngarrindjeri women in South Australia claimed that a secret women's site would be damaged by construction of a bridge across the River Murray to link the mainland with Hindmarsh Island. Following a report by Professor Cheryl Saunders, in July 1994 the then Federal Labor Minister for Aboriginal and Torres Strait Islander Affairs, Robert Tickner, exercised his powers under the *Aboriginal and Torres Strait Islander Protection Act (1984)* and halted the construction of the bridge for a period of 25 years.

The basis on which Tickner did so was perhaps the most embarrassing and intellectually and morally bereft that I encountered in parliamentary life. Tickner deliberately denied himself access to the secret women's business, which contained the 'evidence' that formed the basis of the decision to use Commonwealth powers to ban the building of the Hindmarsh Island bridge. I was ashamed at the rank foolishness of this act and stunned that an otherwise intelligent prime minister, Paul Keating, would not have sacked Tickner on the spot. Tickner had a responsibility to read the material. In choosing to not do so, he ceased to be a minister. His ban on the bridge was overturned in February 2005 by the Federal Court and affirmed by the Full Court of the Federal Court because 'it was not a proper exercise of a power on the part of the Minister to rely so heavily on the subject of women's business, yet deny himself access to the contents of the secret envelopes.'[215]

---

213 Kenny, C. 1996. *It Would Be Nice If There Was Some Women's Business: The Story Behind the Hindmarsh Island Affair*. Duffy and Snellgrove, page 47.
214 Kenny, 1996, p. 71.
215 Chapman v Tickner and ors [1995] FCA 1068 (15 February 1995), para 199.

A major criticism of the secret women's business was that the claims of Aboriginal women had been raised for the first time in about April 1994 and that no Aboriginal woman opposed the bridge in the four years preceding October 1993. Professor Saunders addressed this subject in her report; she noted that there had been 'belated recognition that the area may have particular significance for reasons within the knowledge of Aboriginal women.'[216] The belated claims were heavily criticised in 1995 by a group of Ngarrindjeri women who publicly disputed the existence on Hindmarsh Island of secret sacred women's business. Soon afterwards a Ngarrindjeri man, Doug Milera, who had initially supported the claim, publicly admitted that it was a 'fabrication'. Consequently, the South Australian Liberal Government appointed a royal commissioner to inquire into the Hindmarsh Bridge affair. The royal commission's report was published in December 1995. Its major findings were:

- the 'women's business' was unknown to the twelve dissident Ngarrindjeri women who gave evidence before the commission and who were described by the royal commissioner as 'credible witnesses'
- the claim of the 'women's business' from its inception was a fabrication
- the purpose of the fabrication was to obtain a declaration prohibiting the construction of the Hindmarsh Island Bridge under the Commonwealth's Aboriginal and Torres Strait Islander Heritage Protection Act 1984.[217]

At the completion of the royal commission, and following the overturning of the Commonwealth action, the developers obtained the necessary approvals and proceeded to build the bridge. In 2000 the Chapmans sued Tickner and those who reported to him on the secret

---

216 Chapman v Tickner, 1995, para 124.
217 Hindmarsh Island Bridge Royal Commission, 1995. South Australia.

women's business.[218] Justice von Doussa sat on the case in the Federal Court. Although not asked to address the issue of the existence of the secret women's business, he nevertheless did so. Of particular note is the fact that Justice von Doussa did not submit Doreen Kartinyeri to questions about the contents of the sealed envelopes. Like Tickner he relied on the accounts by Cheryl Saunders and others. He regretted that the original envelopes containing women's business had been destroyed, so he was placed in the same position as Tickner and made the same judgment as Tickner, a judgment criticised by the Full Court of the Federal Court. Nevertheless, Justice von Doussa was not convinced that 'women's business' had been fabricated and advised that he had found four reasons to reject the findings of the royal commission.[219]

Justice von Doussa explained the late emergence of the secret women's business by what he thought was an insufficient consultation process. Earlier judicial inquirers into the Hindmarsh Island Bridge concluded that the Chapmans had sought to consult Aboriginal interests and satisfied the requirements of law. Justice von Doussa found otherwise, based on his experience with native title cases where, owing to physical isolation, eleventh hour disclosure was not uncommon. Geoffrey Partington notes, however, that Doreen Kartinyeri worked in Adelaide, engaged in mapping Aboriginal genealogies. It would be highly unlikely that she would not have known of the events surrounding Hindmarsh Island but apparently chose for years not to disclose her knowledge.

There is no support for women's business at Hindmarsh Island from the standard historical authorities. The Federal Court found that the women had not objected to earlier intrusions by barrages,

---

218 Chapman v Luminis Pty Ltd (No 5) [2001] FCA 1106 (21 August 2001)
219 In this and succeeding paragraphs I have drawn extensively on Geoffrey Partington's brilliant rebuttal of Justice von Doussa's findings. Partington, G. 2003. 'Hindmarsh Island and the Fabrication of Aboriginal Mythology.' *Samuel Griffith Society*, volume15, chapter 10.

the ferry and other cables laid down to connect Hindmarsh Island to the mainland. Earlier anthropological work, especially by Ronald and Catherine Berndt, had revealed no sacred women's traditions; earlier inquiries for other disturbances in the area had not revealed any sacred, secret women's business – nor any traditions of the nature alleged. No evidence before 1994 links Ngarrindjeri infanticide or abortion with Hindmarsh Island. The dissident Ngarrindjeri women indignantly rejected Doreen Kartinyeri's claim that there was such a link. When told by Doreen Kartinyeri that white men took Aboriginal women to Hindmarsh Island to destroy their half-caste babies, one Ngarrindjeri woman replied, 'If that's the case, why are we the colour we are today?'[220] Pinkie Mack, whom Doreen Kartinyeri claimed as the ultimate authentic source of the women's business at Hindmarsh Island, was the daughter of a white Australian, the Sub-Protector George Mason, and received her nickname from her colouring.

The link from ancient times to the present was one woman – Aunty Rosie – who lived distant from Hindmarsh Island but nevertheless, supposedly, knew the stories of old. She allegedly passed the story to Doreen Kartinyeri who shared it with perhaps only three of up to 35 Ngarrindjeri women. The place was one where abortions had taken place. Nevertheless, Justice von Doussa concluded that he was 'not satisfied that the restricted women's knowledge was fabricated or that it was not part of genuine Aboriginal tradition'.[221] He was, moreover, 'not persuaded that the restricted women's knowledge recounted by Dr Kartinyeri is a recent invention, fabricated as an eleventh hour attempt to stop the construction of the bridge.'[222] At the same time that Justice von Doussa dismissed the lack of pre-1993 anthropological evidence for secret women's business, he was impressed by the recall of Stella Newchurch who told him that, on

---

220 Quoted in Partington, 2003.
221 Chapman v Luminis, 2001, paragraph 12.
222 Chapman v Luminis, 2001, paragraph 471.

1 February 2000, she saw a 'very striking photograph of the Murray Mouth' in *The Advertiser*.[223] It reminded her of stories of Aboriginal women who went to Hindmarsh Island to abort babies told to her in her girlhood by Doreen Kartinyeri's Aunty Rosie. It seemed strange that Mrs Newchurch had not remembered Aunty Rosie's words in 1994-95.

Justice von Doussa doubted the evidence of the 'dissident' women because, among other reasons, he thought that it was 'culturally inappropriate to pass on the information [about the 'secret women's business'] if that ... member of the next generation was no longer interested in traditional practices and beliefs.'[224] Justice von Doussa agreed with Doreen Kartinyeri that the dissident women had never been entrusted with the secrets of women's business in Hindmarsh Island because 'they consider traditional Ngarrindjeri culture and practices as historical curiosities that are no longer a part of, or appropriate to, their current lifestyle as Christian members of a wider urban community.'[225]

Partington commented:

> if His Honour and Doreen Kartinyeri are correct in this, we all should pay tribute to the incredible foresight of Aunty Rosie, Nanna Laura and Grandmother Sally, Kartinyeri's three supposed informants, in picking out which of their granddaughters and nieces were likely to be converted to Christianity. An even greater difficulty with Doreen Kartinyeri's claim is that Aunty Rosie, Nanna Laura and Grandmother Sally, the three women she named as her informants, were all Christians.[226]

Whoever was telling the truth, the overwhelming majority of senior

---

223 Chapman v Luminis, 2001, paragraph 465.
224 Chapman v Luminis, 2001, paragraph 383.
225 Chapman v Luminis, 2001, paragraph 384.
226 Partington, 2003.

Ngarrindjeri women had not previously heard of Doreen Kartinyeri's women's business. If the women's business was known to three other women as well as Doreen Kartinyeri, why was it not known to the entire mature female Ngarrindjeri population? Partington thus asked, 'in what way was Doreen Kartinyeri a special bearer of restricted tradition?'[227]

Justice von Doussa did not warm to arguments that it is nonsensical to believe that a bridge was likely to create destruction, when barrages had existed on the Murray for decades without harm to Ngarrindjeri women or anyone else. He stated that 'spiritual beliefs do not lend themselves to proof in strictly formal terms. Their acceptance by true believers necessarily involves a leap of faith.'[228] Nevertheless, in 1994, no Ngarrindjeri women claimed that dire consequences to their health and fertility had resulted from building barrages on the Murray, although these had changed the landscape considerably. According to Partington, the foundations of the Goolwa barrage required 4,770 timber piles of up to ten metres in length to be driven into the river bed. A central line of interlocked steel sheet piling, 10-12 metres in depth, acts as a cut off. The building of the ferry approaches required pylons to be driven into the riverbed, 30-40 metres from each side, to a depth of up to 18 metres. Many Aborigines helped build these barrages. John McHughes, the sole remaining Aboriginal resident in the Goolwa area by the 1990s, took a leading part in that work. He never heard of any objections nor of women's business relating to Hindmarsh Island. Judge Stevens, the royal commissioner, found no foundation for any distinction between the construction of a bridge, a second ferry or the Goolwa barrage in the context of the women's business.

The Hindmarsh Island affair was an unfortunate use of Aboriginal culture to stop non-Aboriginal development. It is not invalid to protect

---

227 Partington, 2003.
228 Chapman v Luminis, 2001, paragraph 391.

heritage or to respect culture, but the recent invention of tradition or its continual reinvention to suit a cause weakens the future adherence to respect in these matters. Kartinyeri has recently gone to her grave swearing her belief in the tradition of secret women's business as it applied to Hindmarsh Island, but a substantial group of Ngarrindjeri women do not agree.

Separation of ATSI Children from Their Families (1997)

The National Inquiry into the Separation of Aboriginal and Torres Strait Islander Children from Their Families was conducted by the Human Rights and Equal Opportunity Commission and produced the report called *Bringing Them Home*. The Inquiry was headed by Sir Ronald Wilson, the President of the Human Rights and Equal Opportunity Commission, former Deputy Chairperson of the Council for Aboriginal Reconciliation, and retired High Court justice. He was assisted by Mick Dodson. It was commonly referred to as 'The Stolen Generations' report for reasons that will become clear. The Commission was heavily influenced by the Deaths in Custody 'finding' that many prisoners who died in custody were removed from their families, as if this was the cause of their troubles despite perfectly acceptable alternative explanations such as poor education.[229] While it is clear that many Aborigines were and are removed from family, proponents of the 'Stolen Generations' never pause to ask why particular children were removed from their family. It is as well they do not because they would be dismayed to know that the reasons would be no less severe than those faced by A. O. Neville who said in 1947, 'if white men had been made responsible for their off-spring

---

[229] 'Empirical studies indicate that the type of crime committed by a certain group of individuals may to a large extent be explained by an individual's human capital (and hence, education).' Gary Becker on crime and punishment. <http://home.uchicago.edu/~gbecker/Nobel/nobel.html#Household>.

... much costly effort [would be] saved.'[230] While Aboriginal children of concern to the Inquiry were not taken because of the intolerance shown 'half-castes' by Aborigines and non-Aborigines in Neville's time, the reasons they were taken are nevertheless important. Aboriginal children were taken because of the risks they faced in remaining with their family. The risks they faced in not being taken were severe.

There is clear evidence that a large proportion of Aboriginal people were affected by children being removed from family. In 1994, 10 per cent of Indigenous people aged 25 years or older reported that they had been taken away from their natural family. The reason for these 'takings' may, however, have included children sent to school or hospital at the request of their parents. The same result was recorded for the closest equivalent age cohort group (35 years or over) in 2002. Both 1994 and 2002 data recorded that eight per cent of Indigenous people aged 15 years or older had been taken away from their natural family. To measure the number of Indigenous people potentially affected by removal of children from their families, in 2002 Indigenous people aged 15 years or older were asked whether they or any of their relatives had been removed from their natural families. Thirty-eight percent reported that they had either been removed themselves and/or had relatives who, as a child, had been removed from their natural family. The most frequently reported relatives removed were grandparents (15 per cent), aunts or uncles (11 per cent), and parents (nine per cent).[231]

The National Inquiry commenced in 1995 aiming to 'trace the past laws, practices and policies which resulted in the separation of Aboriginal and Torres Strait Islander children from their families by compulsion, duress or undue influence, and the effects of those

---

230 Neville, 1947, p. 51.
231 ABS, 2004.

laws, practices and policies.'[232] It was a most serious topic, and there was little doubt that many Aborigines had been removed from their families in earlier generations, in some cases with devastating consequences. Unfortunately, the report was seriously flawed. It was, as my colleague noted at the time, 'one of the most intellectually and morally irresponsible reports to be presented to an Australian government in recent years.'[233]

A crucial fallacy of the report was that it treated all separations as forced, including those that were voluntary or where there was a clear need for the sake of the welfare of the child to be taken. Such all-encompassing definitions enabled the Inquiry to conclude that, 'between one in three and one in ten Indigenous children were *forcibly* removed from their families and communities in the period from approximately 1910 until 1970' [emphasis added].[234] This, despite evidence that many removals were in the interests of the child; in many instances, children were fostered with Aboriginal families, thus undermining the charge of assimilation as the purpose of removals.[235] It also failed to give the historical context of removals, such as the considerable pressure exerted on unmarried Aboriginal and non-Aboriginal mothers, in that era, to give up their children for adoption. Further, the method of the Inquiry was seriously flawed; it did not test any allegations but simply accepted all stories as valid. There was no cross examination.

The most offensive aspect of the Inquiry was its finding that the forcible removal policy constituted 'genocide' and 'a crime against

---

232 Human Rights and Equal Opportunities Commission, 1997. *Bringing Them Home, Report of the National Inquiry into the Separation of Aboriginal and Torres Strait Islander Children from Their Families.*
233 Brunton, R. 1998. 'Betraying the Victims: The Stolen Generations' Report.' *IPA Backgrounder*, Institute of Public Affairs, p. 3.
234 HREOC 1997, Part 2, 10.
235 Australian Bureau of Statistics, 2002. 'Population Special Article: A Profile of Australia's Indigenous People.' *Year Book Australia.*

humanity' in terms of the *United Nations Convention on Genocide*.[236] In the view of the Commission, even assimilation, that is, an attempt to give people a choice to escape poor circumstances, could be genocidal. The Commission maintained this view although, after the Second World War, the International Labour Organisation considered bringing Indigenous people into the modern world to be 'desirable and just'. At the end of the period of the so-called stolen generations in Australia, ILO Convention 107 on *The Protection and Integration of Indigenous and other Tribal and Semi-Tribal Populations* states that the most 'enlightened' international policy was assimilation.[237] To condemn a universally accepted policy from an earlier era may not be unusual but not to acknowledge the policy settings of the time as a reason for actions is a shoddy and disingenuous methodology.

The following illustration is instructive:

> In a letter to the West Australian Commissioner of Native Affairs in November 1943, Inspector Bisley of Port Hedland wrote: I recommend that this child [4 years of age] be removed when she is old enough as she will be probably handed over to some aged blackfellow at an early age.' With respect to the same child, Inspector Neill in Broome wrote to the Commissioner in December 1944, '[t]here may perhaps be an objection to the children being removed from the Hospital without first returning to the Station from which they came as it means breaking faith with the mothers.[238]

Judged by contemporary standards this behaviour was appalling because the child was not reported to be in actual danger and the mother's permission for removal was not sought. Nevertheless, there was an interest in saving the child from a then widely known practice among tribal Aborigines of giving young females to older men.

---

236 HREOC 1997, Part 4.
237 Brunton, 1998, p. 11.
238 HREOC, 1997, Part 1.

Unfortunately, the tendency to replay the past as if later policy had not adjusted to earlier deficiencies makes the problem of the need to enforce standards of care just as difficult today. The contemporary difficulty is that the government is too reluctant to intervene in Aboriginal families for fear of allegations of racism. An Aboriginal advocate for Aboriginal children and women recently stated:

> Departments of community services don't want to create another stolen generation so we find a lot of Aboriginal children are left in a dangerous situation because some white or black worker doesn't want to be called racist.[239]

Some good has nevertheless come from the Inquiry. The Aboriginal corporation Link-Up seeks the reunification of Aboriginal families regardless of cause and is therefore not ideological as was the Commission. Of the Commission's 54 recommendations many, especially the key elements of reparations and a national compensation fund, have been rejected by both sides of politics. Only recently has the apology been given, by the Rudd Government. The apology followed a motion of regret by the Howard Government.[240]

The Stolen Generations has been an exercise designed to extract compensation from the present taxpayer for past government practices, most of which were well-meaning. The Stolen Generations confuses early 20th century institutional practices, which occurred for many groups of children other than Aborigines, with an aspiration for the best present policies. The confusion fails on two counts. First, it unfairly condemns past practices, on the basis that current circumstances, policies and resources, are better. Second, it contains bias towards de-institutionalisation. Institutions are now being revealed not as an inferior solution to providing protection of children at risk but rather, for some, as the best solution. Indeed, the failure

---

239 Pamela Greer, quoted in *The Weekend Australian*, 3-4 May, 2003, 8.
240 Motion of Reconciliation moved by Hon. John Howard Prime Minister, 26 August 1999. House of Representatives Hansard, p. 9205.

to institutionalise the mentally ill, for example, is a major cause of homelessness in Australia. The bias in current practices against foster care and the intensely ideological desire to have Aboriginal children stay with their families is causing death and mayhem. The sensible policy is to decide in the best interest of the child regardless of ethnic or racial circumstances. Only the circumstances relevant to care and safety should be assessed.

The Stolen Generations report has caused an outpouring of grief among damaged families and allowed them to point their anger at a single cause, white institutions, the very institutions they need. Researchers and commentators are busy creating and enhancing the misrepresentation of cause and effect.[241] In 2006, the deeply concerned Phillip Adams, on ABC radio *Late Night Live*, interviewed Dr Sue Gordon, Chair of the National Indigenous Council, about accusations of another 'Stolen Generations' in the continued taking of children for their protection. Adams wondered if the current violence and abuse was 'a legacy of a stolen generation'. Gordon answered, 'Often it's used as an excuse. We can't blame the stolen generations for what's happening now'. The atheist Adams also tried to invoke the Pope's remarks at the time, but Gordon was having none of the 'Sorry' business, suggesting it was irrelevant. Gordon was able to call on the *United Nations Convention on the Rights of the Child*, that the 'best interests of the child [are] served by taking them out of home.' Adams was aghast at the affront to Aboriginal mothers, to which Gordon answered, 'Half the mothers are so drunk they would not know.'[242]

Research into the stolen generations recently published by Keith Windschuttle disproves the so-called evidence of the Royal Commission that large numbers of Aboriginal children were removed

---

[241] Briskman, L. 2003. *The Black Grapevine: Aboriginal Activism and the Stolen Generations*. The Federation Press and Haebich, A. 2000. *Broken Circles: Fragmenting Indigenous Families 1800-2000*. Fremantle Arts Centre Press.
[242] ABC *Late Night Live* transcript, 24 May, 2006.

from their families because they were Aboriginal. After exhaustive archival research, Windschuttle concluded that these 'small numbers of Aboriginal child removals were almost all based on the same child welfare policies that apply to white children. They were neither racist nor genocidal. There were no 'Stolen Generations'.'[243]

Cubillo and Gunner (2000)

The Stolen Generations report and its attempt to press a claim of genocide on past child protection practices has been severely dented by the Federal Court of Australia in *Cubillo v. Commonwealth*.[244] The Stolen Generations Legal Unit and the Commonwealth consented to these two unrelated cases, Lorna Cubillo and Peter Gunner, being run together. Both sides knew that these were test cases for the Stolen Generations. Although the judge was at pains to point out he was deciding only the matters before him, there is no doubt Aboriginal interests would have claimed a victory on behalf of the Stolen Generations had the cases succeeded. For future cases to succeed there will have to be proof that Commonwealth actions were not in the best interests of the child when 'best interest' must be judged in the light of the policy and custom of the day.

In the proceedings, Cubillo and Gunner asserted that, between 1946 and 1966, the Commonwealth engaged in coercive removal of children with the objective of destroying Aboriginal heritage, displacing it with what is variously described as a 'European' or 'white' heritage. The Commonwealth denied that, in the period 1946-1966, a policy was formulated and applied to effect destruction of a person's heritage. It also denied that a policy was formulated and applied for coercive removal of children, save where the child was neglected or its life was at risk.

---

243 Windschuttle, K. 2009. *The Fabrication of Aboriginal History Volume Three: The Stolen Generations 1881-2008*. Macleay Press, p. 618.
244 *Cubillo v Commonwealth* [2000] FCA 1084.

The Commonwealth asserted that until about 1938 it applied a policy of separation and protection of Aborigines on Aboriginal reserves. Thereafter it adopted, for many Aborigines, a policy of assimilation as advocated by the prominent anthropologist, Professor Elkin. The Commonwealth argued that adoption of the policy was a reaction to social change of many Aborigines then taking place and that the social change was not initiated or driven by any policy of the Commonwealth. Assimilation policy was intended to, and did, alleviate or minimise undesirable consequences flowing from the social change. The objective of assimilation policy was to give to those experiencing the social change an opportunity to participate in the community as equals with other Australians, without social, racial or intellectual stigma. An important step in the achievement of that objective was provision of a public education for children, being the same or similar education provided to other Australian children. At the time the educational services in the Northern Territory were under-developed, so that the numbers of schools were few and receipt of a public education necessitated either accommodation in the principal towns or the awaiting of development of schools and provision of teachers in remote areas.

It was perceived that children who were not of full blood Aboriginal parentage, and who had been abandoned by their non-Aboriginal fathers, were at risk (physically, morally and/or intellectually) if left in Aboriginal camps. It was perceived that such children were at risk of exploitation in employment especially in remote stations and of sexual exploitation and abuse, and that by reason of their parentage they were likely to respond positively to, and benefit from, a public education at a school attended by other Australian children without discrimination as to colour or race. It was the intention that this should be done where the mothers of such children consented to them being admitted to hostels at the principal towns where such schools were to be found. Where the children enjoyed both parents, albeit of different races, it was perceived that the presence of both parents lessened or removed the risks that otherwise were feared may exist; that in the case of such children it was expected the parents would make arrangements for their schooling in the public schools in accordance with the policies of compulsory universal schooling adopted throughout Australia.

It was perceived that where the child enjoyed full Aboriginal parentage, it was unlikely such a child was at risk in a physical or moral sense, that it was unlikely such a child would benefit from admission to a public school without extensive educational preparation, and that in such cases special schools should be (and were) established at stations and Indigenous reserves for their education.[245]

Cubillo and Gunner alleged that the Commonwealth's policy was the separation of half-caste children from parents without parental consent, not taking into account but deliberately ignoring individual circumstance by false promises. The alleged purposes were through 'fear' and in pursuit of 'a theory of eugenics' to:

- destroy the child's relationship with his or her family
- assimilate the child into a non-aboriginal society
- provide domestic and manual labour for Europeans
- breed out half-caste people
- protect the primacy of the Anglo-Saxon culture.[246]

Cubillo and Gunner alleged that the Commonwealth acted contrary to Article 2 of the Genocide Convention where it proscribes:

- Causing serious bodily or mental harm to members of a group
- Deliberately inflicting on the group conditions of life calculated to bring about its physical destruction in whole or in part
- Imposing measures intended to prevent births within the group
- Forcibly transferring children of the group to another group[247]

---

245 *Cubillo v Commonwealth of Australia* and *Gunner v Commonwealth of Australia*, *Commonwealth Opening Submission*, p. 2.
246 Cubillo and Gunner, *Commonwealth Final Submission* (Part II), p. 12.
247 Cubillo, *Commonwealth Final Submission* (Part II), p. 12.

The allegation was that the Commonwealth policy was inflicted upon oppressed and vulnerable people in isolated communities and the most desolate parts of the country. It was imposed, supposedly, with unsurpassed cruelty in recent Australian history, causing misery, trauma and abuse. The Commonwealth's policy was characterised as 'scandalous and outrageous, bureaucratic tyranny, contumelious, venal, contemptuous and the worst of conduct, fraudulent, deceitful and treacherous, disgraceful and reprehensible.'[248]

As the Commonwealth stated in its submission, these allegations were:

> a damning attack on the Government and people of this country, calculated to bring the nation into disrepute in the world community. It is an attack upon the person, character and reputation of the various Ministers who formulated the policies, whose number included such highly respected men as John McEwen and Sir Paul Hasluck, who later became a highly respected Governor-General. It attacks the Chief Protectors, Directors of Native Affairs and Directors of Welfare, the patrol officers, the Missionaries who assisted by the conduct of the hostels, and upon all others who lent their hand to its implementation. In all of these cases, the allegation if made out would result in the most serious imputation upon their characters.[249]

The Lorna Cubillo and Peter Gunner cases failed because they lacked merit. Justice O'Loughlin stated, 'I do not think that the evidence of either Mrs Cubillo or Mr Gunner was deliberately untruthful but ... I am concerned that they have unconsciously engaged in exercises of reconstruction, based, not on what they knew at the time, but on what they have convinced themselves must have happened or what others

---

248 Cubillo, *Commonwealth Final Submission* (Part 1), p. 17.
249 Cubillo, *Commonwealth Final Submission* (Part 1), p. 20.

may have told them.'[250]

The loss does not mean that all cases are doomed to fail. But if these were the best cases, what hope for the remainder? Justice O'Loughlin provided the answers. For cases to succeed, there will have to be proof a child was forcibly removed. Only eight witnesses came forth for the applicants. Four of them conceded in cross-examination that they had been placed in the institution at the request of their parents. Speaking of the people at Retta Dixon Home where Lorna Cubillo had been taken, a contemporary, Mrs Harris, said 'Well, my mother didn't want me when I was born but afterwards well, she wanted to do away with me but my grandmother saved me.'[251] The evidence given in the trial on behalf of Peter Gunner bears out this insight and, as the evidence in Box 4 and Box 5 shows, his case.

The hopes of The Stolen Generations report to besmirch the name of earlier administrators failed and future cases would rely on evidence from a small and dwindling number of former officers of 'exceptionally high calibre' of the Native Affairs Branch and the Welfare Branch of the Northern Territory. 'All of them denied the existence of a general or widespread policy of removal of part Aboriginal children and most of them insisted that no child was removed without the consent of the mother of that child.'[252] Plaintiffs will have to prove absence of 'best interest' in the light of the policy and custom of the day. Justice O'Loughlin quoted a fellow judge: 'the events that I am being asked to judge and evaluate commenced in 1942 and finished in 1960. Thus in 1999 I am asked to judge that which took place 39 to 57 years ago ... these are events that occurred in a different Australia, a society with different knowledge, and with different moral values and standards.'[253]

Justice O'Loughlin noted the Bringing Them Home report did

---

250 *Cubillo*, 2000, paragraph 125.
251 *Cubillo*, 2000, paragraph 604.
252 *Cubillo*, 2000, paragraph 28.
253 *Cubillo*, 2000, paragraph 101.

> **Box 4   Gunner's mother Topsy**
>
> By then I was well aware of Topsy's status in the native camp. She was a full blood woman herself but she had a halfcaste child and in those days if you were a halfcaste you didn't belong to the black people and you didn't belong to the white people. Because Topsy had a halfcaste child she was treated as an outcast in the camp. She wasn't being looked after or helped in the camp, she didn't have a husband, which I'm sure she would have by that age if she didn't have the halfcaste baby, and she was dependent on our support and rations to get by.
>
> I was aware that Topsy became pregnant but I have no memory of roughly how pregnant she was when I became aware of it. I do remember clearly that she was still working as my housegirl when I became aware she was pregnant. I don't have any memory of talking to her about it while she was still pregnant and I am sure I never asked her who the father was. I simply assumed at the time that she had married in the tribal way and was pregnant to one of the aboriginal men in the camp.
>
> I do recall that Topsy was working at the house right up until she was due to have her baby. I remember that she was working there one day, heavily pregnant, and the next day she turned up and it was obvious that she had had the baby because her tummy was as flat as a tack.
>
> Topsy was quite young at that time. I don't know what age she'd have been. She wasn't a "girl" but she was definitely of marriageable age. I'd guess she was about late teens. I didn't see the baby after Topsy gave birth. I was quite shocked when she turned up to start work at the house one morning and had obviously given birth since the previous day. I can still remember asking her about the baby. I said "Which way picanniney?" Topsy definitely understood what I meant - what happened with the baby, where is it … She just giggled at me as she always did when I asked her a question. When I asked her again she told me the baby had gone, that it had been put down a rabbit burrow. I understood this to mean the baby had been killed. I had heard of aborigines killing their babies if there was something wrong with the baby or if it wasn't wanted or the mother couldn't manage it. I was quite shocked but I considered that it was tribal business, their way of life and I never interfered in those things.
>
> Source: Affidavit of Dora Hope McLeod sworn 14 December 1998, paragraph. 79. Commonwealth's Final Submission Part IV, pp.52-53.

not inquire into separations that were effected with the consent of a child's family. 'Nor did they require a consideration of cases where a neglected, destitute, sick or orphaned child might have been removed without the consent of the child's parents or guardian.'[254] HREOC and the Commonwealth Government that set the terms of reference left out the crucial matter of the context within which children were removed. It is not clear whether they excluded matters where consent was given, or that the inquiries simply did not ask and/or distinguish the case. Justice O'Loughlin did not make that mistake, quoting from Sister Eileen Heath: 'After the part-aboriginal people achieved drinking rights, alcoholism and violence became larger social problems for them, which often had welfare implications for their children.'[255] The problem with the whole sorry affair is that, once people become compensation-focused, little else matters. 'Mrs Cubillo has, understandably, built up a tremendous sense of grievance and the litigious process has turned that sense of grievance against the Commonwealth to the exclusion of all others.'[256]

What began as an apparently innocent exercise in seeking answers to deaths in custody in 1991 ended with a major exercise to take the moral high ground against the integrity of Australian laws and society. The inquiries were poorly conceived and poorly exercised, in the case of Deaths in Custody, because the answers were known soon after the outset and ignored in preference for setting out a much wider political agenda. The Bringing Them Home report was spawned by Deaths in Custody and was designed to confuse poor circumstances and tragedy with blame for the respondent with the most money to hand over, the Commonwealth.

---

254 *Cubillo*, 2000, paragraph 65.
255 *Cubillo*, 2000, paragraph 110.
256 *Cubillo*, 2000, paragraph 730.

> **Box 5 Saving Peter Gunner's life**
>
> I remember the situation quite clearly. Topsy's baby, Peter, was in the camp and was in a totally neglected state. It was shocking. He was very sick. In general all the babies in the camp were well looked after and healthy, but we could see that this baby was completely neglected and looked to be almost starving. After we saw the baby we called the Alice Springs Flying Doctor Base. My diary note says I spoke to Dr Pryor who told us what to do. The following day, when we went down to check on Peter and give him the tablets, he was even worse. I wrote in my diary on Friday 17 November – 'Peter unconscious today. Jimmy was going to bury him! He dug the grave ready but Alec stopped them from burying him!' I can still remember this clearly. As far as the aborigines were concerned, if someone was sick and became unconscious they were dead. I believe we saved Peter's life at that time in November 1950.
>
> Source: Affidavit of Dora Hope McLeod 1998, pages 55-6.

Hindmarsh Island was brought low by a royal commission. But the Cubillo and Gunner case has destroyed the basis for complaints raised by the political agenda. Unfortunately, the agenda still runs because of ignorance among media and deliberate connivance by some intellectuals to keep the 'Stolen Generations' allegation rolling. The Rudd Government, rather than support the Commonwealth's own case in the Federal Court, preferred the easy appeal to morality and guilt by giving an apology.

Rudd Government Apology (2008)

The Rudd Government Apology to the Stolen Generations on 13 February 2008[257] was an exercise in empty moralising. It deliberately ignored the findings of the Cubillo and Gunner case. It embraced the falsity of the *Royal Commission into Aboriginal Deaths in Custody* and the agenda of the *Bringing Them Home* report save for the fact that it was not so foolish as to establish a compensation scheme or use the word 'genocide'.

The Rudd Government trod the path avoided by O'Loughlin in Cubillo and Gunner. The Rudd Government chose the path of sanctimony, thereby denigrating commonly held beliefs and the intention to do the right thing. More lives were saved in that period than have been by the current policy settings which have let children remain in disgusting and violent circumstances in the name of self-determination and saving a culture. The Prime Minister said in the Apology:

> Some have asked, 'Why apologise?' Let me begin to answer by telling the Parliament just a little of one person's story. ... Nanna Nungala Fejo, as she prefers to be called, was born in the late 1920s. She remembers her earliest childhood days living with her family and her community in a bush camp just outside Tennant Creek. She remembers the love and the warmth and the kinship of those days long ago, including traditional dancing around the camp fire at night...
>
> But then, sometime around 1932, when she was about four, she remembers the coming of the welfare men. Her family had feared that day and had dug holes in the creek bank where the children could run and hide ...
>
> A few years later, government policy changed. Now the children would be handed over to the missions to be cared for

---

257 Hon Kevin Rudd Prime Minister of Australia, 2008. 'Apology To Australia's Indigenous Peoples.' *Hansard* 13 February 2008, p. 167.

by the churches ... She and her sister were sent to a Methodist mission on Goulburn Island and then Croker Island. Her Catholic brother was sent to work at a cattle station and her cousin to a Catholic mission.

Nanna Fejo's is just one story. There are thousands, tens of thousands, of them: stories of forced separation of Aboriginal and Torres Strait Islander children from their mums and dads over the better part of a century.

The Prime Minister conflated forced separations with those where there was consent, of which there were many. And he deliberately ignored the real circumstances which created the need to 'save' children from appalling circumstances. Humbug indeed. He went on to quote the great 'demon',

> The Western Australian Protector of Natives [A.O. Neville] ... expounding ... at length in Canberra in 1937 at the first national conference on Indigenous affairs that brought together the Commonwealth and state protectors of natives.[258]

What was it that Neville expounded?

> [L]ong before the Canberra Conference [1937], we in the West had considered and discarded those other alternatives put forward to absorption or assimilation, referred to as segregation, village settlements and proposals of a like nature, having for their central idea the 'living apart' of the natives from the rest of the community.[259]

Neville's critique of separate development is valid today. The policies of the times need to be understood within the attitudes of the time faced by Neville and his contemporaries. Aboriginal women were treated as chattels in white and black society at the time. In context, Neville was clearly a compassionate man, and within the mores of his time he, for the most part, discharged his duties as compassionately

---

[258] Rudd, 2008, p. 169.
[259] Neville, 1947, p. 27.

as his authority and budget allowed.

> Yet we have had the coloured man amongst us for a hundred years or more. He has died in his hundreds, nay thousands, in pain, misery and squalor, and through avoidable ill-health. Innumerable little children have perished through neglect and ignorance.[260]

Some of his sentiments would not be out of place among the political Left today: 'Who should come first if it isn't the real owners of the land, its first possessors? We are all newcomers to them, dispossessors, despoilers.'[261]

Kevin Rudd was quick to grab the headlines and the applause, but he should know the substance of the issues and these belie his unctuousness. The substance is that many Aboriginal children were taken from dysfunctional families for their protection, just as happened with white children; the only difference was that the numbers of Aboriginal families that were dysfunctional was higher because they had real difficulty in making their way in the modern world for a string of reasons arising from their own culture as well the prejudice and poor treatment by whites. The retreat to collective guilt provides the easy public sentiment for a group apology, it makes the real work of building a bridge into the modern economy harder by constructing programs centred on the 'exceptional' nature of Aborigines and not on the skills of the individual. The Apology will make the work of social workers and others who need to take children for their own safety much harder.

---

260 Neville, 1947, p. 21.
261 Neville, 1947, p. 23.

5
Inquiries into black morality

The 1990s was the decade of confected moral outrage, with the wrongly attributed Deaths in Custody and misdiagnosed Stolen Generations inquiries. The 2000s was, by contrast, the decade of rediscovering outrageous morals. In the 2000s, five inquiries were undertaken into Aboriginal child sexual abuse, in large part the legacy of 40 years of self-determination. The ugly side of Aboriginal society had been known to anthropologists for a very long time, but, with the romanticisation of culture that accompanied self-determination, any discussion of wrong-doing in an 'oppressed' culture was suppressed or, at least, ignored. Taking the high moral ground in the earlier inquiries increased the likelihood of avoiding scrutiny of Aboriginal culture. Had the five inquiries into child sexual abuse been held in the 1990s, many lives may have been spared.

In 1999, Boni Robertson led an inquiry into child sexual abuse in Queensland. This and subsequent inquiries in NSW, WA, NT and SA told a story that was not amenable to Aboriginal claims that all their woes were the fault of the whiteman. The culprits were Aboriginal males; the victims were young Aborigines. Or the culprits and victims were both underage Aborigines who simply had no moral guardians, their parents having abandoned them. As has been suggested, the reasons for this appalling behaviour were related to collapse of Aboriginal society and accompanied loss of power among males and proximate causes such as grog and unemployment.

As valuable as the inquiries were in focusing on the appalling instances of child sexual abuse in Aboriginal communities, the policy suggestions were preconceived and misplaced. In each inquiry there was a reference to collective solidarity and Aboriginal leadership, notwithstanding that some of the leaders were the problem, and that group pride in elements of the culture is a problem. Recommendations that return to culture were to provide the salve to right the wrongs of the past. It seems that every ill was blamed on the whiteman, rather than on the need to adjust to the whiteman's world. Ten years too late, and still coming up with answers that relied on a damaged culture, five inquiries into child sexual abuse nevertheless set a new tone in Aboriginal policy. That in the NT sparked the Emergency Response. In this chapter, each inquiry and the government responses are considered with a special focus on the Aboriginal Child Placement Principles, a typical response to the propaganda of the stolen generation that has caused great harm to Aboriginal children who have been placed with 'kin' but not because it was best for the child.

Five Inquiries into Aboriginal violence and sexual abuse

Robertson - Queensland (1999)

The Aboriginal and Torres Strait Islander (ATSI) Women's Task Force on Violence was established following a meeting of 400 women at Parliament House, Brisbane, to discuss the epidemic of alcohol-related violence against women and children. The ATSI Women's Task Force on Violence was chaired by Associate Professor Boni Robertson. It consisted of 50 Indigenous women. A smaller Working

Group of eleven carried out the research and consultation, visiting communities and conducting interviews throughout Queensland during the first half of 1999.

The Robertson Inquiry found that a majority of the informants believed that the rise of violence in Aboriginal communities could be attributed to the so-called 'Aboriginal industry' in which both Aboriginal and non-Aboriginal agencies had failed to deliver critical services and produce tangible outcomes.[262] The lack of collaboration had hindered progress and the reasons for poor collaboration included:

- lack of coordination of policies and duplication of programs across governments
- under-representation of Aboriginal peoples in senior positions
- absence of Aboriginal people in decision-making processes.

The Inquiry believed that 'economic independence and sustainability' could not be achieved without significant cultural and social development, cultural revitalisation being a priority. The report suggested that 'elders throughout Queensland are calling for the use of cultural lore to address the escalating crime in Communities and the over incarceration of Indigenous people in both adult and juvenile centres. Crime prevention strategies are considered to be deficient with little relevance to traditional lore which provides the most effective deterrent.'[263]

The report appealed to 'a whole of Community/whole of Government approach' to ensure that Aborigines, particularly victims of violence, had access to essential services. It argued that

---

262 Robertson, B. 1999. *Aboriginal and Torres Strait Islander Women's Task Force on Violence Report,* Queensland Department of Aboriginal and Torres Strait Islander Policy.
263 Robertson, 1999.

CDEP should be fully utilised to aid community development and be regularly monitored and assessed by independent bodies. It appealed for subsidies for transport to rural and remote communities so that isolation did not disadvantage Aborigines in accessing food staples and health services.

The report, although important in raising consciousness about the plight of Aboriginal women and children in isolated Aboriginal communities, was threadbare on policy recommendations. There is no evidence the inquirers realised that these places had been subsidised for decades, and that it may be better for Aborigines to leave. No evidence was presented to substantiate the proposition that traditional lore would solve the problem of violence. Just as unproductive, it provided no insight whatsoever into the lack of employment and the failure to adjust to the needs of the people to earn an income. It was all about the government delivering more services. No mention was made about individual agency and difficulties that Aborigines have in breaking collective bad habits.

The Inquiry argued cultural re-integration programs were needed to help redefine cultural identity. Further, local groups needed to be encouraged to develop and facilitate their own programs and governments needed to establish programs and services to enhance 'Indigenous cultures and spirituality'. The proof that government programs can do such things is absent.

The Inquiry acknowledged that excessive consumption of alcohol and drugs was causing grave problems – domestic violence, rape, incest, child neglect – but it could not bring itself to acknowledge that Aborigines find themselves at a serious disadvantage, compared to other Australians, when it comes to dealing with this problem. Aborigines have no blueprint to guide them in their use of alcohol. Any laws now introduced do not carry the "divine" command of the "Dreamtime" and so cannot be enforced by their own societies. Consequently laws brought in by Aboriginal communities are flouted with impunity.

Government response

A major response to the Robertson Inquiry by the Queensland Government was to impose bans on alcohol, either absolute or on certain strengths of beer.[264] The results have been somewhat disappointing. As the data in figure 9 indicates, after an initial fall in the rate of hospital admissions for assault, following the ban on alcohol in Aboriginal communities in Queensland, there was a resurgence; thereafter a small decline beyond original levels.[265]

Figure 9: Hospital admissions and reported offences – post alcohol bans

Year	Reported offences rate per 1,000 (indigenous communities)	Hospital admissions rate per 1,000 (indigenous communities)
2002-03	66	28
2003-04	82	22
2004-05	80	25
2005-06	101	28
2006-07	88	26
2007-08	88	25

Note: Weighted rate across all communities, measured from the year prior to the introduction of restrictions. The reported offences rate and the reported hospital admissions rate for Queensland were 7.4 and 1.3.
Data source: Quarterly Report on key indicators in Queensland's discrete Indigenous communities January-March 2009. (Author's calculations).

---

264 Department of Aboriginal and Torres Strait Islander People Queensland, *Quarterly Reports,* 2002-08.
265 There was a significant decrease in the rate of hospital admissions of Aurukun residents for assault related conditions in 2002-03 compared with the previous year. This decrease commenced prior to the introduction of alcohol restrictions in Aurukun and has been excluded from the analysis.

The data suggest that easy access to alcohol is not the cause of violence in Aboriginal communities although there may well be different consequent injuries requiring hospitalisation under the influence of alcohol. As McKnight remarked of the Mornington Islanders, the violence is less directed or meaningful, and sadly, 'if the Mornington Islanders ever do turn away from alcohol they will discover that only a dim shadow of their traditional culture remains. They will literally have drunk away their culture.'[266]

Gordon - Western Australia (2002)

The Inquiry into *Response by Government Agencies to Complaints of Family Violence and Child Abuse in Aboriginal Communities*, chaired by Aboriginal magistrate Sue Gordon, reported in 2002. The Inquiry visited 44 communities in Western Australia and invited 400 Aboriginal orgnisations and communities to participate. The Inquiry was asked to consider the issues raised by the coroner's inquiry into the death of the young Aboriginal girl, Susan Taylor. On 12 February 1999 Susan Taylor died as a result of hanging at an ablution block at the Swan Valley Nyoongah Community. Susan was 15 years old. She had most recently resided with her grandparents and certain other family members at a residence in Herne Hill. She had not, at any material time prior to her death, lived at the Swan Valley community.[267]

A key issue was the apparent lack of effective coordination of service delivery in the Taylor and other cases examined by the Inquiry. Although up to thirteen different agencies were involved in providing services to Susan Taylor and her family, departments were unaware of 'all the services being provided by each agency and there was a lack of clarity as to a "lead coordinating agency." '[268]

---

266 McKnight, 2002, p. 216.
267 Gordon, 2002, p. 368.
268 Gordon et al, 2002, p. 343.

The case audit of Susan Taylor's death noted that:

> The interagency approach reflects the historical problems in dealing with families who enter and leave the camp from time to time and the problems that causes in delivery services to the family. In taking a whole of family approach to Mairu/Spratt family, the department has endeavoured to work collaboratively with the other agencies who were providing services to the family whilst the children were residing in the camp and in the broader community. The interagency approach was necessary because no one agency had access to the camp and therefore access to all the knowledge and an understanding of the issues confronting the family.[269]

Consistent with others,[270] the Inquiry bundled together all known causes of violence in Aboriginal communities – colonisation, dispossession, loss of land and traditional culture, and the forced removal of children. It noted that these underlying factors were coupled with poverty, racism, passive welfare, drug, alcohol and substance abuse. Persistent assaults on Aboriginal culture, kinship systems and law are said to have created a situation where Aboriginal communities are extremely vulnerable to family violence and child abuse. Despite lack of insight on causes, there were at least some pragmatic approaches to policy. For example, the Inquiry recommended that rather than engage in a further round of dramatic changes to policy and practice, an investment in core child protection skills may provide a better return for governments, agencies and, most importantly, children and their families, in the longer term.[271] 'The Inquiry recommends that key Aboriginal community members be identified for training in sexual assault education and support services so they become a resource in

---

269 Gordon et al, 2002, p. 343.
270 Wild and Anderson, 2007, p. 278.
271 Gordon et al, 2002, p. xxiii.

their own communities.'²⁷² How would this apply in Halls Creek when a very large number of men were responsible for abuse? While this seems to be sensible, it is meaningless if it results in children being placed at risk with Aboriginal families, a basic premise which was not articulated. The Inquiry noted the enormous resources that had been devoted to Taylor, but that the ideologically inspired policy that demanded the child be left with her own caused her death. Moreover, the Inquiry noted that no one agency had access to the camp. Indeed, the camp was run by thugs who held people hostage; this was not made explicit in the findings or the Inquiry recommendations.

The Inquiry noted that non-attendance and truancy were the most significant factors affecting the education of Aboriginal students. It also made a specific request to the Centre for Anthropological Research, University of Western Australia, about traditional Aboriginal violence. The response concluded that

> Our review of the anthropological literature reveals examples of what, on the face of it, might be taken as instances of family violence or child abuse. But the literature also shows that such actions are invariably within the sphere of traditional practice, ritual or the operation of customary law. We have found little material, which suggests that violence or abuse per se are condoned, or took place with impunity, outside traditionally regulated contexts.²⁷³

This carefully worded advice confirms violence in Aboriginal society and, to the extent the Inquiry sought to find a way to re-impose traditional lore, relies on it. But, according to the University of WA anthropologists, to re-impose traditional lore is to support 'instances of family violence or child abuse'. Such a recommendation would be unthinkable if applied to any other group of children. Applied

---

272 Gordon et al, 2002, p. 482.
273 Gordon et al, 2002, p. 68.

to Aborigines it is just as unthinkable. There have been consistent calls for transferring responsibility for and control of Aboriginal child welfare to the Aboriginal community. This view is often linked to the belief that mainstream services have 'failed' both to stem the widespread abuse and stop the over-representation of children in the care system with its echoes of past removal policies.[274] As usual, lack of effective co-ordination is blamed rather than the racism of keeping the culture. This is not to suggest that alternatives are readily available. The Inquiry, for instance, canvassed the possibility that women should escape violence by leaving the community, but concluded,

> Aboriginal women living in remote areas cannot simply leave their homes and start afresh in a new town. Family relations is just one reason that unites them to the communities they live in, both economically and socially. The Aboriginal approach, that the women recommended, is to make the violence go away, not the victim.[275]

There is much truth in the finding of the Inquiry and it would be preferable to find solutions to violence problems *in situ*. Nevertheless, context is important not only in terms of family support, but also in terms of bad influences. As the principal threat to children and women comes from kin, or leading figures in the community,[276] and bad behaviour is reinforced by absence of positive mentors and experiences and unemployment and as these places have no prospects of an economically viable future, the real prospect of moving has to be considered. Nowhere is there a single question about the economy within which communities operate or the viability of the communities, merely conventional rhetoric about equitable services to all. At the very least, children must be able to escape bad influences.

---

[274] Gordon et al, 2002, p. 83.
[275] Gordon et al, 2002, p. 357.
[276] Gordon et al, 2002, p. 444.

Notwithstanding the need for fresh thinking, the recommendations recapitulate old nostrums: solutions need to include 'Aboriginal self-determination' and 'the use of a community development framework';[277] and that the community itself is best positioned to determine whether a child has been neglected.[278] The latter is an especially risky proposition, one not utilised in 'healthy' communities, let alone dysfunctional communities where the Inquiry was finding evidence of systemic child abuse undertaken by community elders.

There was a significant passing remark made by the Inquiry. It related to in-breeding. The Inquiry suggested that the statistical analysis used in analysing samples of DNA must be modified to take account of populations where there is a high degree of interrelatedness.[279] The extent of inter-family marriage is not known. Given, however, the small numbers in each of these remote communities, the chances of inbreeding must be high. This is especially likely as the old marriage system has broken down, although modern transport has facilitated a great deal of (mainly recreational) travel from communities. The Inquiry honestly suspects very unhealthy practices in remote communities and was, unlike any comparable investigation, brave enough to raise the issue. This is a fundamental issue that the culture lobby will probably fight hard to keep hidden from view.

Government response

The Western Australian Government's 'action' plan for addressing family violence and child abuse in Aboriginal communities was predictably bureaucratic; it was wordy and replete with constant

---

277 Gordon et al, 2002, p. 479.
278 Gordon et al, 2002, p. 392.
279 Gordon et al, 2002, p. 480.

references to 'community involvement'.[280] It consisted of a shopping list of programs and expenditure: new remote policing services in four communities, more child protection workers and Aboriginal support workers. The importance of economic development and sustainability of Aboriginal communities was acknowledged but, rather than sensible economic analysis, there was simply an aspirational statement to the effect that 'it is strongly recognised' that secure Aboriginal Land Title provides potential employment and economic benefits for Aboriginal people.[281] The benefits of Aboriginal land title are canvassed below, but it should have been clear to the Inquiry that any benefits are distant.

Ella-Duncan - New South Wales (2006)

The Aboriginal Child Sexual Assault Taskforce was established to examine the incidence of child sexual assault in Aboriginal communities, and to review the effectiveness of government service responses to this issue. The Taskforce, chaired by Marcia Ella-Duncan, visited twenty-nine communities throughout NSW; 300 people were consulted. Its report confirmed that the incidence of child sexual assault in Aboriginal communities was likely to be significantly greater than suggested by the official statistics. The report found that child sexual assault was endemic and intergenerational in some Aboriginal communities in NSW, was poorly understood, and was often affected by that particular community's situation, such as the community standing of the perpetrators, geographic location, and levels of substance abuse. The Taskforce reported that Aboriginal communities perceive government and non-government responses

---

280 Government of Western Australia, 2002. Putting People First: *The Response to the Inquiry into Response by Government Agencies to Complaints of Family Violence and Child Abuse in Aboriginal Communities,* p. 8.
281 Government of Western Australia, 2002, p. 23.

to Aboriginal child sexual assault to be often ineffective, culturally inappropriate or inconsistent. The communities were mistrustful of some government services owing to both historical and present day factors.

The report contained 119 recommendations for government-wide implementation. Almost all related to hiring Aboriginal staff, or training people to be sensitive to Aboriginal ways. What was not made explicit is that there is a real problem with Aborigines meeting their obligations. The recommendation to develop a specific program to support Aboriginal staff and help them to balance the expectations of community, family and the department is a clear indication of the conflict between the requirements of government programs and the demands of Aboriginal kinship.[282] The solution is always the same, that the system has to be changed to accommodate Aborigines, not that Aborigines should learn to work within the system. Placing to one side the rights of Aborigines to special consideration, in terms of simple efficacy it must now be clear, after decades of tweaking services to accommodate Aboriginal culture, that there are no more tweaks to be had. The time has come to call a halt to sensitivities in the delivery of services because those services are, in practice, rewarding people who behave badly.

Participants spoke strongly about the fear of, or actual, repercussions from the perpetrator or the perpetrator's family. If one community member discloses child sexual assault and puts another community member at risk of incarceration, it is possible, even likely, those other community members could ostracise or even harm the family or child who spoke out. One participant reported an instance where a child had disclosed sexual assault; the next day the child's family home was burnt down.[283] Child sexual assault is also having a devastating effect on communities. One consultation suggested that child sexual

---

282 Aboriginal Child Sexual Assault Taskforce, 2006, p. 24.
283 ACSAT, 2006, p. 53.

assault had the potential to 'tear communities apart'. Participants in this consultation suggested that once the extent and detail of child sexual assault emerged, a kind of war would erupt, a war that pitched family against family, community against community.[284] The difficulty in speaking out is a problem with inter-related small communities. It begs the question, why is 'community' such a prize when the problems of tight-knit communities are often horrendous?

During consultations, participants continually mentioned the historical experiences of Aboriginal communities and expressed the view that the levels of violence and child sexual assault in Aboriginal communities cannot today be separated from the effects of colonisation. An attempt to blame sexual assault on events two centuries ago and echoes of continuing 'colonisation' is not convincing. In any event it provides no solution to sexual assault or, indeed, any other problem suffered by Aboriginal people. While participants frequently referred to the devastating government practice of removing Aboriginal children from their families and the inability of communities to cope with the associated stress, it is clear from Cubillo and Gunner that removals were often in the best interests of the child. It may be that many of the children who were removed (now mothers and grandmothers, fathers and grandfathers) experienced sexual abuse while they were in institutions or foster care[285] but those risks could never excuse the risk of leaving the child in dysfunctional circumstances. The reluctance to reach beyond the welfare intervention of an earlier generation has blinded policy-makers to some substantial underlying problems in Aboriginal society, albeit not helped by poor government and charitable institutions in some instances.

Although the Inquiry paid due deference to the Aboriginal Child Placement Principles (discussed below), it nevertheless recognised that there is a clear argument that in a situation where sexual assault

---

284 ACSAT, 2006, p. 56.
285 ACSAT, 2006, p. 61.

of a child is occurring, the removal of the offender (by criminal justice agencies) must be the response which is preferable to removal of the child.[286] The Inquiry observed that there is little evidence-based evaluation of what actually works to reduce the incidence of child sexual assault in Aboriginal communities.[287] The observation did not dissuade them from suggesting that Aborigines should be hired into more positions, suggesting confusion between the goal of soaking up whiteman's resources and seeking to restore cultural integrity and older ways. Nowhere is there a willingness to acknowledge that Aborigines have to adjust to the actual circumstances in which they operate, and not to try to build a fantasy world with others' money that in a most incomplete way recreates a society that is not only ill-suited to the times but was never particularly bountiful or satisfying in the first place.

Government response

By contrast with some of the aspirations of the Inquiry, the NSW Government undertook to roll out in stages a number of pragmatic programs, beginning with priority communities that show acute levels of disadvantage and dysfunction. Key proposals included additional resources for witness assistance programs and forensic examinations; culturally appropriate awareness-raising programs to target the causes and address the consequences of abuse, and to inform communities of government services; additional legal education resources and support for victims, and expanded provision of sexual assault counselling by NSW Health to provide more timely and culturally appropriate responses to victims and their families. Compliance with mandatory child protection reporting requirements in communities at risk was also encouraged.

---

286 New South Wales Government, 2007. *New South Wales Interagency Plan to Tackle Child Sexual Assault in Aboriginal Communities 2006-2011*, p. 15.
287 NSW Government 2007, p. 5.

A key focus of the NSW Government's child protection response is improving the way Joint Investigation Response Teams (JIRT) operate. Importantly, JIRTs ensure that the service response reflects the circumstances of each case by providing a mechanism for investigation and assessment that incorporates the child protection assessment by the Department of Community Services, the criminal investigation by Police, and Health's assessment of appropriate support services, including medical examination, counselling and therapeutic services.[288] These measures are entirely sensible. They are, however, responses to crises, not solutions to the underlying causes for which there seems to be a romantic patina and unwillingness to understand that a people have reached their endgame in staying outside the main society without a way of supporting themselves with dignity. The response is practical but does not address the Inquiry's challenge to the 'cultural hegemony' of the dominant society. The reason why this and every other inquiry needed to address the cultural hegemony thesis is to demolish it. The thesis does not allow for any proper or comprehensive response to Aboriginal distress. It allows, instead, the collective to wallow in self-loathing and hatred of the dominant society. In setting hatred running it does not produce a positive exit strategy for Aborigines.

Wild and Anderson - Northern Territory (2007)

The Board of Inquiry into the Protection of Aboriginal Children from Sexual Abuse held more than 260 meetings with interested parties around the Northern Territory.[289] One of the most serious accusations at the time expressed by the then Federal minister, Mal Brough, was that paedophile rings operated in some remote communities. While the Inquiry found no evidence of 'paedophile rings' operating in the Northern Territory, there was enough evidence to conclude

---
288 NSW Government 2007, p. 15.
289 Wild and Anderson, 2007, p. 44.

that a number of individual non-Aboriginal 'paedophiles' had been infiltrating Aboriginal communities and offending against children. A small number of offenders did fit the stereotypic 'paedophile' category. As is often the case, these offenders appeared to have offended against many victims. They were often known to the community (and the child and her/his family) and often held positions of influence or trust in a community rather than being a 'stranger'.[290] By way of contrast, the Australian Crime Commission National Indigenous Violence and Child Abuse Intelligence Task Force Special Intelligence Operation[291] uncovered two systemic issues that contribute to criminality within remote communities: poor sharing of information and reporting on violence and child abuse, and abuse of power that facilitates violence, child abuse and other crime. Abuse of power occurs because of the closed nature of small communities and the nepotism of Aboriginal organisations that run them.

This is a case of seeing what you want to see, in which case the Wild and Anderson Inquiry preferred to defend traditional practices and then sought evidence, such as it was, to justify its stance. Although the Inquiry reflected deep-seated attitudes of senior bureaucrats in the NT government, the Inquiry relied on one source for its insights into the relationship between Aboriginal law and Aboriginal dysfunction. Professor Judy Atkinson of the Gnibi College of Indigenous Australian Peoples, Southern Cross University, was the sole expert, and her advice was very contentious. The following extract illustrates the lack of credibility of the report:

> The Inquiry's experience was that there was generally more overall dysfunction in urban centres and those communities where Aboriginal law had significantly broken down. In the more remote, 'traditional' communities, there was still dysfunction

---

290 Wild and Anderson, 2007, p. 58.
291 The interim report of the Task Force *Picture of Criminality in Indigenous Communities* has been finalised and was endorsed by the ACC Board in June 2009, but will not be made available to the public. Australian Crime Commission.

but often on a lesser scale.[292]

Despite the level of disclosed intra-familial sexual abuse, the unanimous view among Aboriginal community members throughout the Northern Territory who participated in the Inquiry's consultations was that incest was an extremely serious breach of traditional law and punishable by death. One reason for complex and intricate traditional 'skin' systems being developed was to prevent incest. Any breach of that 'skin' system was treated with the utmost seriousness. This observation may be true, but how does the introduction of long disregarded laws overcome such behaviour. The disciplines and brutality which enforced those laws are gone.

The Inquiry suggested that, although episodes of sex offending were reported to be occurring in communities where Aboriginal laws were still strong, the prevalence of incest and other intra-familial offending appeared to be higher in communities where Aboriginal law had significantly broken down.[293] This is more hope than evidence. It implies that recapturing tradition will stop the abuse. The skin system broke down almost everywhere years ago. Where it remains in some form it is at the convenience of the powerful. As McKnight has pointed out, the traditional law was often breached when it suited the most powerful old men. The Inquiry cannot explain how reviving law can stop child abuse. Reinstating customary practice, which has condoned violence, is not a solution.

The Inquiry's experience essentially reflected views of advocates such as Jon Altman of the ANU and Olga Havnen of the NT Chief Minster's Department (now working as Head of Indigenous Strategy for Robert Tickner at Red Cross) that, no matter how abysmal the lives of Aborigines in remote Australia, the whiteman's dream of the true Aborigines living on country is worth pursuing, no matter the consequences or cost. The data is clear and is set out in Chapter 3

---

292 Wild and Anderson, 2007, p. 36.
293 Wild and Anderson, 2007, p. 58.

above and below at Chapter 7; Aborigines sitting on their own land are the poorest, most miserable Australians. Instead, the Inquiry lapped up the standard fare that, prior to colonisation, sexual abuse of children and family violence were rare. The Inquiry heard that the present level of sexual abuse and family violence resulted from a combination of the erosion of traditional restraints and behaviour that has been 'learnt' from the treatment received at the hands of the colonisers.[294]

Professor Judy Atkinson contended that the violence, dispossession of land and disempowerment inflicted upon Aboriginal people during colonisation had a profound impact on community structures and relationships.[295] This may be true, but two questions arise, why are many Aborigines similarly dispossessed not so traumatised, and why are some of those not removed from their land traumatised? The answers are plainly that the former are integrated; in the case of the latter, the land and culture did not provide protection or, indeed, meaning, to Aboriginal people facing an entirely new way of life. Those who have been unable to adjust are as likely to have failed because of clinging to inappropriate ways as of forgetting them.

The Inquiry also formed the view that much of the failure to address the dysfunction in Aboriginal communities successfully has its roots in the 'language barrier' and the 'cultural gap'.[296] Failure to understand the Aboriginal 'world view' has apparently resulted in many culturally inappropriate practices and programs that failed to achieve the desired outcomes. The endemic confusion and lack of understanding about the mainstream world was reported to be preventing many Aboriginal people from being able to contribute to solving problems such as child sexual abuse effectively.[297] It would be more sensible for Aborigines to learn English and then decide

---

294 Wild and Anderson, 2007, p. 139.
295 Wild and Anderson, 2007, p. 139.
296 Wild and Anderson, 2007, p. 50.
297 Wild and Anderson, 2007, p. 52.

for themselves if they want the whiteman's money, than to plead ignorance continuously, based on culture. There does not seem to be any problem in understanding the need for moneys from mining royalties and government programs, neither is there a shortage of material desires to be satisfied; every part of the whiteman's world is desired by some – except the necessity to generate wealth and live by decent rules.

The Inquiry was master of consultation routines. It believed its meetings were a success due to pre-planning consultations and using 'previsits' to make contacts, utilising existing resources such as Aboriginal organisations and non-government organisations, interpreters, seeking advice from 'cultural brokers' and holding consultations in places where community members felt comfortable. Apparently, many communities also told the Inquiry that they were rarely, if at all, consulted about programs, policies or structures affecting their community, and they often felt that they had been ignored.[298] This claim is incredible as it is well known that communities are consulted endlessly – it is part of the income of communities that either elders are paid to attend meetings or their organisations are paid to organise them. These meetings, if anything, seem to be in lieu of anything ever being decided; indeed, they seem to be a ruse to ensure nothing is ever decided. Where is the dignity in that? Wild and Anderson, assisted by Michael Dillon and Neil Westbury[299] who now advise Jenny Macklin, the Commonwealth Minister for Families and Indigenous Affairs, seem to believe that engagement of itself achieves wonders. In fact, it achieves little other than keeping people out of work.

An important theme of the Inquiry's consultations was that Aboriginal communities should not be viewed as a 'whole'. Within

---

298 Wild and Anderson, 2007, p. 52.
299 Dillon, M. and N. Westbury, 2007. *Beyond Humbug: Transforming Government Engagement with Indigenous Australia.* Seaview Press.

each community there is a division between different language groups and, within those language groups, there is a division between clans or families.[300] This is an accurate reflection of the real situation. The Inquiry was told that members of one clan may be prevented from speaking out in the presence of a separate clan. Certain clans may also dominate certain resources to the exclusion of other clans. An awareness of the clan and family structures in each community is essential to ensure effective delivery of services. The Inquiry was told that failure to recognize and act through these structures was a core reason for failure of shared responsibility agreements in some communities.[301] The policy response is 'recognition and respect of Aboriginal law and empowerment and respect of Aboriginal people'.[302] The Inquiry suggests that aspects of Aboriginal law 'that effectively contribute to the restoration of law and order within Aboriginal communities and in particular effectively contribute to the protection of Aboriginal children from sexual abuse'[303] be incorporated into Northern Territory law.

Fortunately, the Inquiry also recognised that aspects of Aboriginal culture discourage some Aboriginal people from disclosing abuse, in particular obligations under the kinship system.[304] But the kinship system, which lies at the heart of Aboriginal custom and law, is ruled by old men. Even if such rule could restore law and order, it is doubtful it could do so in a way acceptable in a liberal and enlightened society. Much more is needed than handing over money to Aboriginal organisations without proper accountability and without the need to provide the best service.

One theme presented by both men and women throughout the Inquiry's consultations was that young people were often committing

---

300 Wild and Anderson, 2007, p. 53.
301 Wild and Anderson, 2007, p. 54.
302 Wild and Anderson, 2007, p. 53.
303 Wild and Anderson, 2007, p. 179.
304 Wild and Anderson, 2007, p. 58.

the sexual abuse. The Inquiry believed that this situation stems from a combination of inter-generational trauma, breakdown of cultural restraints and the fact that many of these children (if not all) have themselves been directly abused or exposed to inappropriate sexual activity (through pornography or observing others).[305] If juvenile sex is not condoned by either culture but is a consequence of the breakdown of norms, whose norms will replace the absent ones? For example, the Western Australia Police were investigating allegations that a man had made a 15-year-old Aboriginal girl pregnant. In a letter of complaint to the Police, the Yirrkala Dhanbul Community Association said the girl had been sexually assaulted. The letter said:

> We are strongly opposed to young girls being raped and our culture being used as a reason for this to be overlooked.[306]

A reasonable point ...

> Why does the government stand by and let underage sex happen? In our law the promise system is a very highly respected system but from the white perspective if an old man takes his young promised wife then there is immediate and serious action. But when young people who are under-age have sex with one another, which in Aboriginal law is seen as a very serious breaking of law, there is no action from the white law.[307]

The statement seems to imply that the whiteman's law condones child sex; in fact it expressly forbids it. How did the Inquiry handle this accusation by the Aboriginal community that the 'white society' condones underage sex, or at the very least fails to police it? The Inquiry suggested that action needed to be taken to establish a new set

---

305 Wild and Anderson, 2007, p. 63.
306 Wild and Anderson, 2007, p. 64.
307 Wild and Anderson, 2007, p. 67.

of moral 'norms' within Aboriginal communities that do not fetter the freedom of choice but encourage the young to make appropriate and healthy choices in relation to sex and make certain behaviours socially unacceptable. In stating the obvious and extant situation in white law, it then went on to suggest that traditional marriage practices could still exist but the age difference between husband and wife would need to be reduced (otherwise the girl would not consent to be with the man) as the 'marriage' could not be consummated until both parties were 16 years or older, and the sex must be consensual. In other words, the girl must enter the marriage of her own free choice.[308] These new rules obviate the need for traditional law. They are not traditional law; they are, in fact, whiteman's law. It is hard to see what the Inquiry is recommending.

Concern was expressed that women experience a high level of physical and sexual violence, which goes unreported or is not acted upon. It is unrealistic to expect that child abuse will be reported where community violence is high.[309] A newspaper reporter for *The Age*, Russell Skelton, followed the progress of the Inquiry. He provided a damning critique of its conduct.

> When Rex Wild and his team visited the Ali Curung, a closed community with a long history of violence against women and children, they stayed little more than two hours. After being assured by the men over tea and biscuits that child abuse was not a problem, and faced with silence from the women, the team left.
>
> The visit by the author of the landmark *Little Children are Sacred* report into sex abuse of Aboriginal children in the Northern Territory dismayed some of those present who had been fighting a losing battle to contain a generation of violent young men. In Ali Curung, followers of gangsta rap have

---

308 Wild and Anderson, 2007, p. 71.
309 Wild and Anderson, 2007, p. 78.

imposed a mindless culture of terror on women, the elderly and children.

'They have no interest in tradition or culture; it's all about booze,' said a long-term resident who declined to be identified for fear of reprisals. 'Houses get smashed up every couple of weeks, they are heavily into payback.'

It seems age offers no protection. *The Age* was told by a social worker familiar with the community of an 80-year-old woman who was 'beaten to a pulp' and had her arm broken by a young man. He had been demanding money and access to a granddaughter. In the school yard there have been incidents of older boys inappropriately touching young children.

A Northern Territory Government official, who asked to remain anonymous, said he was shocked at how short the visit by the Wild team to Ali Curung had been and at its failure to thoroughly investigate violence that had plagued the community for years.

'It seemed to me the women, who were spoken to separately, were just starting to loosen up, when suddenly it was all over,' he said. 'Perhaps it didn't matter in the end, because the Wild report highlighted the appalling levels of abuse everywhere, but it did not touch the surface of what goes on at Ali Curung.'

Jenny Walker is an anthropologist familiar with Ali Curung and many of the surrounding communities of the central desert, including Yuendumu, where local women were the first to organise night patrols. She said the older women of Ali Curung had had a hard time trying to contain the violence but had made some progress. After 'downing tools' the women had been provided with a night patrol vehicle by the NT Government and things improved. But the change was short lived when the men commandeered the vehicle, which was in turn confiscated by the police when men were caught smuggling grog.

'This was an unfortunate development, because effective night patrols can reduce domestic violence by as much as 80 per cent,' she said. 'Loss of the vehicle meant the women were effectively disempowered.'[310]

Wild and Anderson acknowledge the pitfalls in self-determination in a footnote in the Inquiry report. They noted 'anecdotal evidence that some male elders, in particular, have hindered violence prevention initiatives because of their own involvement in family violence'.[311] But Wild and Anderson, nevertheless, could do nothing more than suggest that the cultural track was the path to salvation.

Government response

The Northern Territory Government response was a process of, in the main, more talking and 'engagement'. The Commonwealth response, by contrast, was massive and radical – physical intervention on the ground. It is analysed further, below.

Mullighan - South Australia (2008)

The Commission of Inquiry *Children on Anangu Pitjantjatjara Yankunytjatjara Lands Commission of Inquiry: a Report into Sexual Abuse* was perhaps the most formal of the inquiries. The Inquiry was not prepared to act only upon indirect or anecdotal evidence of the existence of sexual abuse of children. It investigated allegations to ascertain what other evidence existed. There are about 2,700 Anangu, including about 1,000 children, living in small communities and many homelands.[312] The Inquiry visited eight communities on the Lands and held 147 meetings. It found that 141 particular children had been sexually abused on the Lands. The majority, 113 cases, were girls. Of

---
310 Russell Skelton, 6 July 2007. 'Violence Behind the Silence.' *The Age*.
311 Wild and Anderson, p. 275.
312 Mullighan, 2008, p. xi.

The Whiteman's Dream 189

these cases the Inquiry was able to investigate 133 from records and other evidence. The other nine cases involved sexualised behaviour. These cases indicated 269 allegations of sexual abuse of children. Three occurred during the 1980s, 18 occurred in the 1990s and the remainder were reported since the year 2000. In all, 248 of those allegations involved 119 children. In some cases there were multiple allegations involving the same child.[313]

The recommendations were a mixture of the immediate and practical to the wildly idealistic and downright harmful. In an example of the latter, the Centre for Restorative Justice informed the Inquiry that:

> It is recognised that Indigenous Australians are very well versed in the notions and practical implementation of restorative justice, as is the case in many First Nation communities around the world.[314]

The Restorative Justice Centre was, in effect, advocating payback, which the Aboriginal people know only too well. It is bad behavior, and illegal. Given an intellectual underpinning and named 'restorative' does not make it any more acceptable. It was a proposal nevertheless given mild support in the Inquiry.

More sensibly, the Inquiry found that there were about 600 school-aged children; however, Department of Education statistics show only about 250 children are regularly attending school.[315] A key recommendation was to enforce school attendance.[316] The Inquiry recommended that the SA Government 'continue to assess ways and means of ensuring that all children on the Lands of compulsory school age attend school and that adequate resources are provided for that

---

313 Mullighan, 2008, p. xiii.
314 Mullighan, 2008, p. 240.
315 Mullighan, 2008, p. 195.
316 Mullighan, 2008, p. 198.

assessment.'[317] The Inquiry noted some schools had systems in place where the children would be given breakfast and clean clothes when they arrived at school. Children have also come to rely on school as a safe environment.[318] There was also the vexed question of tailoring the curriculum to traditional cultures. The Inquiry also recommended that consideration of the teaching of numeracy and literacy 'in a manner suitable to Anangu children' continue to be assessed and implemented and that principals and teachers at the schools on the Lands 'consult with senior Anangu and consider whether traditional Anangu skills and law should be introduced into the curriculum.'[319] But, at the same time as the desire to introduce Anangu skills and law, the Inquiry heard opinion of the attitude that condemns children to remain on the Lands,

> what school teachers were doing is thinking these people won't want to leave the Lands, so we will train them up to get a job here; collecting rubbish, or those things. It's a life sentence. They will never be able to leave the AP Lands. They can't transfer. ... These people get a life sentence from the Education Department.[320]

The apparent dilemma of cultural sensitivity was expressed by a teacher who suggested that while families want their children to complete year 12, they don't understand that there is a 'cultural cost' to that – which means the students have to attend classes all term and might miss funerals and ceremonies sometimes.[321] There are well tested ways to use the school curriculum to lift attendance. These involve drawing on the culture in a utilitarian way so as to attract children. Once the pattern of attending has been consolidated,

---

[317] Mullighan, 2008, p. xiiv.
[318] Mullighan, 2008, p. 196.
[319] Mullighan, 2008, p. xiiv.
[320] Mullighan, 2008, p. 199.
[321] Mullighan, 2008, p. 200.

teachers may then concentrate on the standard and serious curriculum which is compulsory for all students. The matter is further considered at Chapter 7.

The great failing of this and, indeed, of all the inquiries, is that at no time was the need for an actual economy on the lands mentioned. It is as if a better serviced community, with no purpose, especially no productive work, would ever succeed. But this and all of the inquiries proceeded in this ignorant vein. All that mattered was to reflect the undoubtedly genuine desire of some Aboriginal people to restore what they thought they once had – an idyll. Except, there never was an idyll. These inquiries are no more than a recitation of opinions voiced during proceedings with little analysis. The Inquiry model as a legal process should be overturned in favour of a scientific approach. Measures should be tested, not opined. These children cannot read and write; most end up in gaol, the root cause of Deaths in Custody. It is the end of the road for people not because they are stolen but because they are ignorant.

Government response

In responding to the *Children on APY Lands Commission of Inquiry* report (and coincidentally the *Children in State Care Commission of Inquiry* report), the SA Government voted an extra $2.24 million to prosecute child abuse cases arising from the Mullighan Inquiry. More police and social workers were posted to the communities on the APY Lands. An additional $190 million over four years was allocated for the child protection system.[322] The *Children's Protection (Implementation of Report Recommendations) Amendment Act 2009* was enacted. The focus was on practical measures for protection of children and young people accessing services. It required a broader range of organisations to have criminal history checks on employees working with children,

---

322 South Australian Government Response to the Children in State Care Commission of Inquiry Report 2009, p. 1.

additional protection for mandatory notifiers, and strengthening the role and powers of the Guardian for Children and Young People and the Health and Community Services Complaints Commissioner.[323]

New directions despite the Inquiries

Each of these five inquiries into child sexual abuse has bowed in the face of Aboriginal culture as if it were a remedy. None challenged the concept of cultural separation implicit in their recommendations. Governments accepted the sentiments of the various inquiries but actually delivered relatively straightforward practical measures centred on child safety, with a large dose of consultation and engagement. Fortunately, despite the fact that the inquirers could not bring themselves to confront the intellectual stranglehold of cultural identity as the holy grail of Aboriginal policy, three measures did begin to gain favour with governments, probably as a result of the evidence presented to the inquiries. The three most important were the Northern Territory Emergency Response, income management, and the beginnings of a reassessment of the Aboriginal Child Placement Principles.

The NT Intervention

The origins of the Australian Government's Emergency Response into 73 Aboriginal communities in the Northern Territory, more commonly called the Intervention, were straightforward. The Wild and Anderson Inquiry had caught Prime Minister Howard's attention. The result was that the Prime Minister mentioned to his minister, Mal Brough, shortly before a Monday question time in the House of Representatives, that he was thinking of 'cutting off the grog' in Aboriginal communities in the Northern Territory. The matter was

---

[323] *Children's Protection (Implementation of Report Recommendations) Amendment Act 2009*, p. 4.

raised by Howard in Cabinet the same afternoon. As a stand alone measure, Brough was opposed. He was asked to bring a package of measures to Cabinet later that week. He sat down after Cabinet and wrote at the top of a sheet of paper, 'How to fix a town'; he proceeded to build a 'to do' list. He took his thoughts to senior officers in the Department of Families, Housing, Community Services and Indigenous Affairs. By Thursday's Cabinet meeting the intervention was well under way. The intervention took place in June 2007 and accompanying legislation was introduced in August 2007.[324]

Prime Minster Howard wished to make some form of dramatic move on Aboriginal communities. The wish presented Brough with an opportunity to intervene in a bold manner. He did so with a military model in mind, using logistics – people who could do things on the spot: no meetings, no permits, no obligations and no engagement – the things that strangle resolve. The background to Brough's conception of the intervention was that in May 2006 Nanette Rogers, a Deputy Crown Prosecutor in Alice Springs, had bravely revealed the widespread nature of child sexual abuse in the Northern Territory. Subsequently, Brough secured agreement from a national summit of the states to work on child sexual abuse. Nothing happened, however. As is often the case, an old agenda was brought forward at the propitious moment; the Wild and Anderson report was used as the pretext. While the report was the catalyst for the Intervention, it was never the intention of the Howard Government to implement its recommendations. As mentioned above, implementation was left to the Northern Territory Government.

Three pieces of Commonwealth legislation provided the legal basis for the intervention. These related to alcohol restrictions, pornography bans, changes to the permit system and township leasing, and to

---

[324] For a longer account see Johns, G., 2008. 'The Northern Territory Intervention in Aboriginal Affairs: Wicked Problem or Wicked Policy?' *Agenda*, 15(2).

quarantining of welfare payments. *The Northern Territory National Emergency Response Act 2007* (Cth) provided a statutory framework for:
- Alcohol restrictions
- Computer audits to detect pornographic material
- Five-year leases
- Land-tenure changes
- Appointment of government business managers
- Removal of customary laws as a mitigating factor for bail and sentencing, and
- Better management of community stores.

The *Social Security and Other Legislation Amendment (Welfare Payment Reform) Act 2007* combined three elements: welfare reform specific to the Northern Territory (NT), welfare reform specific to Cape York, and a broader welfare-reform package announced earlier. The Government proposed to quarantine various income-support payments and direct Aboriginal families to provide basic necessities such as food, clothing and shelter for their children, rather than supporting substance abuse and gambling. The *Families, Community Services and Indigenous Affairs and Other Legislation Amendment (Northern Territory National Emergency Response and Other Measures) Act 2007* amended existing legislation to include imposition of bans on pornography and lifted the requirement for permits to visit Aboriginal land in townships and access roads and airstrips.

The Emergency Response[325] brought significant additional funding and government effort to the Northern Territory's Aboriginal communities:
- To ensure a better range of healthy food, 83 community

---

325 Department of Families, Housing, Community Services and Indigenous Affairs, 2009a. *Submission of Background Material to The Northern Territory Emergency Response Review Board* and *Future Directions for the Northern Territory Emergency Response: Discussion Paper*.

stores (and four new stores) were licensed
- School nutrition programs were set up in 69 communities providing breakfast and lunch to school-aged children. These programs encourage children to go to school, providing better nutrition, and employing around 130 local Aboriginal people
- Five new crèche facilities were established and six existing crèches have been upgraded
- More than 13,000 child health checks were completed, with over 2,500 children receiving follow-up hearing services and over 2,100 receiving follow-up dental services
- Up to 66 extra police are now working in remote communities
- Four permanent police stations have been upgraded and 18 temporary stations set up
- Sixty-nine active community-run night patrols have been set up
- There are 13 new safe houses to provide protection from violent situations
- A mobile child protection team is working across the Territory
- New Remote Aboriginal Family and Community Workers are working in eight communities
- Around 2,000 new jobs have been funded in government service delivery. Much of this work was previously done by people on CDEP. The new jobs provide award wages, superannuation and access to training and professional development
- Sixty Government Business Managers (GBMs) were appointed in 73 remote communities as well as town camps in Darwin, Tennant Creek and Alice Springs
- 20 Indigenous Engagement Officers were appointed to

support GBMs and to help government talk with local communities.[326]

In October 2009 the Rudd Labor Government removed the provisions in the three pieces of legislation that excluded the operation of the *Racial Discrimination Act* and the Northern Territory anti-discrimination laws.[327] While an evaluation of the Intervention may take some years, what is plainly apparent is that the Intervention, coming as it did after five Inquiries into child sexual abuse, and earlier Inquiries into deaths in custody and separated families, tried a direct and massive physical intervention into the lives of Aborigines in remote communities. The Intervention contained elements of the old missions, with emphasis on personal oversight of behaviour and the use of money; elements of the modern economy with its emphasis on land tenure; and elements of government service provision with its emphasis on extra police and child protection workers. Each of these is probably essential to change Aboriginal behaviour. How these work with broader considerations, especially economic development on Aboriginal lands, is examined in Chapters 6 and 7.

Income management

Following the Intervention in the Northern Territory, more than 15,000 people were subject to income management. It applies to people in the 73 prescribed areas and associated outstations in the Northern Territory who receive income support and family payments. It also applies to people who live in town camps in and around major centres.[328] This means that half of people's Centrelink money (and all of most advances and lump sum payments, and Baby Bonus) can be spent only on essential items and expenses. Money set aside includes half of most income support and family assistance payments and all of most advances and lump sum payments, and of Baby Bonus (which

---

326 FaHCSIAa, 2009a, p. 4.
327 FaHCSIAa, 2009a, p. 8.
328 FaHCSIA, 2009a, p. 10.

is paid in instalments). Centrelink staff help individuals to work out their priorities in spending their income managed funds. Income-managed funds can be made available on the BasicsCard for buying essential and everyday items. Other income-managed funds can be used to pay bills, rent and other expenses. Funds that are income managed cannot be used to buy excluded goods such as alcohol, tobacco, pornography and gambling products. During the first 20 months of income management, 71 per cent of income managed money was allocated to food.

Income management was established together with new arrangements to license and improve community stores. Prior to the Intervention there was a very poor range of food available in many communities, and very few food outlets. Income management has given people the means to spend more on food and household items. As a result community stores have been able to stock a greater variety of priority goods. A number of communities now have new stores or they get regular fresh food drops.

The great surprise is that a Labor government would contemplate extension of income management not only to other remote areas for Aboriginal people, but to a much wider array of poor areas and applying to all welfare recipients. The Rudd Labor Government extended the income-management scheme contained in the Emergency Response legislation to Wadeye in the Northern Territory and the Kimberley and parts of Perth in Western Australia. The Noel Pearson-inspired Family Responsibilities Commission will be the vehicle to expand income management to Cape York in Queensland. It is refreshing that areas in Aboriginal policy should lead to wider reform. Families in the Brisbane suburbs of Woodridge, Kingston, Logan Central and Eagleby; the communities of Doomadgee and Mornington Island will take part in a trial linking school enrolment and attendance with welfare payments.[329]

---

[329] Joint Media Release, Anna Bligh and Jenny Macklin, 'Increasing school attendance and enrolment in Queensland.' 18 September 2009.

The issue is whether income management is to remain compulsory or whether there would be an opt-out clause, a position espoused by the Australian Council of Social Services[330] and widely held within the service community. As to the level of compulsion applicable to income management, a matter being debated presently in the Parliament, there are two broad options available. Option one is that individuals may apply for an exemption from income management based on an individual assessment. This option would continue income management in its current form, that is, income management would still be compulsory for all welfare recipients in prescribed communities, outstations and town camps, but individuals could apply to Centrelink for exemption. Getting an exemption would require an assessment of the person's circumstances against set criteria. People who can show that they do not need income management would then be able to exit.

Centrelink would take a number of factors into account to assess whether a person should remain on income management, including:

- level of financial literacy and budgeting skills
- extent of family responsibilities
- evidence of participation in or exposure to antisocial behaviours, and
- vulnerability to violence, coercion or 'humbugging' if the person is not income managed.

Option two would mean that income management would continue to be compulsory for all welfare recipients in the areas where it currently applies.

The recent evaluation of compulsory and voluntary income management in the Kimberley region and metropolitan Perth suggests a good outcome. There have been 1131 Centrelink clients who have participated in income management. Under the program,

---

330 Martin, C. *The Australian*, 9 March 2010.

income-managed funds cannot be used to purchase excluded goods such as alcohol, tobacco, pornography or gambling products. The evaluation suggests that clients, public servants, financial counsellors, welfare organisations and community leaders agree that income management had 'delivered significant positive impacts on child and family wellbeing'. More than 90 per cent of income-managed funds allocated to BasicsCard, used by Centrelink clients to make purchases, were allocated to food (73 per cent), clothing (16 per cent) and fuel (5 per cent).[331]

There were complaints; one client said: 'I lost my kids and my house and I'd just got out of prison and I didn't want my money locked up any more.'[332] 'Her money' is in fact taxpayers' money, and increasingly, both major political parties are viewing the matter of welfare moneys far more seriously than has been the case for many years. There is a longer-term risk that some clients may become dependent on the system and not take personal responsibility because their money is being managed for them. It is also true that the BasicsCard used by clients may be misused to purchase drugs or alcohol. These are slippages in the system, but before income management, grog, smokes and gambling made up a big part of some recipients' spending.

The evidence is that children and families are better off as a result of income management. In fact, some clients wanted 70 per cent of their income managed, when the government had recently moved to 50 per cent. Better still, about six in 10 current compulsory income-management clients reported that they would consider going on to voluntary management at the conclusion of their compulsory period.

---

331 Department of Families, Housing, Community Services and Indigenous Affairs, 2010. *Evaluation of the Child Protection Scheme of Income Management and Voluntary Income Management Measures in Western Australia*, p. 241.
332 FaHCSIA, 2010, p. 57.

Aboriginal Child Placement Principles

The Gordon Inquiry endorsed continuation of the Aboriginal Child Placement in Western Australia and sought its expansion to provide additional support to and monitoring of Aboriginal foster families. The Aboriginal Child Placement Principles have operated since 1985 in Western Australia and control the placement of Aboriginal children with Aboriginal families when they are placed outside their own family. The Principles 'firstly focus on the best interests of the child being paramount' and that it may not be appropriate to place a child with certain carers. The Principles state that the order of preference, if these options are available, is for Aboriginal children to be placed with the child's extended family, followed by the child's Aboriginal community or kin; the third is with other Aboriginal persons and the last preference, with non-Aboriginal persons sensitive to the needs of the child.[333]

More than 80 per cent of Aboriginal children in Western Australian who were in out-of-home care at 30 June 2003 had been placed in accordance with the Aboriginal Child Placement Principles. Out-of-home care provides care for children who 'are placed away from their parents or family home for reasons of safety or family crisis', which may include abuse, neglect or harm, illness of a carer or the inability of parent(s) to provide adequate care. Normally, children placed in out-of-home care are also on a care and protection order.[334] Nevertheless, the recommendation on monitoring Aboriginal foster families suggests some concerns in the implementation of the Principles when the enthusiasm of public servants and Aboriginal advocates override common sense and decency and put children in danger by placing them with kin or other Aboriginal families without adequate checking.

---

333 Gordon et al, 2002, p. 152.
334 Department of Indigenous Affairs, Western Australia, undated, *Overcoming Indigenous Disadvantage*, pp. 169-188.

The *Children and Young Persons (Care and Protection) Act 1998* in NSW provides principles for placement of Aboriginal children and young people who are in need of care and protection. The Aboriginal and Torres Strait Islander Child and Young Person Placement Principles[335] are essentially the same as for WA and NT[336] and elsewhere. The NSW Inquiry sought to extend them as follows:

- Aboriginal communities are the primary decision makers
- Education about child sexual assault is provided to all communities
- Aboriginal communities identify the issues at a local, regional, state level and are involved in developing service responses
- Service delivery models are tailored to suit the local community
- Responses to child sexual assault are delivered in a holistic way, including understanding Aboriginal communities holistically as well as providing coordinated responses and addressing child sexual assault at the same time as addressing social and economic disadvantage
- Communication protocols are developed and agreed on, outlining the responsibilities of service providers and communities to share information as required and keep each other informed about what is happening
- Anyone working in Aboriginal communities or with Aboriginal people must have an understanding of the community dynamics and the potential impacts that a disclosure of child sexual assault may have on them
- Support is provided to Aboriginal communities as required for them to develop and implement solutions to child

---

335 Aboriginal Child Sexual Assault Taskforce, 2006, p. 124.
336 http://www.nt.gov.au/health/comm_svs/facs/foster_care/indigenouscare.shtml.

sexual assault.[337]

It is doubtful that there is anything particularly useful in these recommendations. They play with the emotions of Aboriginal ownership and provide little insight into how to stop bad behaviour.

By contrast, recent insights into the NT administration of the Aboriginal Child Placement Principles are instructive and may herald some sensible changes. The report by Howard Bath in 2007 to the Northern Territory Government, although couched in careful language, was despairing of the prospects for the safety of Aboriginal children under the placement arrangements. He recommended a return to institutional care in some instances. He recommended that the NT Government, as part of an overall strategy for responding to the needs of young people with high and complex needs, 'consider the development of a small-scale "secure care" facility to provide a temporary containment and treatment option for young people at extreme risk. Secure welfare facilities are operated by Human Services in Victoria, are under development in Western Australia, and are being considered by other states. Planning around secure care options might be undertaken in the context of a broader high-risk youth strategy.'[338]

He also urged a far greater scrutiny of carers, this scrutiny being presently ignored quite possibly because of the Aboriginal Child Placement Principles:

> It is recommended that FACS institute a plan to substantially improve the compliance rates relating to the requirements around the assessment and training of carers, with a particular emphasis on ensuring that relative and 'other' carers offer a

---

337 ACSAT, 2006, p. 292.
338 Bath, H. and D. Boswell, 2007. *Northern Territory Community Services High Risk Audit, Executive Summary and Recommendations.* Northern Territory Department of Health and Families, p. 9.

comparable standard of safety and care to that provided to the children in regular foster care placements ... It is recommended that FACS develop and implement a plan to significantly reduce its reliance on care providers who have not been appropriately assessed, licensed or trained.

And further,

It is recommended that FACS investigate the possibility of instituting a risk-based foster family classification system. Such a system might help identify foster families that need higher levels of supervision and support. Updated risk classifications could be included as components of the regular annual case reviews.[339]

Although the Bath report does not allude directly to the Aboriginal Child Placement Principles, it comments that, 'The present data suggests, as do some of the decisions in the case studies [from the report], that in some cases this principle appears to be given primacy over basic child protection consideration.'[340] In the final report to the Northern Territory Government, Inquiry into the Child Protection System, the Aboriginal Child Placement Principles were endorsed but the inquiry recommended that it be 'interpreted and applied in such a manner that the safety of the child is paramount.'[341]

---

339 Bath and Boswell, 2007, p. 9.
340 *The Weekend Australian* 6-7 February, 2010.
341 Northern Territory Government, 2010. *Inquiry into the Child Protection System in the Northern Territory 2010*, volume 1, Department of Health and Families, p. 27.

6

Pretend economy

Economic independence is a shared policy goal among the political parties and Aboriginal people. It is a concept which obscures profound differences. To self-determination advocates, economic independence means Aboriginal ownership first, and economic viability second. The key activity is governance of pseudo-business entities, economic 'independence' in a pretend economy. To integrationists, economic independence means economic viability for individuals and companies, and ownership not judged by reference to race. The key variable is market viability. This is economic independence in a real economy.

Writing in 1972, Charles Rowley observed, 'with what has been spent on establishing settlements out of the way of economic enterprise, perhaps a real stake could have been acquired by the purchase of cattle stations offering real chances for training and management. ... But the Aboriginal was to remain on the fringe of the economy indefinitely.'[342] Rowley posed the question, 'whether the logic of welfare or the prejudice of White Australia is to prevail'?[343]

---
342 Rowley, 1972, p. 331.
343 Rowley, 1972, p. 340.

Rowley would be dismayed (one hopes) that prejudice was replaced by idealism, even though welfare remained.

Wild and Anderson mused that one area of potential work identified in a number of communities was that of community mediator/monitor, where elders and other identified people would be employed in such positions because of their standing and cultural knowledge. An added benefit of this employment would be reinforcement of the status of the elders and culture.[344] Essentially they recommend that people be paid to be an Aborigine, surely the ultimate insult to both Aborigines and the economies. The Aboriginal economy is an internal, redistributive economy that creates no value. It is for managers of grant-distributing agencies and artists. The Wild and Anderson conception of Aboriginal economic development is a contradiction in terms.

The creation of a pretend Aboriginal economy, mostly but not exclusively in remote Australia, has led to decline in the circumstances of remote area Aborigines and other Aborigines because it has induced Aborigines to wait for the whiteman's gifts. The pretend economy consists of land held in collective ownership, making commercialisation difficult, a bias against mining and in favour of strong environmental preservation. It is underscored by work disincentives. A great deal of intellectual and real capital has been expended in returning land to Aborigines and creating jobs to keep them there. How has it ended up?

A number of factors combined to ensure Aborigines failed to enter the modern economy. One was land rights. Land rights legislation was structured for collectives which did not reflect Aboriginal clan society based on patrilineal or other forms of descent groups[345] but instead was a mimic of socialism with an overlay of race. Land rights delivered the power to extract rent and prevent development.

---

344 Wild and Anderson, 2007, p. 193.
345 Albrecht, 2008, p. 56.

It did not provide the wherewithal necessary to make markets work. By placing land councils between traditional owners and their land it undermined traditional authority,[346] although that was hardly something to cherish.

> The Land Rights Act is being used to wrest control of land from certain Traditional Owners. The justification is that more Traditional Owners will get their say under the Land Rights Act. That may be true but it does not reflect traditional ownership in the traditional sense, and it defies private ownership in any sense. Collective ownership has failed the owners.[347]

Albrecht reflects, for a number of clans the *ALRA* makes a return to a traditional life of hunting and gathering possible; none has chosen to do so.[348] In this regard, the history of the homelands or outstations movement is instructive. The movement was caused by the desire of Aborigines to escape settlement strife which occurred with the loss of control within Aboriginal mission settlements after missionaries departed. The control was essential because Aboriginal clans (however defined) did not live together at least in permanent arrangements; they were often enemies. At the first chance some escaped to outstations, returning to their country. But they could no longer live on it. People thought that they could easily live off the land as did their forefathers. They forgot that to do so requires much effort and detailed knowledge of fauna and flora. As McKnight observes, there have been pleas from one or two outstations after a stay of only a few days for someone to come and get them because they were starving. People now have to bring supplies with them to be able to live in the bush. They need transportation to and from the

---

346 Albrecht, 2008, p. 19.
347 Elferink, J. 2001. 'Land Rights: Why the Potential Hasn't Been Reached and What To Do About It.' *The Bennelong Society Conference.*
348 Albrecht, 2008, p. 56.

outstations; only under dire circumstances would they ever walk.[349]

The Northern Land Council recently audited 55 Community Living Areas (pastoral excisions) granted in the NLC's area. This highlighted the poor state of infrastructure on many pastoral excisions and the difficulties residents face in their day-to-day lives. A substantial number of pastoral excisions do not have year-round road access, are far from schools, stores and medical clinics, and face enormous difficulties in maintaining existing infrastructure and obtaining new facilities such as houses and water pumps. Almost half do not have a functioning public telephone.

Despite the poor living conditions many Aboriginal people choose to continue to live on the excisions because of the strong attachment traditional owners have to their land. The NLC asserts that Aboriginal residents of pastoral excisions derive substantial benefits from living on their country with their own kin; 'Aboriginal elders living in proximity to their own country are able to more easily pass on knowledge about the country to their children and grandchildren.'[350] Interviews conducted as part of the audit revealed that one of the key benefits for Aboriginal people living on pastoral excisions was provision of a refuge from the culturally destructive impact of town living, 'marred as it is by easy access and abuse of alcohol and drugs as well as in-fighting between different Aboriginal tribal groups.'[351]

The NLC also asserts that Aboriginal people living on their land are much more likely to be involved in natural and cultural resource management than their town-based kin. More of their food comes from traditional bush tucker. The effort required to obtain bush tucker and keep country healthy also results in a fitter population less prone to chronic disease. A recent study by the Menzies School of Health Research found that 'higher levels of participation in

---

349 McKnight, 2002, p. 175.
350 NLC, 2008, p. 58.
351 NLC, 2008, p. 58.

Indigenous [natural and cultural resource management] are associated with significantly better health outcomes'.[352] The study also concluded that a cross-sectional analysis cannot determine if natural and cultural resource management prevents chronic diseases or if chronic diseases preclude such participation.

As important, these activities do not determine their income but are a mere supplement. The comparison is also invidious. People living in town camps are very unhealthy because they are unemployed. If the choice is between homeland poverty and scrounging for food and living on the dole in fringe dwellings, then the comparison reveals a great deal about the mind-set of the researchers. Is that all Aborigines are fit for? Even the NLC has to admit that 'the obstacles to establishing a functional living area are enormous.'[353] At another level, how can keeping young girls (and young men) in these isolated areas for prescribed marriage partners be healthy?

Promise of land rights

Hope still abounds that Aborigines can make a living sitting on their land. Mr Justice Toohey's remarks at the granting of lands to the Walbiri under the *Aboriginal Land Rights (NT) Act 1976* (Cth), that 'there will be benefits to the people of a spiritual and psychological nature, mainly I think in the impetus it will give to the movement away from centres of high population and the opportunities to return to a more traditional way of life', were badly mistaken.[354] Writing in the early 1980s, Kenneth Maddock declared, 'Aborigines have suddenly found themselves in positions of great economic power, with all the

---

352 Burgess, C.P. and F.H. Johnston, 2007, 'Healthy Country: Healthy People: Stakeholder Debriefing Paper.' Menzies School of Health Research, Northern Territory, p. 1.
353 NLC, 2008, p. 58.
354 Quoted in Maddock, 1982, p. 160.

political implications of this. What a dramatic development from the stirrings of Elcho Island in the 1950s and Yirrkala and Wave Hill in the 1960s!'[355] The optimism continues; in 2005 the Human Rights and Equal Opportunity Commission claimed that 'the Aboriginal Land Rights Act (NT) can be said to have been an unqualified success in achieving its primary aim of granting traditional Aboriginal land for the benefit of Aboriginal people'[356] Benefit is a much contested word.

Table 3: Indigenous land tenure and associated rights, June 2006

Ownership	As proportion of all Aboriginal land	Character	Legislation in major
Freehold (inalienable, lease only)	61 % (94 % in NT, 93% in SA)	99% in very remote areas	ALRA (NT) 1976 Pastoral Land Act (NT) 1992 APY LRA (SA) 1981 MT LRA (SA) 1984
Freehold (inalienable, perpetual or fixed term lease)	3% (46% in Qld)	85% in very remote areas	Aboriginal Land Act 1991 (Qld), esp. Cape York
Leasehold (lease in perpetuity to Aborigines)	19% (53% in Qld, 45%WA)	97% in very remote areas	ATSI Land Holding Act (Qld) 1985 Land Administration Act 1997 (WA)
Aboriginal reserve (sell, lease to Aborigines)	16% (56% in WA)	99% in very remote areas	Aboriginal Affairs Planning Authority Act 1972 (WA)

---

355 Maddock, 1982, p. 21.
356 Human Rights and Equal Opportunity Commission, 2005. *Native Title Report 2005.*

Ownership	As proportion of all Aboriginal land	Character	Legislation in major
DOGIT (lease less than 30 years)	<1% (Qld only)	100% in very remote areas	Community Services (Aborigines) Act 1984 Land Act 1994
Native Title			
Native Title (cannot sell or mortgage)	9% (24% in WA) WA constitutes 93% of all determinations	73% in very remote, 13% in remote areas	Native Title Act 1993 (Cth)
ILUAs (lease only)	11% (30% in Vic)	73% in very remote, 18% in remote areas	Native Title Act 1993 (Cth)

Data source: Productivity Commission, 2007. Overcoming Indigenous Disadvantage, Tables 11.A.3.1-6. Australian Human Rights Commission, 2006. Native Title Report 2005, AIATSIS, Native Title Resource Guide.

The numbers look impressive. Nationally, in 2008 land owned or controlled by Aborigines comprised 17 per cent of the area of Australia. Almost all of this land was in remote or very remote areas of the country. It had been determined that native title existed in full or in part in 11 per cent of the total area, and registered Indigenous Land Use Agreements (ILUAs) covered 13 per cent of the total area of Australia. About 1300 claims have been dealt with under the *Native Title Act 1993* (Cth), 473 applications for recognition of native title, and 121 registered native title determinations.[357] Between 1995 and 2008, the Indigenous Land Corporation acquired 221 properties in remote, rural and urban locations covering 6 million hectares, at a total cost of approximately $216 million.[358] These holdings are reaching their peak as the *Aboriginal Land Rights (NT) Act 1976* (Cth) (ALRA) specified a 20-year period for claims to be lodged, which closed in

---
357 National Native Title Tribunal, 2009. *Native Title in Australia*.
358 Productivity Commission, 2009. *Overcoming Indigenous Disadvantage: Key Indicators 2009*, chapter 8.2.

1997; in time native title will also be exhausted.

Broadly, there are two types of land rights legislation used to recognise Aboriginal interests in land.[359] There is land rights legislation that generally grants an inalienable freehold title to traditional owners and/or Aboriginal residents of an Aboriginal community. Second, the *Native Title Act 1993* (Cth) provides for recognition of the communal group or individual rights and interests of people under traditional laws and customs over land or waters. These two forms of land rights are represented in Table 3 with their prominence and preconditions for commercialisation.

The land base acquired under the ALRA is inalienable. Reeves found inalienable title to be 'a source of deep reassurance to Aboriginal Territorians'[360] and that the inalienability of Aboriginal land held under the ALRA did not significantly restrict the capacity of Aboriginal Territorians to make commercial use of inalienable freehold land. Nevertheless, little appears to be happening. This likely stems from the difficulties of joint decision-making, and possibly also an anti-commercial mindset. Whilst the ALRA allows for leasing for any purpose and to anyone, in practice the provisions are most commonly used to lease land for community and governmental purposes. Medium term leases are granted for health clinics, hospitals, schools, and for medical staff and teacher accommodation.

Residential leases are rarely granted. The Central Land Council suggests that this is because communities are concerned with increasing the availability of housing rather than increasing individual

---

359 Excluding earlier legislation to control and protect Aboriginal peoples including some legislation that provides for a title to former Aboriginal reserves that cannot be sold without the consent of the Minister and authorisation of Parliament. Australian Human Rights Commission, 2006. *Native Title Report 2005*.
360 Reeves, J. 1998. *Building on Land Rights for the Next Generation: The Review of the Aboriginal Land Rights (Northern Territory) Act 1976,* Aboriginal and Torres Strait Islander Commission, pp. 479,481.

home ownership in particular.[361] Increasing the availability of housing basically means more public housing. The required legal and traditional customary processes are complex and time consuming. Decision-making processes for Aboriginal land-holders that must be followed when an Aboriginal Land Trust is considering the grant of a lease are designed to ensure that traditional owners retain control over decisions about what happens on their land. A lease cannot be granted unless the relevant land council is satisfied that the group of traditional owners understand the nature and purpose of the proposed grant and, as a group, consent to it. Group consent need not be unanimous but must be given in accordance with either an agreed or a traditional decision-making process. These pre-conditions to the grant of a lease of Aboriginal land are a hurdle that must be jumped by individual Aboriginal people, organisations or other developers when seeking approval for a lease of Aboriginal land.

Leases proposed to be granted for particular purposes for particular terms currently require the consent in writing of the Commonwealth Minister. Such consent is not currently required for a residential lease to an Aboriginal person, but it is required for a lease to a non-Aboriginal person for a business purpose for a period longer than 10 years. Leases to Indigenous people for residential purposes are subject to less stringent requirements than leases to non-Indigenous people. The requirement for ministerial consent to dealing with Aboriginal land has been described as an important part of the principle of inalienability of freehold title,

> [A] fundamental principle [is] that Aboriginal land [is] to be held under inalienable freehold title. Any dealing that effectively alienates Aboriginal land, though not transferring title, is contrary to that principle. A lease or licence for an unduly

---

361 Central Land Council, 2005. 'Communal Title and Economic Development.' *CLC Policy Paper*, p. 3.

long term may offend the principle, hence the justification for ministerial consent.[362]

Fortunately, some of these matters are being addressed. As part of the NT Intervention the Commonwealth took head leases over settlements for five years to ensure that it could effectively run the settlements. Further, 99 year leases were insisted on by the previous government (the Rudd Labor Government reduced these to 40 year leases), which is, nevertheless, a significant breakthrough in increasing the possibility of enhanced commercial interest in Aboriginal land.

The situation with respect to native title is significantly different to that applying under land rights legislation. The *Native Title Act 1993* (Cth) left the common law position with respect to Indigenous peoples' use of native title largely untouched. The native title rights and interests held by particular Indigenous people will depend on both their traditional laws and customs and what interests are held by others in the area concerned. Generally speaking, native title must give way to rights held by others. The capacity of Australian law to recognise the rights and interests held under traditional law and custom will also be a factor. Native title rights and interests may include rights to:

- live on the area
- access the area for traditional purposes, like camping or undertake ceremonies
- visit and protect important places and sites
- hunt, fish and gather food
- use traditional resources like water, wood and ochre
- teach law and custom on country.

In some cases, native title includes the right to possess and occupy an area to the exclusion of all others (often called 'exclusive

---

362 See Bauman, T. 2006. *Final Report of the Indigenous Facilitation and Mediation Project July 2003-June 2006: research findings, recommendations and implementation*, Australian Institute of Aboriginal and Torres Strait Islander Studies Report No. 6.

possession'). This includes the right to control access to, and use of, the area concerned. This right is restricted to certain parts of Australia such as unallocated or vacant Crown land and some areas already held by, or for, Aborigines. Native title rights and interests differ from Aboriginal land rights in that the source of land rights is a grant of title from government. The source of native title rights and interests is the system of traditional laws and customs of the native title holders themselves.

Native title can only be surrendered to the Crown. Native titleholders cannot grant leases. Further, in many cases, native title will only be recognised as comprising non-exclusive rights in land and waters. Native title is held and managed by a Prescribed Bodies Corporate (PBC) made up of some of the native title holders. Native title cannot be used as collateral for a mortgage. The Act does, however, provide two means by which a lease for commercial or residential purposes could be granted by a PBC that could be used as security for finance: the native titleholders could consent to the grant of a statutory title (freehold or leasehold, for example) through an Indigenous Land Use Agreement (ILUA); or the government could compulsorily acquire the native title for a third party.[363]

An ILUA can authorise government to grant freehold or a lease either to the PBC or to a third party. The agreement would effectively suspend operation of the native title, and allow the statutory title to be used in the normal way. Unless the ILUA provides for surrender of native title that is intended to extinguish it, native title is not extinguished. If it does not, native title would continue to be the underlying title to the land. If the government issued a freehold title to the PBC pursuant to the ILUA, it could then issue leases on its own terms. The freehold or a lease could be used as security to raise finance, given appropriate capacity in the PBC. Such a process requires the consent of the native title group, and the active participation of

---

[363] NNTT, 2009.

the government in granting the freehold title.

The other mechanism is compulsory acquisition of the native title, and grant of a freehold title in its stead. Compulsory acquisition of native title under the processes of the NTA would result in extinguishment of native title. Compensation would be payable on just terms for loss of native title. Part of that compensation could be met by provision of freehold title. While the right to negotiate provisions of the NTA would apply in such a case, it is likely that such an approach would be generally unacceptable to many Aboriginal people as it entails permanent loss of their native title.

ILUAs also play an important part in the native title process. ILUAs are generally agreements that, once registered under the Act, allow for an agreed act to be done over land subject to a native title claim or positive native title determination. They can explain how native title co-exists with other interests in the determination area. They can 'top-up' the native titleholders' rights or they can stand alone as an alternative to a native title determination. Currently, there are 389 registered ILUAs.[364] Examples are available for scrutiny[365] but not in sufficient detail to understand the impact of ILUAs.

A recent Native Title Discussion Paper[366] canvasses options to improve outcomes from native title agreements, in particular through increased transparency including registration of agreements. Limiting the assessment of agreements is the fact that many agreements and their terms remain confidential. Increased transparency of provisions in and benefits provided under agreements have the potential to affect significantly the opportunities for traditional owners. The obvious difficulty in promoting transparency is whether and how to protect sensitive or confidential information of the parties to agreements.

---

364 See National Native Title Tribunal, *Indigenous Land Use Agreements Register*.
365 National Native Title Tribunal.
366 Department of Families, Housing, Community Services and Indigenous Affairs, 2009b. *Native Title Discussion Paper*.

Western Australia has, however, published native title agreements; and New Zealand has a policy of publishing all settlement agreements.[367] Even if some provisions might warrant confidentiality, at least for a period, current practice in many areas is not to publish any features.

One way to increase transparency, while still enabling people to protect sensitive information, is to require registration of agreements on a public register which only discloses certain 'relevant' details. Alternatively, such a register could publish selected 'best practice' agreements. A central repository of agreements would provide a single point of reference to negotiators and drafters looking for best practice examples and provide a more effective means of evaluating the capacity of agreements to provide meaningful outcomes and durable benefits.

Second, and closely aligned to the insuperable problems of governance, Aborigines collectively hold land that crosses traditional lines of authority. The moves to arrange long term leases over Aboriginal title land (see Table 3) and other instruments such as Indigenous Land Use Agreements governing native title rights inevitably create collectives where none existed. Moreover, land councils and registered claimant groups reinforce the artificial group solidarity which is at odds with traditional authority and which means that traditional and historic owners are locked into family feuds. The best way to release this tension is to convert land rights by granting traditional owners title to their lands, with all the rights and responsibilities that attend freehold land ownership under Australian law. Even so, it may be too late to unscramble this egg and the cost of so doing compared to the few benefits to be had from land rights (discussed below) may make pursuing it unwise and unlikely to yield much benefit.

---

367 See http://www.nativetitle.wa.gov.au/ and http://www.ots.govt.nz/.

Iconic land rights battles

The roll call of the great battles by Aboriginal people for land rights sends shivers of delight through the spine of the Aboriginal rights movement. Key events in the political struggle for recognition of land rights were the 1964 destruction of the Cape York Mapoon community by the Queensland Government for a Comalco mine; the 1966 walk off at Vesteys' Wave Hill cattle station in the north-west of the Northern Territory; the 1968 Yirrkala Arnhem Land fight against Nabalco; and the 1980 battle at Noonkanbah in the Kimberleys to halt AMAX drilling for oil there. In all cases, Aborigines gained rights to land through political struggle and by legislation, including native title following the Mabo judgment.

If Justice Toohey and other judges sympathetic to Aboriginal demands such as Murray Wilcox formerly of the Federal Court[368] and Robert French, formerly of the National Native Title Tribunal and the Federal Court, and now Chief Justice of the High Court, were to revisit earlier decisions and accompanying declaratory remarks, they would be shocked that their handiwork has produced little or nothing, and possibly the opposite of what they had hoped. The landmark land rights cases provide a tale of the unintended consequences of the law as a remedy in matters of political economy.

Mapoon

Comalco was granted a lease to mine bauxite in Cape York. The lease included the land occupied by both Weipa and Mapoon missions. In 1964 Presbyterian missionaries planned to relocate residents to make way for a mine. Mapoon residents were assured that they would not be forced off the mission. Many agreed to move. About 40, however, wanted to stay and be given a chance to establish local

---

368 See Ron Brunton on Wilcox's appalling final judgment in Brunton, R. 2007. 'A Bombshell in the Centre of Perth: An Anthropologist Considers the Single Noongar Judgment.' *The Bennelong Society Occasional Papers.*

industries. These 40 were forced from their homes and the town was razed. From the late 1970s, people began returning to Mapoon. They returned with little expectation that an economy would follow. In 2000, Mapoon was formally recognised as a Deed of Grant in Trust Community with status similar to a shire council.[369]

Mapoon is situated in the primary labour market catchment of Weipa and is within an hour's drive of Weipa. Rio Tinto Alcan is the primary employer; Weipa's very existence is due to the development there of bauxite mining. Unfortunately, the children of the Mapoon returnees have different expectations and, whether because of welfare dependence or lack of employment in Mapoon (but not in Weipa), have succumbed to drugs. Drug and alcohol dependence were the primary factors preventing Aborigines from being employed by Rio Tinto Alcan or its contractors in a recent Rio recruitment intake. Of 57 applicants, most of whom were Mapoon residents, only 11 passed; the remaining 46 failed mandatory drug and alcohol screening.[370]

Wave Hill/Wattie Creek

In August 1966, Gurindji pastoral workers walked off the job on the Vesteys' cattle station at Wave Hill in the Northern Territory. The next year the group moved to Wattie Creek, a place of significance for the Gurindji people.[371] Under Whitlam Government legislation, the original Wave Hill lease was surrendered and two new leases issued: one to the Vesteys and one to the Murramulla Gurindji Company. The Gurindji lease of approximately 3300 square kilometres included important sacred sites.

In 1975, Prime Minister Gough Whitlam came to Daguragu and, in an historic act of conspicuous compassion, poured a handful of

---

369 National Museum of Australia: http://indig<enousrights.net.au/document.asp?iID=677.
370 DFD, 2009, p. 22.
371 Hardy, F. 1968. *The Unlucky Australians*. One Day Hill.

soil into claimant Vincent Lingiari's hand. Whitlam said:

> Vincent Lingiari, I solemnly hand to you these deeds as proof in Australian law that these lands belong to the Gurindji people, and I put into your hands part of the earth as a sign that this land will be the possession of you and your children forever.[372]

Wattie Creek Station is now held by the Daguragu Land Trust. The area of the property exceeds 3,000 sq kilometres. Of this only, 700 sq kms are leased (McDonald Yard); 5,000 head of cattle are run; there is very little employment associated with the lease. The traditional owners do not live on the property. They simply receive rent from the pastoral lease.

Yirrkala

In 1963, the Commonwealth Government approved Gove Bauxite Corporation's plans to mine in the vicinity of the Yirrkala Methodist Mission in north-east Arnhem Land.[373] In 1968 the Yirrkala people launched a legal challenge against the Gove bauxite alumina project. In 1971 Mr Justice Blackburn ruled against the Yirrkala claimants in *Milirrpum and Others v Nabalco Pty Ltd and the Commonwealth of Australia*. The Yirrkala people eventually received title to their land in 1978 under the *ALRA*. However, the mining leases to which they had objected were excluded from the provisions of the Act. In the intervening years, 4000 white Australian mining employees and their families settled in the area.[374]

Meanwhile, Laynhapuy Homelands Association, a major player in the region, wanted to keep Yolngu people on country and connected to their cultural and social foundations. They are not in favour of

---
372 National Museum of Australia: http://indigenousrights.net.au/subsection.asp?ssID=85.
373 Wells, E. 1982. *Reward and Punishment in Arnhem Land*, Australian Institute of Aboriginal and Torres Strait Islander Studies, Canberra.
374 National Museum of Australia: http://indigenousrights.net.au/subsection.asp?ssID=63.

economic development through mining. Instead, they wanted to manage their 'estate' and be engaged in border and environmental protection, bio-diversity conservation and production of arts crafts, music, dance, and the general maintenance of culture.[375] To this end there are 34 government-funded designated Ranger positions for Yirrkala Rangers.[376]

> In the long term, if the small business sector of the remote economy can grow, it will generate a genuine income stream for homelands communities, and their dependence on government monies for their survival will correspondingly decrease. At best, remote Australia will be home to networks of thriving, functioning small communities, where thousands of people continue to balance, in a creative way, their sense of being uniquely themselves with the demands of being part of the wider polity and economy.[377]

The Laynhapuy Homelands Association dreams of a 'milk bar' economy based on CDEP jobs, the dream of many anthropologists and others oblivious to the importance of economics. It does not support the elevation of mainstream jobs to the 'top of the hierarchy'.[378]

Noonkanbah

The Yungngora people were employed by the station owners at Noonkanbah in the Kimberleys, Western Australia, until 1971 when they walked off over a pay and conditions dispute.[379] In 1976 the

---

375 Laynhapuy Homelands Association Incorporated, 2008, *Submission to Northern Territory Government on the CDEP Discussion Paper*, p. 4.
376 LHAI, 2008, p. 9.
377 Morphy, F. 2008. 'The Future of the Homelands in north-east Arnhem Land', quoted in LHAI, p. 8.
378 LHAI, p. 9.
379 Kolig, E. 1990. 'Government Policies and Religious Strategies: Fighting With Myth at Noonkanbah.' In Tonkinson, R. and M. Howard (eds) 1990. *Going It Alone: Prospects for Aboriginal Autonomy*. Aboriginal Studies Press.

station was purchased by the Aboriginal Land Fund for development by the traditional owners. Since then, it has been run by the people of the Yungngora Community. A few years later, the station was the scene for an intense political dispute when the WA Government allowed exploration company AMAX to drill for oil in sacred sites in 1980, a convoy of 45 drilling rigs entered the site. Violent confrontations between police and Noonkanbah protesters ensued, culminating in the drilling rigs forcing their way through community picket lines.[380]

In April 2007, the Yungngora people had their native title over the Noonkanbah land recognised. Noonkanbah Pastoral Lease is managed by Noonkanbah Rural Enterprises. It is a wholly owned subsidiary of Yungngora Association Incorporated, the owner of the lease. Even with an enormous variety of sources of government support, the property is not self-supporting. A recent report contained the very sad comment, that there is '[d]iminishing commitment of local people to Station employment.'[381] According to local graziers,[382] the property runs 3,000 head of cattle but is capable of running up to 30,000 head of cattle.

Yungngora's Community Development Employment Project is one of the largest stand-alone CDEPs left in the region. It has 165 on CDEP which includes participants who work on the three outstations under their control. In 2008 it had no non-CDEP jobs and no viable businesses.

On a more positive note, agreement has been reached on the $20 billion Browse Basin LNG project. The reason for agreement is a combination of a sensible Martin Ferguson, Federal Minister for

---

[380] Smith, T. 2002. 'Indigenous Accumulation and the Question of Land in the Kimberley Region of Western Australia: Pre 1968-1975.' *International Economic History Association, XIII Congress.*
[381] Kimberley Indigenous Management Support Services, 2008, *September Quarterly Report*, Noonkanbah Station, p. 2.
[382] My source is well placed in the area and is a member of the Pastoralists and Graziers Association of W.A.

Resources, a change of state government from Labor to Liberal, and the realisation of Wayne Bergmann of the Kimberley Land Council that he was too ambitious in the previous Inpex deal. A traditional owner, Frank Sebastion, who was involved in the original Noonkanbah protests, stated, 'I'm doing the same thing here that I did in Noonkanbah, but the opposite way ... at least we are treated as equals.' Asked his opinion of environmentalists opposed to the project, he responded, 'They're dickheads, a mob of arseholes.'[383] The interesting aspect of this dispute is the growing split between environmentalist interests and Aboriginal interests. Some local Aboriginal traditional owners have accepted the Commonwealth Government proposal that Muckaty Station near Tennant Creek in the NT should be the preferred site for a national nuclear waste dump.[384]

Land rights played their part in the maturation of the relationship between Aboriginal and non-Aboriginal Australia, but they did not produce much change for Aborigines. Armed with government money and ample avenues for legal redress, land councils have attempted to sting developers for rent. No doubt they will do so again, using any and all means to do so, but precious few viable jobs have ever come from Aboriginal land rights.

NT Land Rights Act mining veto

The ALRA had its origin in the findings of the 1973-1974 Woodward Royal Commission, appointed by the Whitlam Labor Government. Among other reasons, Woodward described the provision of land holdings 'as a first essential step for people who are economically depressed and who have at present no real opportunity of achieving

---

383 Reported in *The Australian* 28 April 2009.
384 Reported in the NT News, 24 February 2010.

a normal standard of living.'[385] In terms of land area accumulated under ALRA and other forms of land title, Whitlam's and Woodward's aspiration for Aboriginal people has fared quite well.

John Reeves, when reviewing the ALRA, concluded that land is an economic *cul de sac*. In his view, economic development would be best assured through investment and use of royalty monies from mining on Aboriginal land:

> [F]ar more important modern sources of economic advancement than the possession of land are the possession of productively useful skills, technology and capital of the kind in demand in the mainstream Australian economy.[386]

The ALRA sets out terms and conditions upon which mineral exploration licences, mining interests and other leases and interests can be granted over land held by an Aboriginal land trust. Depending upon the nature of the interest granted over Aboriginal land and the nature of the agreement negotiated, there are various ways in which money is eventually received, whether by the relevant land council, or the relevant Aboriginal person or group on whose land the activity takes place. In the case of royalties paid by mining companies to the Northern Territory or the Commonwealth governments, the ALRA established the Aboriginals Benefit Reserve. The Reserve consists of funds taken from the Commonwealth Consolidated Revenue Fund, equal to any royalties received by the Commonwealth or the Northern Territory in respect of a mining interest in Aboriginal land. A percentage of the funds in the Reserve is distributed to the land councils for administrative purposes. A further percentage is paid to Aboriginal councils whose areas are included in the area affected by the relevant mining operations, or to Incorporated Aboriginal Associations whose members live in or are the traditional Aboriginal

---

385 Woodward A.E. 1974. *Aboriginal Land Rights Commission*, Second Report, Australian Government Publishing Service, p. 2.
386 Reeves, 1998, p. 544.

owners of, the area affected by the relevant mining operations. The ALRA controls entry onto Aboriginal land and prohibits a person (other than an entitled Aboriginal person or group) from entering onto or remaining on Aboriginal land without a permit. The *Aboriginal Land Act 1992* (NT) operates concurrently with the ALRA and deals with entry onto Aboriginal land and control of entry into seas adjoining Aboriginal land.[387]

As at 2006, there was 594,000 square km of ALRA land in the Northern Territory, about 44 per cent of the Northern Territory; a further 10 per cent is subject to claim.[388] Under the ALRA, traditional owners who are granted land are able to exercise considerable control over mining and other activities on their land. For example, Part IV of the Act allows traditional owners to veto minerals exploration for ongoing five-year periods or, alternatively, to negotiate the terms and conditions of exploration licences and mining interests.[389] These provisions were amended in 2006 to provide for a core negotiating period of two years allowing the Northern Territory Government to set deadlines to bring negotiations to a conclusion and to withdraw a company's consent to negotiate where it has not seriously pursued negotiations and providing for the lifting of the five-year moratorium period at any time that traditional owners agree.[390]

---

[387] Agreements, Treaties and Negotiated Settlements Project at http://www.atns.net.au.
[388] Department of the Chief Minister (NT), *Detailed Joint Submission to the Commonwealth. Workability Reforms of the Aboriginal Land Rights (Northern Territory) Act 1976.*
[389] *Aboriginal Land Rights (Northern Territory) Act 1976.*
[390] *Aboriginal Land Rights (Northern Territory) Amendment Act 2006.*

Figure 10: Mineral exploration expenditure NT and Australia, 1988-2007

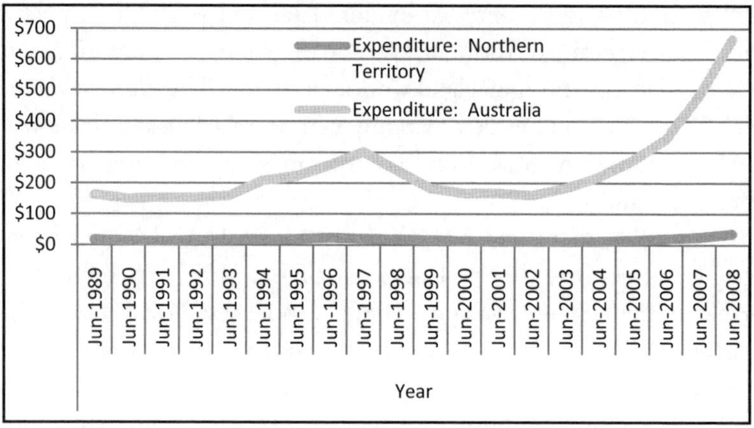

Note: $ Millions. Data source: Australian Bureau of Statistics, 8412.0 - Mineral and Petroleum Exploration, Australia, Dec 2008.

The ALRA established the land councils, among other things, to 'assist Aboriginals ... to carry out commercial activities (including resource development, the provision of tourist facilities and agricultural activities).'[391] Precious little development, especially resource development, has proceeded (Figure 10). The NT has not had major discoveries in minerals or on-shore petroleum for a generation. The lack of discovery has affected perceptions of prospectivity of highly prospective geological terranes. The NT has the longest delays in access to the most prospective terranes of any state/territory (up to 20 years) and delays of two years or more over large prospective areas. This neutralises the NT Government's initiatives to attract exploration. More broadly, the NT has the lowest intensity of exploration, that is, expenditure per prospective area, of the large jurisdictions.[392]

The most important factor in attracting exploration is perceived unexplored prospectivity. '[One of the] main elements necessary to

---

391 *ALR (Northern Territory) 1976, section 23*.
392 ACIL Tasman, 2007. *Bring Forward Discovery: Review of NT Exploration Investment Attraction Programs 1999-2007*.

increase mineral and petroleum discovery in the Territory [is] making key land available for exploration.'[393] A survey of current and potential exploration investors conducted for a recent review found that 'the reputation of the Northern Territory for access to land is very poor. This was reinforced by the latest results of the authoritative survey by the Fraser Institute. It rated the NT 56th worst out of 64 global jurisdictions in 'Uncertainty of Native Land Claims'; 41 per cent of respondents claimed this is a disincentive to exploration in the Territory. This view is supported by other discussion with companies around Australia. Land access and investor perceptions of it are thus critical factors to resolve if the NT is to lift its ranking as an investment destination. Problems of access to Aboriginal land are the major issue for explorers. There are some positive signs that attitudes and approaches of Aboriginal people are becoming more oriented to economic development. Discovery is a key to this, and the lack of major discovery in the Territory, for many reasons, is starting to affect its promotion despite agreement on its geological prospectivity.

The Fraser Institute report also showed that:

- The Northern Territory ranks 24th out of 64 world jurisdictions (and 6th out of 7 in Australia) in Current Mineral Potential Index, considered by Fraser to be the best overall measure for investment attractiveness. This ranking was down from 8th globally for the previous two years
- It ranks 20th globally (and 5th in Australia) in the Policy Potential Index, a composite measure of the attractiveness of its policy climate. This improved from a 25th ranking in 2004-2005
- The NT ranks very highly in certainty of regulations and environmental regulations, and equal best in the world for political stability (ahead of SA and WA).[394]

---

393 ACIL Tasman, 2007, p. ix.
394 ACIL Tasman, 2007, p. 40.

An Australian survey of 22 companies[395] with experience of exploring in the NT, or who have expressed an interest in doing so, reiterates the importance of access to prospective land and security of land title as key drivers of exploration activity. Respondents cited Aboriginal land access regimes, legislation and procedures, and the risk of delays arising from entrenched processes and institutions, as significant impediments to Territory exploration. While responses also suggest that the degree of concern over these obstacles varies, the consensus opinion is summarised in a statement by one respondent that 'serious mining companies do not waste money on exploration in jurisdictions that cannot deliver security of tenure'.[396]

The message from oil exploration companies is similar. Certainty of title and access to prospective areas are viewed as the most important factors in considering and conducting exploration activity. Like mineral explorers, access issues and land title administration are also cited as major inhibitions on exploration in the Northern Territory. The Central Land Council's continued lack of co-operation in providing information on sacred site clearances to the Aboriginal Areas Protection Authority (AAPA) is viewed as counter productive. Additionally, the recent push for separate applications over Aboriginal freehold land and pastoral leases in favour of single conjunctive applications is viewed as running the risk of making applications even more tedious and complex to administer.[397]

Despite the 2006 changes, the average time taken (in years) from the date an application is received under both the ALRA and the *Native Title Act* by the Central Land Council to either consent or refusal has increased from 1.5 years to 3.5 years between 2005 and 2008. There is now a large backlog.[398] Exploration licence applications are generally running at 100 per year; the number consented to is 10 per year,

---

395 ACIL Tasman, 2007, p. 33.
396 ACIL Tasman, 2007, p. 33.
397 ACIL Tasman, 2007, p. 42.
398 Central Land Council, 2008. Annual *Report 2007-2008*, p. 50.

falling from 40 per year in 2005; the number refused has fallen from 40 to 25 in the same period. A large number of applications lapse. In the financial year 2007-08, 77 out of 96 exploration applications received by the CLC were solely or primarily aimed at discovering uranium,[399] indicating that the CLC is coming under pressure to respond positively for the first time since the mid 1980s to allow mining of uranium. Fortunately, there are signs that there may be support forthcoming, though these signs are no more positive than that a number of information sessions are being held with traditional owners and industry associations (but not proponents).

As at June 2005, the area of mineral titles granted on Aboriginal freehold land was 21,400 square km, and 74,600 square km on non-Aboriginal land. The grant of exploration licenses on pastoral lease (native title affected land) is now relatively routine and few objections are experienced. However, the number of grants of exploration licenses on Aboriginal-owned land (i.e. subject to ALRA) is still a concern; the rate of approvals is very low compared with other land. As at 31 January 2006, there were 325 outstanding applications on Aboriginal land. This included 229 in the negotiating process, 58 pending grant of deed and 38 awaiting proposals to land councils. There were 152 in moratorium and 53 new applications pending. These numbers have not improved significantly during the past few years.[400]

The ACIL Tasman review concluded that significant improvements depend on changes in Aboriginal attitudes to mining and the ability of government, companies and Aboriginal people to develop partnerships. Mining should be seen not as an imposition but a benefit from an endowment in the land that is vitally important to Aboriginal people. In the past, they relied on the surface of the land and its waters, flora and fauna. Underground mineral wealth can now be as important for their futures.

---

399 CLC, 2008, p. 52.
400 ACIL Tasman, 2007, p. 42.

Cape York Wild Rivers

The fight between the Aborigines of Cape York and the Queensland Government over the Cape York Wild Rivers legislation is a recent significant development in Aboriginal policy. It demonstrates that the interests of Aborigines are not the same as those of environmentalists. This fight has significant implications for the future state of Aboriginal policy. Indeed, the Leader of the Opposition, Tony Abbott, is seeking to override the Queensland legislation with the Wild Rivers (Environmental Management) Bill.

Cape York is majority owned and/or controlled by Aboriginal people. More than six million hectares will be under Aboriginal management, representing 45 per cent of Cape York's 13.7 million hectares. The composition of Aboriginal ownership and control is shown in Table 4. More than a third of the total Cape York Aboriginal estate is designated for conservation purposes. Cape York Peninsula contains the largest areas of natural environment in eastern Australia within a land space slightly larger than the state of Victoria. Unlike Victoria, where five million people reside at a very high standard of living, Cape York accommodates only 13, 000 people, most of whom live on welfare. It faces environmental challenges too great for such a small number of poorly resourced people to handle, particularly from feral animals, weeds and poor fire management. The strategy of the Queensland Government and some conservation groups for handling the future of Cape York is profoundly pessimistic and risky. The strategy is to lock away much of the land by means of various legislation, in particular the Wild Rivers legislation, with its connotations of land being devoid of human activity. This strategy assumes that the future of Cape York will be based on tourism and government transfers (green welfare) and that future residents will be unable to manage and develop land both to create wealth and preserve or, indeed, enhance the environment of Cape York.

The politics of the environment movement's power over the future of Cape York, and more generally over much Aboriginal land in remote Australia, is that voters are more prepared to 'preserve' an environment for which they bear few costs of adjustment than one that affects them directly. Conservation is cheap at distance because there are no apparent trade-offs. Most of Australia's consumer wealth is centred on southern Australia while most of its mineral and other resource wealth is located in the north. The corollary of the north-south resource divide is a north-south division in Australia's environment conscience. A wealthy, prosperous and consuming south demands the protection at any cost from development of whatever form of great tracts of sparsely populated northern Australia. Typically this protection takes the form of reservation of land in the conservation estate, where it can be used only for conservation purposes and for a limited range of other activities. This protection does not usually allow for the full exploration of all of the options for wealth creation and conservation. The southerly penchant for conservation at distance applies to the Wild Rivers legislation and the Cape York Aborigines.

Four Wild River basins have been declared in Cape York comprising more than 13 individual wild rivers.[401] The Act establishes an entire water catchment as a single entity for the purpose of maintaining the rivers' natural values. Specific attention is paid to individual impacts and the aggregate impact on the river resulting from activities within the basin. Within the catchment of a declared wild river there are various preservation zones and activities are either prohibited or subject to restriction. Restrictions are greatest in the High Preservation Area which is an area extending up to one kilometre from the river or tributary subject to declaration.[402]

---

401 Initially six Wild River Basins were declared in Queensland with most situated in the Gulf of Carpentaria. Declarations and consultation reports are available for the Archer, Lockhart, Stewart and Wenlock basins at Queensland Government, Department of Environment and Resource Management.
402 See for example, Queensland Government, 2009. *Stewart Basin Wild River Declaration*.

Table 4: Cape York Peninsula Aboriginal estate (hectares)

	Current	Proposed	Total
National parks	193,918	1,692,532	1,886,450
State land dealings	580,650	403,278	983,928
DOGIT	1,967,985	-	1,967,985
Indigenous pastoral leases	757,744	-	757,744
Land trust	147,600	431,988	579,588
TOTAL	3,647,897	2,527,797	6,175,695

Note: DOGIT: Deed of Grant in Trust; ILUA: Indigenous Land Use Agreement.
Data source: Balkanu Cape York Development (unpublished correspondence).

The criticism of the Wild Rivers legislation is that it restricts the future options of Aboriginal people in the Cape by exceeding the agreed arrangements for environmental protection applying to other parts of Australia with similar environmental values. It also contradicts a number of other instruments and agreements by the Queensland and Commonwealth governments. The *Wild Rivers Act* is precautionary, with a stated aim to minimise adverse effects on known natural values and reduce the possibility of adversely affecting poorly understood ecological functions.[403]

> The Acts that regulate these resources and activities generally do not set development limits at the catchment scale. Those Acts that do set limits, generally do so under the principles of ecological sustainable development (ESD), which permits a loss in natural values to achieve economic and social benefits. The level of preservation sought for wild rivers, which have all or almost all of their natural values intact, is higher than for ESD but below that generally provided in a national park.[404]

---

[403] Wild Rivers Bill 2005 s3, 3, (b).
[404] Wild Rivers Bill 2005. *Explanatory Notes*.

The *Wild Rivers Act* specifically disassociates itself from Ecologically Sustainable Development. This disassociation effectively unbundles the three equally important core principles of the National Strategy for Ecologically Sustainable Development, that is, economic development, intergenerational equity and biological diversity. The Act is therefore in clear violation of the Queensland Government's Council of Australian Government commitments.

The Explanatory Notes recognise that pressure to develop Cape York is 'limited' and 'little' development has historically taken place. Not only are there few expected threats of damage, but these threats are currently being constrained by existing legislation and regulation. The Act fails to acknowledge the potentially significant impact that welfare reform will have on Cape York. Welfare reform's focus on individual responsibility, reciprocity and incentives are designed to break widespread passive welfare dependence and boost individual economic independence. In support of this major reform, the Queensland and Australian governments have contributed $100 million over four years. This commitment includes specific encouragement to communities and individuals to develop businesses that will broaden the Cape's economic base, in line with the consistent ESD principles detailed in the Cape York Heads of Agreement.

The Explanatory Notes to the Act explicitly preclude consideration of ESD cost-benefit analysis by stating that, while wild rivers may contain or support other values, such as economic, social, scientific, educational and Aboriginal, the Act establishes the primacy of preservation, rendering other values secondary and outside the scope of the legislation.[405] The Explanatory Notes introduce the concept of 'necessary development'. In the absence of cost-benefit analysis, necessary development is understood on purely conservation grounds. The aim of the Act is to ensure that a declared wild river's environment is maintained largely in its natural state, and the impact

---

405 Wild Rivers Bill 2005. *Explanatory Notes.*

of necessary development minimised.[406] This underscores the earlier observation that the Act unbundles the ESD package of equally important core objectives specified in the National Strategy and the Cape York Heads of Agreement. The Act removes any consideration of elements outside natural preservation, including cost-benefit analysis. It is heavily restrictive legislation in a number of ways.

The Wild Rivers Code is very explicit in its application of precaution. The assessment manager must take a precautionary approach when determining whether an application meets the required outcome. That is, the manager must not use the lack of full scientific certainty as a reason for not imposing requirements or conditions to minimise potentially adverse effects on the natural values. The onus lies with the applicant to demonstrate that a proposed development or activity meets the required outcomes of the Code.[407] The proponent must both demonstrate that no harm will arise from the proposed development and that there will be a 'beneficial impact' on conservation values. This narrowly defined beneficial environmental impact is well outside the scope of ESD. Well-defined and accepted Australian interpretations of ESD place no requirement of proof on proponents. The Act is clearly highly restrictive, a finding reinforced with reference to ministerial decision-making. Any proposed amendment is subject to the consideration of public submissions and ultimately ministerial decision. Once a property development plan is considered by the relevant minister, the minister is required to ensure that the proposed amendment: 'will not have an overall adverse impact on the natural values of the wild river.'[408] And that further: 'the environmental benefits of the plan justify the approval of the plan.'[409]

The proposed amendment must demonstrate that the property development plan has positive environmental benefits and not simply

---

406 Wild Rivers Bill 2005. *Explanatory Notes*.
407 Queensland Government. 2007. *Wild Rivers Code*. Department of Natural Resources and Water.
408 Wild Rivers Code (s31E(b)).
409 Wild Rivers Code (s31E(c))

an absence of harm.

Wild Rivers implicitly acknowledges intergenerational equity but only inasmuch as it seeks to preserve amenity for future generations. It seeks to conserve Cape York's river catchments for future generations but ignores the economic and social well-being of these for future generations. Heavily restrictive conservation policy that is disassociated from ESD eliminates current development opportunities; it also eliminates all future opportunities. ESD gives full voice to future generations by limiting current and future development that does not maximise welfare. The singular focus on future enjoyment of the environment, at the expense of their future economic and social welfare, heavily circumscribes the Act.

There are currently two certain and serious threats to Cape York's biodiversity – invasive weeds and feral animals. Cane toads, wild pigs and invasive grasses from Africa impose great current cost on Cape York. In large measure, Wild Rivers relies on existing legislation and regulation to deal with these environmental costs.[410]

The established Australian statutory and regulatory practice of ESD specifically seeks to minimise costs by allowing broad consideration of costs and benefits attributable to conservation, development and intergenerational equity and selecting options that maximise total benefits, net of costs. Consistent application of ESD principles has, among other forces, contributed to the refinement of a range of economic valuation methodologies in the context of properly valuing the environment, including market-based techniques. Without the requirement to articulate costs and benefits clearly, the development and application of enhanced valuation methodologies may stifle adoption of best practice developments in ESD and valuation. Development of 'improved valuation, pricing and incentive mechanisms' is identified as one of the key principles

---

410 A trial of 20 Wild River Rangers is underway across the Gulf and the Cape with a total commitment of 100 rangers to eventually cover the entire Gulf and Cape declared Wild Rivers.

of the Intergovernmental Agreement on the Environment. Of more obvious impact are the costs associated with setting aside the application of well-founded and universally agreed principles of ESD-derived regulation.

Ignorance of cost effectiveness and a reliance on mandated and inflexible precaution may lead to perverse consequences where costs of precautionary measures exceed the costs of waiting to clarify uncertain impacts. There is a general failure to recognise that regulation under the legislation imposes costs as well as promised benefits. In the case of Cape York, the Explanatory Notes make clear the limited extent of development pressure. Some types of developments can pose serious and irreversible harm to the environment, but other types of developments pose reversible and temporary harm. Consultations on the Stewart Basin declaration discuss this very concept as 'misdirection of resources'.[411] Instead of referring to cost-benefit assessment on a case-by-case basis, the departmental response asserted that:

> Experience in other parts of Australia has shown that it is extremely expensive to rehabilitate degraded river systems. It is far more cost effective in the mid to long term to protect existing natural values than to rehabilitate or seek to replace lost natural values.[412]

Such a claim cannot be substantiated in all instances without reference to case by case assessment of costs and benefits. In some instances the cost of rehabilitation may be significantly lower than the opportunity cost of precautionary preclusion. Simply, the Act may make society worse off, including the remote and very poor people of Cape York. The *Wild Rivers Act* is heavily restrictive. These findings are supported by the Act's explicit dissociation of well defined Australian legislative and regulatory commitment to ESD.[413]

---

411 Queensland Government, 2009.
412 Queensland Government, 2009.
413 A full discussion is found at Iles, S. and G. Johns, 2010. 'An Economic Unravelling of the Precautionary Principle: the Queensland Wild Rivers Act 2005.' *Agenda* 17(4).

Community Development Employment Projects

Community Development Employment Projects (CDEP) is a training program to assist people to gain non-CDEP employment.[414] At its peak in 2002-03, it delivered services to 35,000 participants through 260 providers in hundreds of communities throughout Australia. At the end of June 2008, there were 18,800 participants and 152 providers at an annual cost of $223.2 million in remote and very remote regions. Previous participants have moved into mainstream labour market programs. Despite major increases for the rest of the labour force, Aboriginal labour force participation has increased only marginally in the last 30 years, and only in non-remote areas and among the most educated of the Aboriginal population. The labour force participation rate for Aboriginal people (59 per cent) is about three quarters of that for non-Aboriginal people (78 per cent); the unemployment rate for Aboriginal people (13 per cent) is about three times the rate for non-Aboriginal people (four per cent).[415]

Except in high-end employment among graduates and the public sector, Aboriginal employment has been stagnant for decades.[416] CDEP has masked this appalling outcome in public policy. Until very recently, CDEP participants were a major part of the labour force in some remote and very remote areas especially, as noted earlier, in the Northern Territory. The Australian Bureau of Statistics classifies CDEP participation as a form of employment and, by subtracting those on CDEP from the employment figures, the real level of unemployment among Indigenous people (Figure 1) is

---

414 Department of Families, Housing, Community Services and Indigenous Affairs, 'Changes to the CDEP programme 2007', announcement 9 May 2008.
415 Productivity Commission, 2007a, 3.46.
416 Gregory, B. 2004. 'Asking the Right Questions?' in Austin-Broos D. and G. Macdonald (eds) 2004. *Aborigines, Culture and Economy*. ANU, p. 4.

revealed.[417] The real level of unemployment among Aborigines in remote Australia is extraordinarily high. By contrast, non-Aboriginal employment declines with remoteness.[418] This observation is not to underestimate the dangers of discounting or abolishing CDEP. Bob Gregory has observed,

> If there is a significant long run rejection rate of mainstream jobs because of CDEP this must be against the long run economic interests of the Indigenous community. ... On the other hand, if CDEP is a scheme where community life is made better for people who really have no employment alternatives then we should be less willing to restrict its further growth.[419]

Gregory does not explain what he means by a better community life. His admission, however, that there really is no employment in many Aboriginal communities raises the question of the future of such communities. CDEP would want to be making an extraordinary contribution to 'community life' to justify its existence if, indeed, it was holding people out of the economic mainstream. As McKnight observed,

> Unemployment money was known as 'sit-down money'; in contrast CDEP money became known as 'stand-up money'. The community was given a block sum to pay people to work ... what was important was that women were employed as well

---

417 Care should be exercised when using CDEP participation as its collection was limited to people enumerated on the Indigenous Household Form and who answered 'Yes' to the question on whether 'they had a job last week'. The limited collection in the 2006 Census of this variable means it cannot be used as a count of people who are participating in the CDEP program but it does provide the best estimate in a form comparable to Census data.
418 If CDEP did not exist, the increase in unemployment benefits would not be the same as the numbers who were on CDEP, as some would receive benefits not related to the labour force, but nevertheless, the degree of substitution would be very high.
419 Gregory, 2004, p. 10.

as men and they received the same rate as men. This gave them economic independence, and, of course, it gave them their own beer money.[420]

In the inflated language of self-determination, the overall aim of CDEP is to 'assist Indigenous Australians to achieve economic independence.'[421] In fact, CDEP is designed to help Aboriginal job seekers find and keep jobs. The trouble is there are few jobs in the areas in which it operates; even when there are jobs, the skills of the locals are so poor they are often unemployable.

Much of the problem with CDEP stems from its beginnings and its confused rationale. The impetus for CDEP arose from a decision by the Commonwealth Arbitration and Conciliation Commission in 1965 to include Aboriginal workers in the Cattle Station Industry (Northern Territory) Award 1951. The decision created widespread unemployment among Aborigines in remote areas of Northern Australia. The 'solution' was to grant Aboriginal people access to unemployment benefits. Unfortunately, when access was granted, the absence of realistic work prospects created a real disincentive to work.[422] The observation from Aboriginal communities at the time was that their people should not be paid 'sit down'[423] money because of the harmful effects of this payment on motivation. The Commonwealth Government's Interdepartmental Working Group's opinion in May 1976 was that the 'only real long-term solution' to these problems was 'creation of useful employment against which a realistic application of the "work test" could be applied to applicants for unemployment benefit'. Creation of 'useful employment' was

---

420 McKnight, D. 2002, p. 95.
421 Department of Families, Housing, Communities and Indigenous Affairs, 2009c. *Portfolio Budget Statement 2008-09*, p. 46.
422 Altman, J.C., Gray, M.C. and R. Levitus, 2005. Policy Issues for the Community Development Employment Scheme in Rural and Remote Australia, *Centre for Aboriginal Economic Policy Research Discussion Paper* No. 271/200, p. 27.
423 Altman et al, 2005, p. 27.

resolved by the suggestion that unemployment benefits, rather than being paid to individual beneficiaries, be paid to community councils 'to fund work projects'.[424] The CDEP program was thus developed as an alternative to payment of unemployment benefits to Aborigines in communities where there was little prospect of unsubsidised employment or economic development. Aborigines have thus remained 'uselessly' employed for 30 years. Communities have not developed and participants have become less motivated.

The assumption, closely related to land rights, was that Aboriginal people would not move from their land in order to search for work. The key assumption, not moving to work, remains. The often unspoken part of the CDEP story is that there has always been a very strong sentiment towards economic development *in situ*[425] There are two problems with this. There is the mistake that Bob Gregory appears to make in assuming that community development is somehow a substitute for economic development. Second, the misperception that CDEP operates in what the Australian Government terms 'emerging'[426] or 'limited' economies.[427] This is typical political 'spin' that will not admit that some regions fail or are in decline. As the economic development officer of Burke Shire (NSW) remarked, 'one of my tasks is to help business, mainly "helping them to fail gracefully."'[428] Many labour markets and economies in remote Australia are not limited; they are 'contracting' or 'stagnant', basically

---

424 Australian Council of Social Services, 2004. *Congress Selected Papers*, p. 77.
425 A history is provided by Altman, et al, 2005.
426 'growth is occurring and there will be opportunities to link Indigenous people to employment, education and participation with the right strategies.' Australian Government, 2008. *Increasing Indigenous Employment Opportunity; Proposed Reforms to the CDEP and Indigenous Employment Programs*, attachment C.
427 'enterprise, cultural activities and community are strong, ... but where the development of a fully-fledged labour market and full range of services may not be realistic.' Australian Government, 2008, attachment C.
428 DFD, 2009, page 20. The author was the principal researcher for the CDEP evaluation.

'failing' economies. Traditionally, in failing economies, people leave; in Aboriginal communities, foolishly, they do not. The whiteman keeps adding more and more helpers so that there is less and less to do in these non-economies, except 'engage' the whiteman.

CDEP operates in markets where few jobs are available locally that are not government-funded positions, usually supplied by Aboriginal service organisations,[429] and where the problems of distance are too great to overcome. Areas in the Kimberley, non-metropolitan South Australia and much of the Northern Territory exhibit this characteristic. There are regions, however, where jobs exist in the private sector, usually in mining or tourism, and this is especially evident in parts of Cape York and in some larger centres in the Kimberley and NSW.

Where opportunities are present, participants are often not able to take advantage of them because of lack of capacity. The capacity of participants is a crucial determinant of their success. For example, evidence from the recent evaluation of CDEP revealed in the Kimberley 75 jobs for mobile plant operators were unfilled at a local mine because of poor job readiness among Aboriginal applicants.[430] In broad terms, a better educated participant is more likely to find work;[431] the evidence is clear that the level of education among Aboriginal people in remote areas is poor.[432] There is evidence that lack of education is of recent origins. While 'adults in employment over 35 have good literacy and numeracy the younger generation lacks this education through poor school attendance and poor outstation

---

[429] Northern Territory Government 2008. *Maningrida Study*. Department of Regional Development, Primary Industry, Fisheries and Resources, p. 10.
[430] DFD, 2009, p. 21.
[431] Productivity Commission, 2007c. 'Men Not at Work: An Analysis of Men Outside the Labour Force.' *Staff Working Paper*, p. 247.
[432] Indigenous students scoring at or above the national minimum standard on a range of tests for reading, writing and numeracy at years 3, 5 and 7 ranged between 15 and 40 per cent in very remote and remote regions compared with 70 per cent in cities. National Assessment Program Literacy and Numeracy 2008.

education opportunities'.[433] More broadly, CDEP participants often have problems with alcohol and drugs. One CDEP manager pleaded that CDEP participants should be drug tested, and reported that of 57 tested, 46 failed on a recent entry exam for a local employer. Criminal records, particularly for violent crimes, were reported among applicants. Loss of drivers' licences among applicants was also reported for things like unpaid fines or the accumulation of demerit points, thus complicating the problems of access to opportunities in the labour market in other areas.[434]

CDEP operates in an environment where 'humbugging'[435] – family demands to share income – is intense. The presence of 'family obligations that flow from collectivist culture'[436] and family pressures prevent work benefits accruing to the individual and weaken the incentives to work. Worse still, there is no work culture. In a recent survey CDEP managers were asked whether there were any difficulties in willingness to work among participants. Nine answered 'Yes', two 'No'. Also, 'general lethargy' was reported, as was the perception of the 'lack of relevance of a job in their lifestyle'.[437]

A study of the work culture of the APY lands in South Australia published in 2008 found that generally few Anangu were sufficiently skilled for complex tasks and that a culture of work was lacking in many of the communities. Further, it found that there were too few people in full employment to act as role models for children and adolescents. It also noted that too many adolescents were leaving school without acquiring work-related skills, or with an understanding

---

433 DFD, 2009, p. 21.
434 DFD, 2009, p. 22.
435 Martin, D. 1995. 'Money, Business and Culture: Issues for Aboriginal Economic Policy.' *Centre for Aboriginal Economic Policy Research Discussion Paper* No. 101, p. 19.
436 DFD, 2009, p. 22.
437 DFD, 2009, p. 22.

of the reciprocal nature of employment.[438] These matters are the real culture, and yet too many of the intelligentsia have their minds turned by romantic aspects of ancient cultures that no longer exist and were never romantic. If such advocates encouraged the work ethic inherent in hunter-gatherer peoples they may just have an argument.

Employment outcomes for CDEP participants are poor. In 2007-08, only 11 per cent of participants were placed in employment; of these, only three per cent remained in that placement after 26 weeks. The cost of these outcomes provides a sobering reminder of waste in Aboriginal policy. The cost per non-CDEP placement was $15,515 in 2007-08. Because few Aboriginal participants stay in the job beyond 13 and 26 weeks, the cost per placement at 13 and 26 weeks is huge – nearly $100,000 and nearly $200,000 respectively. Labour market programs are expensive, and comparisons are difficult – Job Network programs[439] cost $6,370 a placement.[440] This is not to argue that another labour market program would do better, but to highlight the fact that labour market programs for people outside of the market, but inside a culture of dependence, are completely misplaced.

Measuring the effectiveness of labour market programs is generally very difficult because many job seekers would get jobs for themselves even if nothing were done to assist them. It is important, therefore, to differentiate clearly between employment outcomes and net impacts. Net impacts represent the *improvement* in outcomes a program delivers compared to what would have happened in the absence of assistance. In a study of the Intensive Assistance program for Aboriginal job

---

438 Vickery, D. 2007. 'Culture of Work and Community: Consultations on the Anangu Pitjantjatjara Yankunytjatjara Lands in South Australia.' *Report prepared for the Department of Education, Employment & Workplace Relations*, p. 9.
439 These range from those as intense as CDEP, for example, Work for the Dole and Job Search Customised Assistance, while others, the bulk, are simply Job Search which requires fewer resources and less contact time than CDEP.
440 Auditor-General, 2009. 'Performance Audit Administration of Job Network Outcome Payments Department of Education, Employment and Workplace Relations.' *Audit Report* No.17 2008–09, p. 20.

seekers the gross measure of outcome for participants was 21.5 per cent but the net impact of Intensive Assistance measured from commencement, the difference in outcomes for the participants and the control group – those who did not participate but were unemployed – was just 6.5 percentage points.[441]

Even when assistance does help people get jobs, it may be at the expense of other job seekers who would otherwise have been successful. Consequently, composition of the unemployment queue may change but, overall, unemployment may be relatively unchanged. Nevertheless, such 'churning', by building up the skills and employability of more disadvantaged job seekers, can increase overall employment.[442] The Evaluation results are entirely consistent with research that indicates generally poor returns in labour market programs,[443] especially among long-term unemployed where there are incentives in place to remain on welfare and where the price of labour is too high to justify employing people with limited skills.[444]

CDEP may well have the wrong candidates. As a recent study of 50 self-employed urban Aboriginal entrepreneurs found, 'around 88 per cent of survey participants have Year 12 or better education, over half have tertiary qualifications',[445] a group very unlike the CDEP participant profile. The entrepreneurs generally stated that 'traditional

---

[441] Department of Employment and Workplace Relations, 2003. 'Indigenous Employment Policy Evaluation Stage Two: Effectiveness Report.' *Evaluation and Programme Performance Branch Report* 1/200, p. 75.
[442] Productivity Commission, 2002. *Independent Review of the Job Network Inquiry Report.* Number 21, 5.3.
[443] Heckman, J. 2003. 'Human Capital Policy.' *National Bureau of Economic Research Working* Paper No. 9495, p. 1.
[444] 'The 'iron law' of income support policy indicates that high guaranteed incomes and strong work incentives are incompatible objectives.' Haveman, R. 1996. Reducing Poverty While Increasing Employment: a Primer on Alternative Strategies and a Blueprint. *OECD Economic Studies* No. 26. 1996/1, page 35.
[445] Foley, D. 2006. 'Indigenous Australian Entrepreneurs: Not all Community Organisations, Not all in the Outback.' *Centre for Aboriginal Economic Policy Research Discussion Paper* No. 279/2006, p. 9.

values' no longer existed for them, which also probably distinguishes the group from CDEP participants, but also indicates the absence of factors such as entrepreneurship among CDEP participants, thought to be essential for successful business. As one of the interviewees in the case studies remarked, 'Education is required on what a job is before starting a business should be considered.' Further, 'it usually starts with an existing activity, difficult with people with no work history, and work it up from an existing activity.'[446]

The communities in which CDEP operates are economies substantially characterised by the recirculation of public income and the consumption of public goods and services. Value is created in a few instances sufficient to justify the income and goods and services consumed but few goods and services of value are traded beyond the communities. CDEP has been operating in the same communities for more than 30 years. It has provided three generations of participants with a major link to the labour market; in many communities the CDEP is the labour market. And that is the problem; CDEP acts as a sop to the real business of getting Aborigines access to real jobs.

The Evaluation makes abundantly clear that there is a need to be clear about what outcomes are sought from CDEP. For most of its existence CDEP has worked with two major objectives – employment outcomes and community development outcomes. The actual priority of these outcomes is mixed. It is possible to identify an intent that CDEP increasingly focuses on employment outcomes and labour market preparation but it is not clear whether this is the case in practice.

The Evaluation found that the outcomes from CDEP are modest and relatively expensive for three main reasons:

- participants have a poor capacity for employment
- the cultural and community context, including the intergenerational context, makes success difficult

---

[446] DFD, 2009, p. 59.

- there are limited opportunities in most of the labour markets in which CDEP operates.

As a result, for many participants, CDEP has become a destination in itself rather than a stepping stone to employment.

The combination of part-time, lightly scrutinised CDEP activity (compared to a real job or self-employment), low emphasis on job search, and pressure to supply labour to Aboriginal corporations will keep the focus internal to the community where the labour market is weakest. In the long run an internal focus will make CDEP's role in economic development inappropriate.

The intergenerational and cultural aspects and context of CDEP in remote communities make adjustment to the labour market very difficult. CDEP must address these challenges directly if it is to improve. CDEP has a dual challenge: on the one hand, to maintain the intensity of the job readiness experience; and, on the other, to minimise the opportunity cost implied in creating activities that hold participants out of the labour market. In the latter respect, Job Network programs concentrate on job search activities which are less intense and rely on mobility for real jobs.

Mobility may hold the key to behaviour change and in preparing participants for real jobs by explicitly overcoming intergenerational expectations. Aboriginal people rarely move for economic reasons. This is not surprising given that they have been paid to stay outside of the workforce for several generations.[447] Nevertheless, CDEP will add value if it adds to the range of training activities available to labour market aspirants. CDEP can be improved and become more appropriate to the goals of real jobs and viable business enterprises if the following are addressed.

- the cost of training and job support must be transparent

---

[447] Biddle N. and B.H. Hunter, 2005. Factors associated with internal migration: A comparison between Indigenous and non-Indigenous Australians. *Centre for Aboriginal Economic Policy Working Paper* No. 32/2005.

so that different jobs strategies are compared fairly
- providers should be focused on preparing participants for real jobs, wherever these are offered by the labour market
- CDEP must be sufficiently intense to overcome entrenched poor behaviour
- CDEP must address intergenerational unemployment in remote communities by assisting participants to experience workplaces outside of the communities in which they operate
- CDEP is not well-suited to address community development issues or economic development issues as these are not the same as labour market preparation issues.

These changes to CDEP are also occurring in a broader context of other welfare-related reforms such as the Cape York Welfare Reform Trials[448] and Income Management.[449] The Coalition and the Australian Government have recently agreed to legislation to extend income management to all areas in Australia.[450] All of these reforms are likely to have major implications for the effectiveness of participant incentives.

The trouble with the pretend economy is that its rationale is not clear. If Aborigines are not living a traditional life, what is it that Aborigines are meant to do? Or is it that they are just meant to be? Aborigines are not living by the script. Instead, the promise of land rights has been empty. Despite the iconic land rights battles of the last 40 years, all is not peace and love on Aboriginal land. Aboriginal land title has been structured so that it throws together those who

---

[448] http://www.facsia.gov.au/internet/facsinternet.nsf/family/wpr_cape_york_wf.htm..
[449] http://www.facsia.gov.au/nter/income_mngmt.htm.
[450] http://www.abc.net.au/news/stories/2010/03/31/2860977.htm.

historically had little collective interest in, and no means of, working together.

Most Aboriginal land in the Northern Territory came with a veto over mining and this has been used to thwart wealth that Aborigines could have shared. That which has been agreed with mining companies, mostly outside of the NT, has been wasted through present consumption and with no thought to investing in the future of Aboriginal people. The mindset that pitched Aborigines against miners was partly seeded by environmentalists who built a myth around Aboriginal culture that it had something to do with protecting the environment. Instead, it had everything to do with protecting sacred objects, not the environment. As Christopher Anderson found, sacred sites are sometimes a commodity to be traded at the right price, in some cases for the sake of 'development'. In the Daintree region on Cape York, a proposed road threatened a number of sacred sites. The local Aboriginal community was keen to obtain the benefits the road would bring, so it denied the existence of sites that he himself had recorded five years previously, much to the ire of environmentalists, whose reaction was that the community had 'lost their culture'.[451]

---

[451] Anderson, C. 1989. 'Aborigines and Conservationism: the Daintree–Bloomfield Road.' *Australian Journal of Social Issues*, August.

7

Real economy

The sole hope for the future of Aborigines lies in entering and adjusting to the real economy. Any expenditure that slows the adjustment is an investment in misery. To aid in this essential direction, those who romanticise Aboriginal culture would do well to recall the industriousness of the Aboriginal hunter-gatherer economy. At the heart of the Aboriginal economy was the absolute necessity to work. As a hunter-gatherer, an Aborigine either worked or he or she would die of starvation.

In the transition from hunter-gatherer to the modern economy many have failed to gain a foothold and have been forced into idleness. It was this idleness that created strife, as much as the loss of some immutable culture. The historical observations on the work habits of Aborigines and the loss of culture and the idleness are not at all controversial. Donald Thomson spent at least two years working with the Aboriginal tribes in Eastern Arnhem Land, mainly east of what are now Milingimbi and Ramingining. His 1949 book, *Economic Structure and the Ceremonial Cycle in Arnhem Land*, described the life of a hunter-gatherer:

> The first impression that any stranger must receive in a fully organised group in Eastern Arnhem Land is of industry. He

cannot fail to see that everybody, man or woman, works hard, and that the work is well organised and runs smoothly. And he must also be impressed by the fact that with the exception of very young children who engage earnestly in play, much of which is imitative and based on the activities of adults, there is no idleness. Even the young men are engaged fully in hunting and fishing activities and work hard, in marked contrast with the conditions in similar groups close to white settlement, where the organisation is breaking down.[452]

The Australian anthropologists Ronald and Catherine Berndt completed a survey of conditions among Aboriginal workers and their families in the Northern Territory in 1944-46, in particular work on the cattle properties and in the Army.[453] In the light of labour shortages, the Berndts were called in by Australian Investment Agencies (Vesteys) and the Department of Aboriginal Affairs to assist in surveying the diminishing Aboriginal population on the cattle stations, and to advise on the future of bush people and of Aborigines released from military employment. The Berndts made a number of important observations at a point of immense change in the lives of among the last Aborigines to face the full force of modernity. Until this point the Arnhem Land Aborigines had known only the comparative discipline and protection of the missionaries, the cattle stations and the Army.

They noted a number of changes to culture. They observed that while there was pride shown in the display of song and dance ceremonies from the different language groups on each station, the traditional commitment was out of 'memory' and not of a 'living' kind.[454] They concluded that traditional knowledge had to

---

452 Thomson, D. 1949. *Economic Structure and the Ceremonial Cycle in Arnhem Land*, Macmillan, p. 34.
453 Berndt R.M. and C.H. Berndt. 1987. *End of an Era: Aboriginal Labour in the Northern Territory*. Australian Institute of Aboriginal Studies.
454 Berndt and Berndt, 1987, p. 207.

be regarded as constituting a memory rather than a living culture.[455] They also concluded that the Indigenous form of education was gradually collapsing, and had not been replaced by any real substitute. Information picked up by children from camp life and from glimpses of the life led by Europeans around the stations was 'not only insufficient for their future needs but in a number of cases definitely harmful'. Most acutely, they concluded, 'in view of their increasing contact with Europeans, and their more rapid absorption into a non-Aboriginal context, it appeared that these children would eventually have little use for much of the Aboriginal background that remained to them.'[456]

The critical issue for the Berndts was how Aborigines who had little or no direct contact with Europeans, and whose society's structure had been only partially modified, were to maintain or have restored to them an interest and a faith in life and living, and a belief that they had something worthwhile to pass on to their children. The Berndts thought it imperative that such a belief should not be undermined during the slow process of adapting themselves to change.[457] They were right to think in terms of adjustment but perhaps naïve to think that much traditional thought could survive the transition. Underlying much of the desire to protect and preserve culture was the fear that Aborigines would drift into town. In 1946, the Acting Director of Native Affairs 'was concerned with attempting to stem the drift of Aborigines into town'.[458] So much of Aboriginal policy since has been crudely based on keeping Aborigines separate from the town. The separation denied Aborigines the opportunity to replace their understanding of life with something substantial instead of a dead and wholly inappropriate set of rules and customs.

McKnight recalls a more recent case of the breakdown in discipline

---

455 Berndt and Berndt, 1987, p. 210.
456 Berndt and Berndt, 1987, p. 237.
457 Berndt and Berndt, 1987, p. 250.
458 Berndt and Berndt, 1987, p. 259.

and production following the departure of a white supervisor at Mornington Island.

> The market garden looked as if it was going to be a great success under the talented supervision of Maurie James, a horticulturalist. He established a nursery [1985] and cultivated seven acres where he grew a variety of vegetables ... The cattle industry looked promising. It finally seemed as though Mornington was going to reach some degree of economic self-sufficiency. Alas, within a year of James' departure, the splendid market garden collapsed. And so did the cattle industry. It is of interest why these two enterprises failed. After James left a Mornington Islander took charge and initially the workers followed James's regime but gradually in the mornings they arrived later and later and departed earlier and earlier in the afternoon. ... The person in charge lacked the presence to get his fellow Mornington Islanders to work. The values of autonomy and egalitarianism were too strong for him to impose authority ... The workers well knew that they would be paid regardless of how much they did.[459]

The Thompson, Berndts and McKnight observations suggest that in the transition from a traditional economy to a modern economy Aborigines were at risk of falling idle. So much of current policy, while acknowledging the fact, remains committed to saving an ancient culture in the name of political stability, while ignoring the parts of the culture that act as an impediment to work. Those who concentrate on recapturing culture seem content to ignore the essential need for Aborigines to work and to reap the rewards of work to survive and prosper.

Efforts to take the economy to Aborigines in the hope they could have both work and culture have failed. Unfortunately, for three

---

459 McKnight, 2002, p. 102.

generations, Aborigines in remote Australia especially have been paid to not work. The effect on their discipline and self-esteem has been devastating. Programs such as CDEP and land rights have prevented Aborigines from adjusting to the actual circumstances in which they find themselves. Many Aborigines are now less equipped than their elders to create a decent life. Three closely related major programs – settlement, housing, and education – indicate some positive movement towards a more rational stance but their true (in contrast to their stated) intent is yet to be revealed because governments are unable to articulate the necessary path.

Back to the mission

The entire edifice of separatist Aboriginal policy has been challenged in the Northern Territory with the abandonment by the Australian Government of its responsibility for homelands and outstations. Homelands are generally a common location occupied by the traditional owners or people with a direct link to the traditional owner of the land. These have few services and may or may not be permanently occupied. Outstations are similar but residents may not be able to demonstrate traditional ownership and may only have a general association with the area.[460]

Homelands and outstations established in the late 1970s and early 1980s carried the weight of expectations that Aborigines could escape the whiteman's world. They are sustained by the whiteman's

---

460 Phillpot, S. 2007. 'The Future Of Remote Aboriginal Communities: A Series of Relic Settlements of People Created by the Ebb and Flow of Contact with non-Aboriginals.' *The Bennelong Society Conference*, p. 3.

taxes. They have their supporters in very high places,[461] still singing their praises, still gathering the political support that will only leave Aborigines in limbo for many years yet, trying to live the impossible dream of being an Aborigine on traditional land in a modern world. The same irresponsibility has been demonstrated in the recent film, *Samson and Delilah*. It portrays two young Aborigines who escape both the whiteman's world at Alice Springs and their own community outside Alice Springs to settle on her people's country, driving there in a borrowed four-wheel drive with a box of tinned food, as if this was a realistic way to survive. The shame is that so many regarded the film as optimistic.[462] The significant question, however, is to decipher what abandoning outstations is likely to achieve. It is most likely an attempt to consolidate Aboriginal settlement for the ease of providing services. An essential part of those services is establishment of law and order and to have children attend school full-time. Although no government would admit it, in effect they are re-establishing the missions, in most cases on the original site as Tables 5 and 6 demonstrate.

The decision by the Australian Government to abandon outstations has been taken in two parts. First, the Howard Government made an explicit offer to the Northern Territory Government to pay it $20 million per year to take over outstations, as it chose to intervene in only the largest of the remote communities; second, the Rudd Government decided to continue the new settlement policy by funding a consolidation of the largest Aboriginal settlements in the NT.

---

461 In October 2009 the Academy of Social Sciences in Australia and the Centre for Aboriginal Economic Policy Research convened a workshop at the Australian National University in Canberra on Homelands/Outstations. Invited to the workshop were homeland/outstation residents, their resource agencies, peak Aboriginal organisations, social and physical scientists, educationalists, medical practitioners and bureaucrats. There was an endorsement of a communiqué in support of the continuation of homelands. Academy of Social Sciences in Australia, *Dialogue* 28 (2).

462 See review by Johns, G. 'Myth of Outback Escape is Unrealistic.' *The Australian*, 4 June 2009.

Aboriginal settlement policy is rarely explicitly stated, but the emergency intervention and other housing-policy initiatives of the Howard Government provided some indications. There seemed to be a covert policy of physical consolidation of Aboriginal communities because the 73 'intervention' communities were quite simply chosen on the basis of size (any community over 100), the inference being that the Australian Government would no longer service any smaller community. Wadeye in the NT, for example, was funded not because it deserved the same infrastructure as any town the same size (the public rationale), but because of the fear that if the largest Aboriginal community could not survive, then none would. The entire edifice of discrete Aboriginal communities would collapse.

More recently, the Australian Government announced that it would supply new housing to a subset of the 1,100 remote discrete Aboriginal settlements throughout northern Australia. Under the Australian Government's *National Partnership on Remote Indigenous Housing*[463] $5.5 billion will be spent over ten years in 26 priority settlements. All but two of these settlements are former missions or government ration stations (see Table 5 and Table 6) and each is almost wholly or predominantly Aboriginal. Fourteen of these communities are in the Northern Territory. In addition, the Northern Territory Government's initiative, *A Working Future*,[464] has designated 20 settlements as towns. They receive infrastructure funds though a number have not been chosen for Australian Government housing funding.

---

463   http://www.fahcsia.gov.au/sa/indigenous/progserv/housing/Pages/RemoteIndigenousHousing.aspx.
464   http://www.workingfuture.nt.gov.au/.

Table 5: National Partnership on Remote Indigenous Housing, Northern Territory

Communities Northern Territory	Location	Contact history	Total population Aboriginal clan	Economic base
Galiwinku	Elcho Island N E Arnhem Land	1947 Methodist Overseas Mission	2200 Yolngu	No base
Nguiu	Bathurst Island nth of Darwin	1911 Missionaries of the Sacred Heart	1500 Tiwi	Plantation forest industry
Numbulwar	Opposite Groote Eylandt	1952 Church Missionary Society(Rose River mission)	1200 Nunggayinbala	No base
Angurugu	On Groote Eylandt	1943 Church Missionary Society	800 Anindilyakwa	Gemco manganese mine
Umbakumba	On Groote Eylandt	1921 Church Missionary Society at Emerald River	300 Anindilyakwa	Gemco manganese mine
Milingimbi	Island near Maningrida N E Arnhem Land	1923 Methodist Overseas Mission	900 Djambarrpuyngu and Gupapuyngu	No base
Maningrida	N E Arnhem Land	1957 ration station/ trading post ' to quell the post-war migration of Aboriginal people into Darwin'	2600 includes 30 outstations Kunibídji and ors	No base
Gapuwiyak	N E Arnhem Land	1960's outstation of Galiwin'ku	1000 Yolngu	No base
Yirrkala	Near Nhulunbuy (service centre) East Arnhem Land	1935 Methodist Mission	800 Yolngu	Alcan bauxite Nhulunbuy
Ngukurr	Roper River 330km sth-east of Katherine SE Arnhem	1908 Church of England Roper River Mission	1300 Ngukurr	No base

Communities Northern Territory	Location	Contact history	Total population Aboriginal clan	Economic base
Lajamanu	Hooker Creek between Tennant Creek and Katherine	1948 ration station 1962 Baptist church 1970s Gurindji people from Wave Hill area 'handed over' to Warlpiri	700 Warlpiri	No base
Yuendumu	294 km north-west of Alice Springs on the Tanami Road	1928 Coniston massacre 1946 ration station 1947 Baptist mission	1300 Warlpiri	Granites Gold cattle stations
Hermannsburg	Nataria 125 km west of Alice Springs	1877 Lutheran missionaries	600 Arrente	No base
Wadeye	Port Keats 220 km south-west of Darwin	1941 Our Lady of the Sacred Heart School	2215 seven different clans	Blacktip Gas Trans-Territory Pipeline

Data source: various, compiled by author.

The broader context of the settlement consolidation strategy is change to the social contract between government and Aboriginal people. Remote area exemptions for welfare benefit obligations are being abolished; CDEP are being wound down or converted to training and job brokerage. Communities and the individuals within them will, in many cases, have to change the way they function. Parents will be expected to take responsibility for their family well-being including their children's health, safety and education. The restoration of social norms is also a focus of the current welfare reform pilots being conducted around Australia: income management in the Northern Territory; Cape York Welfare Reform; and the Child Protection Measure in the Kimberley and in Cannington, Midland, Mirrabooka and Joondalup in Perth. Similarly, the School Enrolment and Attendance Measure being piloted at a number of locations in the Northern Territory is also aimed at increasing personal responsibility and improving the welfare of children. In so many ways the Australian Government has decided to re-missionise remote Australian Aborigines. It is as if the policy cycle has started over again.

The attempt to re-missionise through change to personal behaviour and to consolidate the location of services into fewer settlements has taken place unannounced. There is no explicit acknowledgement or plan as to the purpose of these two significant changes to policy. It is unclear whether governments are pursuing a strategy for Aboriginal economic development or a strategy for Aboriginal integration in the wider economy, or a service consolidation strategy, or maybe all three. The intention to develop a formal Aboriginal economic development strategy has been announced by the Australian Government (previous strategies concentrated on home ownership and enhanced training opportunities[465]) but no strategy has as yet emerged.[466] The Northern Territory Aboriginal economic development strategy[467] consists merely of aspirations and targets. There is no strategy other than to link 'economic development' with the growth towns. One positive insight into the strategy is an implicit acknowledgement that the *Aboriginal Land Rights (Northern Territory) Act* is an impediment to development. After years of lauding separate development and self-determination, governments are very reluctant to mention integration as an explicit goal, but it is difficult to discern whether this strategy is behind the consolidation.

Are these 26 towns likely to develop or die? Will they become 26 launching pads to the wider economy or 26 well-serviced ghettoes? Well-serviced towns will probably not only act as a magnet for those

---

[465] Australian Government, undated. *Achieving Indigenous Economic Independence: Indigenous Economic Development Strategy.*
[466] Department of Families, Housing, Community Services and Indigenous Affairs, 2009d. *Increasing Indigenous Economic Opportunity: a Discussion Paper on the Future of the CDEP and Indigenous Employment Programs,* p. 5.
[467] Northern Territory Government Department of Regional Development, Primary Industry, Fisheries and Resources, 2009. *Indigenous Development Strategy 2009-2012,* p. 17.

on outstations, but also from fringe dwellers in established centres. As a result, they may well grow much more quickly than anticipated. The issue is not ease of service but the reason why people are provided service. Services are not a static element in a person's life. By and large they are meant to change people by restoring health, bringing law and order or by education in order that they may fend for themselves.

Table 6: National Partnership on Remote Indigenous Housing, Elsewhere

Communities Elsewhere	Location	Contact history	Total population Aboriginal clan	Economic base
Fitzroy Crossing WA	400 km east of Broome Kimberley	1951 United Aborigines Mission	900 Junjuwa	Tourism, cattle stations and mining
Halls Creek	Kimberley	Gold town 1880s	1200 Jaru and Kija	Cattle stations
Ardyaloon	Broome Dampier Peninsula	Settled permanently 1970's	500 hub for outstations Bardi-Jawi	No base
Beagle Bay	90 km north of Broome	1892 established by Trappist Monks	300 Djarindjin, Bardi, Bobeiding and Ngardalargin	Tourism
Mornington Is. Qld	Gulf of Carpentaria	1914 Presbyterian mission	1000 Lardil and Kiadilt	No base
Doomadgee	Gulf of Carpentaria	1931 Christian Brethren 'moved from the fringes of Burketown'	1000 Gundalita	No base
Hope Vale	East side Cape York north of Cooktown	1886 Lutheran mission and again 1949	700 Warra	No base
Aurukun	West side cape York	1904 Presbyterian Church of Australia	1000 Wik Munkin	Bauxite mining
Amata SA	Anangu Pitjantjatjara Yankunytjatjara Lands	1961 SA Government 'take pressure off Ernabella'	300 Anangu	No base
Mimili	APY Lands	Cattle station	300 Anangu	No base

Communities Elsewhere	Location	Contact history	Total population Aboriginal clan	Economic base
Walgett NSW	Western NSW	1859 town established 'Freedom Rides in the late 1960s'	1700 Gamilaraay, Yuwaalaraay and Ngayiimbaa	wool, wheat and cotton
Wilcannia	Western NSW	1850s pastoral settlement	600 Barkindji	Sheep

Data source: various, compiled by author.

Instead, the services provided in the new towns or, more accurately, the new missions, are as likely to maintain poverty and dysfunction as to relieve them. The service consolidation strategy is not explicitly stated other than in terms of 'equity', which is that, all towns of the same size, but presumably not the same remote locality, should receive the same services expected in other Australian towns of comparable size and circumstances. A recent NT Government study identified the essential characteristics of the Maningrida community and its economy, and contrasted such characteristics with a similar-sized 'mainstream' community located elsewhere in Australia.[468]

The program will see construction of up to 4,200 additional houses and major upgrades and repairs to around 4,800 houses in remote communities. Unfortunately, the prospects that these will be delivered are not positive as a component of the *National Partnership on Remote Indigenous Housing Program, Strategic Indigenous Housing and Infrastructure Program*,[469] a $672 million jointly funded housing program in the Northern Territory, struggled to deliver any houses to similar areas in the first twelve months since inception.

The initial housing investment is said to focus on these 26 larger communities which the Australian Government claims 'have the potential for economic development'. Nowhere is the term, 'economic development', defined, or is evidence adduced to suggest how this

---

[468] NTG, 2008, p. 2.
[469] http://www.fahcsia.gov.au/sa/indigenous/progserv/housing/Pages/sihip.aspx.

economic development might occur, other than 'through increased local training and employment opportunities in construction and housing management.' Such training schemes rarely result in development or even in a secure entry to the labour market.[470] Almost all of the 26 preferred settlements are mission stations or ration stations settled early last century. Almost all have little economic prospects. The Government's criteria for selecting them are scattergun:

- significant concentration of population
- anticipated demographic trends and pressures
- the potential for economic development and employment
- pre-existing shortfalls in government investment in infrastructure and services.

No data to justify the selection accompanied the announcement. Australian governments have provided income and infrastructure support to Aboriginal settlements in remote Australia as if permanent settlements could be made on the foundation of government expenditure alone, that is, in the absence of a real economy. Even when there was real economic activity, such as a mine, local Aborigines did not necessarily have the skills to apply, nor could these skills necessarily be acquired *in situ*. In short, there is limited scope for most remote settlements to thrive. Moreover, reconstruction and revitalisation of remote Australia is not on the Australian Government's agenda notwithstanding that it funds Desert Knowledge Australia which makes the bold claim, 'the reconstruction and revitalisation of Remote Australia could be considered the last great task of Australia's structural reform project and one of the grand challenges for the national commitment to cooperative federalism.'[471] Australia will witness, as it did until the 1960s, a movement into town. When the

---
470 DFD, 2009, p. 31.
471 Desert Knowledge Australia 2008: 'remoteFOCUS: Revitalising Remote Australia', *Prospectus*, p. 12.

difficult issues of the abandonment of remote settlements and the growth of town camps arise, policy-makers will need to be able to remain focused on the principal job – adjustment.

These townships inevitably comprised Aborigines with different land and family affiliations. The more traditional Aboriginal people do not always have mechanisms for co-operation in day-to-day matters beyond the bounds of the extended language group. This is largely why there is not one functioning Aboriginal township in the Northern Territory. It is not possible to have effective Aboriginal local government for cultural reasons, and governments should therefore directly run all essential services in Aboriginal townships. It is probably at the base of the service strategy, which is an implicit recognition that Aborigines cannot govern themselves and that these towns will be governed by non-Aborigines as was the case in the mission period. The unstated assumption of the study is that all towns should be propped up regardless of their prospects.

No job, no house

Settlement policy and Aboriginal housing can only be understood in the context of economic development. Policies aimed at stabilising Aboriginal communities *in situ* will, all things being equal, lessen the impact of the economic imperatives operating in northern Australia. In a choice between economic development on Aboriginal lands and the incentives to search for work and services away from those lands, the latter will almost certainly win unless governments continue to stop adjustment by making services and monies available to those who are prepared to sit and wait as opposed to those who are prepared to search for opportunity. In short, if you pay people to stay in a poor area, they are less likely to escape poverty.

The factors influencing change in remote Aboriginal Australia are:

- The artificial labour market will unravel, driven by the removal of Remote Area Exemption on Centrelink programs, and the shift in CDEP to employment services
- Education authorities are beginning to re-impose authority to ensure attendance at school and the teaching of literacy and numeracy
- Changes to the *Northern Territory Land Rights Act* may encourage some people to sell their interest in the land and leave
- Chronic poor health is driving people to seek long-term medical attention, which is available only in regional centres
- Women are seeking physical protection; hostels are more likely to be available in regional centres
- Economic development is unrealistic for more than a handful of communities
- Local populations do not necessarily have the skills to take advantage of economic development. Acquiring skills is unlikely to take place in the community.

Governments also fund stabilising programs, which may have the effect of keeping people away from opportunity:

- Alcohol and substance abuse programs. dry communities
- Service agreements for utilities. telephone, sewerage
- Shared Responsibility Agreements no school, no pool
- Infrastructure programs housing
- New settlements from Native Title and Indigenous Land Use Agreements claims
- Investment in school facilities and staff
- Investments by the Indigenous Land Fund and Indigenous Business Australia
- Investment in law and order.

Both sets of factors and programs send confused signals. In the end they drive up the cost and delay adjustment. At present, Aborigines are mobile, but they are not necessarily adjusting. Aborigines move about as part of community activity; and they sometimes 'orbit' in the sense in which Noel Pearson means children who leave their communities for education, and perhaps to return on graduation, but insufficient people leave communities permanently for work. And yet the purpose of building 26 new missions is presumably to attract people. If they are attracted for reasons of servicing their needs, but have no work prospects, they will simply camp on the outskirts. How people adjust and how their needs are to be met will be a challenge, as will management of the communities they leave behind but there is a point to the adjustment. Self-sufficiency, not self-determination, is the end point. If Aborigines are not to become, once again, refugees in their own land, governments and citizens must prepare for the next chapter in the Aboriginal story.

Government-supported housing for Aborigines is in danger of ignoring these drivers and falling into the trap of simply chasing apparent need. Apparent need is the crucial element of this debate on housing. There is a need for more housing for Aborigines who live in remote Australia. It would be folly to assume immediately, though, that the houses should be built in remote Australia, given there is little economic opportunity in the regions. Further, it must not be forgotten that the default position with public support for housing in Australia is that each person should purchase their own accommodation. If they are unable to do so, consideration is given to various forms of support. The support may be temporary, to allow the person to save for purchase or to subsidise rent until the person's income improves. Where the person remains unable to support themselves public housing may be long term, but the presumption remains. Once the presumption is removed, however, trouble follows. If a family receives a house regardless of their effort to secure one, those who try to secure one by their own efforts inevitably lose heart. There has never been an unqualified right to housing in Australia. The presumption must be in favour of people buying or renting their own house so that any housing assistance must never undermine the presumption of self-provision.

There is a direct link between Aboriginal housing shortages in remote areas and job shortages in remote areas. While some jobs exist in remote areas they tend to be highly skilled jobs in the mining sector. These jobs have not gone to Aborigines. Despite training opportunities being offered to Aborigines they have not taken advantage of them. Alternatively, Aborigines live in remote areas where these jobs are not available. Further, the behaviour of Aborigines who live in remote communities means that they are not ready to enter the shallow employment markets that exist in remote areas. Nor are they in a position to take responsibility for renting a house or paying a mortgage like Aboriginal and non-Aboriginal people in other parts of Australia.

Many of the remote communities have failed. The communities are in many cases beset by major social problems: high rates of sexually transmitted disease, domestic violence and homicide combined with poor health, education, housing and child care services, low job prospects and a culture of humbugging. Aboriginal people are starting to abandon these communities in search of a better life. Younger people in particular are leaving these communities for better educational and employment opportunities. The decline of these communities both in a social and population sense raises serious doubts about the level of government assistance that should continue to be provided to them.

Governments should cease building permanent housing for Aborigines in remote communities where they do not have a job in the real economy and where they are unable, like other Australians, to pay rent or service a mortgage. In the interim, temporary housing only should be supplied. Building more houses is not a solution. As Phil Bevan of the housing company, New Future Alliance, established to build houses in Tennant Creek and elsewhere in the NT as part of the $672 million Strategic Indigenous Housing and Infrastructure Program, said, 'you could build a thousand homes out there and it doesn't mean each family is going to go and live in each one of them. Only a small number would be used because families … like to be together and love having their relations around them ... the refurbishments ... will not address the overcrowding, it never will.'[472]

Public expenditure on Aboriginal housing has been long term, large and targeted to service states and territories with significant Aboriginal populations. In 2005-06, the Australian and state governments spent $2.4 billion[473] in dedicated housing and accommodation support programs for Aborigines. In addition, like other Australians, Aborigines have access to a range of accommodation support services provided on a needs basis.[474]

The Northern Territory and Western Australian governments have been granted extra monies from the Commonwealth Grants Commission (CGC) on the basis of their Aboriginal populations and servicing obligations in remote areas. A special CGC report on Indigenous funding concluded, 'the current distribution of Indigenous specific funds broadly accords with relative need – a larger share of these funds is allocated to remote regions that have the greatest need.'[475] More recently, the Northern Territory Indigenous Expenditure Review of 2006 concluded that in 2004-05 an estimated 49.7 per cent of the Northern Territory Government's expenditure was related to its Indigenous population ... an estimated 42.3 per cent of the Northern Territory Government's revenue [including tied grants and GST revenue] was related to its Indigenous population over the same period ... Indigenous related expenditure exceeded a per capita share by 73 per cent and represents 2.44 times the per capita expenditure related to non-Indigenous persons in the Northern

---

472 *The Weekend Australian*, 15-16 August 2009.
473 Productivity Commission, 2007b. *Report on Government Services 2007 - Indigenous Compendium*, page *228*; Secretaries' Group, 2007. *Annual Report 2005-06*; Department of Families, Community Services and Indigenous Affairs, 2007. Office of Indigenous Policy Co-ordination, *unpublished data*.
474 Department of Families, Community Services and Indigenous Affairs, 2007. *Housing Assistance Act 1996: Annual Report 2005-06*, p. 4.
475 Commonwealth Grants Commission, 2001. *Report on Indigenous Funding 2001*, p. xxi.

Territory.[476] The review found that 'the estimated total proportion of Indigenous related expenditure in the NT Department of Local Government, Housing and Sport was 69 per cent.'[477]

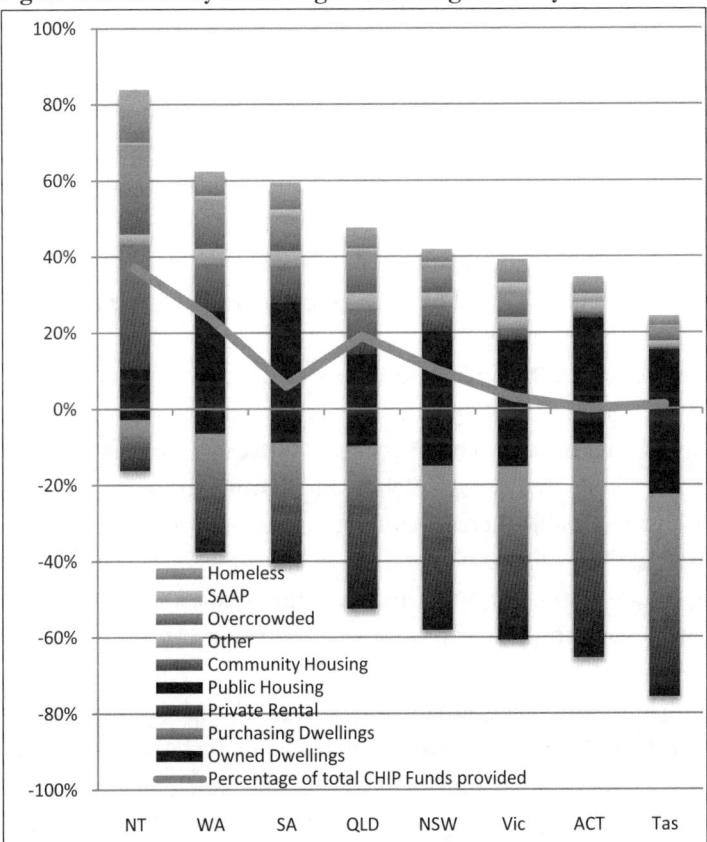

Figure 11: Hierarchy of Aboriginal housing needs by state

[Stacked bar chart showing housing categories across NT, WA, SA, QLD, NSW, Vic, ACT, Tas with y-axis from -100% to 100%. Legend includes: Homeless, SAAP, Overcrowded, Other, Community Housing, Public Housing, Private Rental, Purchasing Dwellings, Owned Dwellings, Percentage of total CHIP Funds provided.]

Note: SAAP, Supported Accommodation Assistance Programme. CHIP, Community Housing and Infrastructure Programme.
Data source: Department of Families, Community Services and Indigenous Affairs, 2007. Indigenous Housing: Findings of the Review of the Community Housing and Infrastructure Programme 2006, p. 56.

---

476 Northern Territory Treasury, 2006. *Indigenous Expenditure Review*, p. 3.
477 NTT, 2006, p. 44.

Further evidence of targeting housing assistance is shown in Figure 11. It shows both the percentage of Aborigines in each state and territory who require housing assistance (above the line), and those who are more self-sufficient (below the line). The data indicate that overcrowding and homelessness are relatively bigger problems in the Northern Territory, in particular, but also in Western Australia, South Australia and Queensland compared to the south-eastern states. The figures probably reflect the number of Aborigines in remote, discrete communities. The percentage of total Community Housing and Infrastructure Program funds provided to each state (with the possible exception of SA) more or less reflects the housing need of their population. An important element of Figure 11 is not so much the Aboriginal need displayed in some places, but the independence of Aborigines in the southern states.

While there is clearly an inadequate stock of houses for Aboriginal people,[478] a housing shortage does not necessarily prove insufficient government investment. The Australian Government has invested around $2 billion in Aboriginal housing during the past 10 years without an appreciable increase in the number of houses. In the past five years, the Aboriginal housing stock has only increased by two per cent, or an extra 471 houses, bringing the total to 21,758. Despite increased investment, in the Northern Territory there are 271 fewer houses than there were five years ago.[479] In the recent analysis of a major Indigenous housing and infrastructure policy, *Indigenous Housing: Findings of the Review of the Community Housing and Infrastructure Program*, the absence of material improvement in the stock of Aboriginal housing is attributed, among other things, to corruption in local

---

478 Confirmed by the Northern Territory Emergency Response Taskforce, 2008. *Final Report to Government*, p. 18.
479 Brough, M. 2006. Minister for Families, Community Services and Indigenous Affairs, 'Blueprint for Action in Indigenous Affairs' Press release, 5 December.

housing management and appalling tenant behaviour.[480]

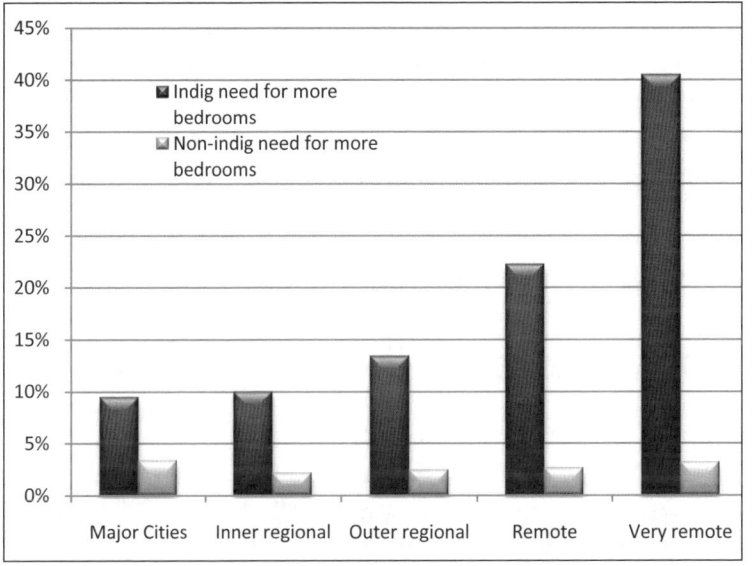

Figure 12: Households require extra bedroom, by remoteness areas, 2006

[Bar chart showing Indigenous need for more bedrooms vs Non-indigenous need for more bedrooms across remoteness areas: Major Cities (~10% Indig, ~3% Non-indig), Inner regional (~10% Indig, ~2% Non-indig), Outer regional (~13% Indig, ~2% Non-indig), Remote (~22% Indig, ~3% Non-indig), Very remote (~40% Indig, ~3% Non-indig)]

Note: 'Households' defined as occupied private dwellings. 'Require an extra bedroom' based on the Canadian National Occupancy Standard for housing appropriateness.
Data source: Australian Bureau of Statistics, 2008. Population Characteristics 2006, Aboriginal and Torres Strait Islander Australians. 4713.0 table 9.4, p. 143.

Even with substantial targeted funding, Aboriginal housing shortages exist in all areas, but most acutely in remote Aboriginal communities. 14 per cent of Indigenous households live in dwellings that require at least one extra bedroom (based on the Canadian

---

480 Department of Families, Community Services and Indigenous Affairs, 2007. *Living in the Sunburnt Country - Indigenous Housing: Findings of the Review of the Community Housing and Infrastructure Programme*, p. 16.

National Occupancy Standard for housing appropriateness),[481] compared with three per cent of non-Indigenous households. For Indigenous households (Figure 12), average household size and the proportion of households requiring an extra bedroom escalated as remoteness increased. The proportion of households requiring at least one extra bedroom varies from nine per cent in major cities to 40 per cent in very remote areas. The need for at least one extra bedroom in non-Indigenous households was much lower, with less than four per cent requiring an extra bedroom in any remoteness area.

Figure 13: Population housing need, discrete Indigenous communities, 2006

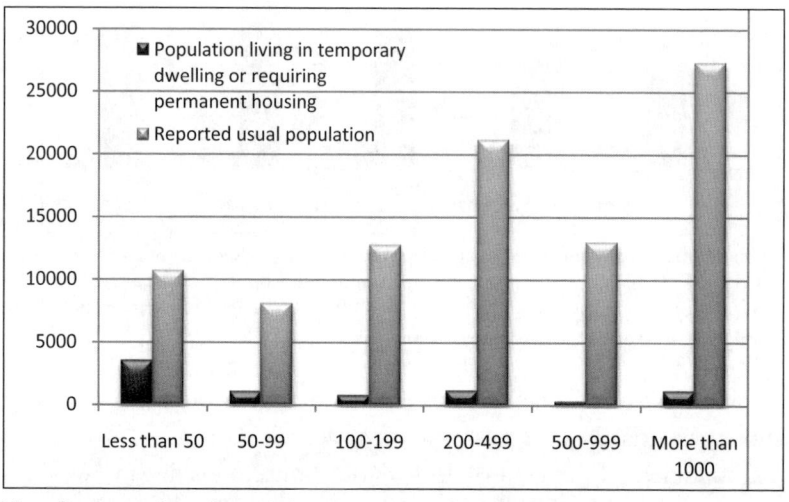

Note: By reported usual population. Data source: ABS, 2007 Housing & Infrastructure in Aboriginal and Torres Strait Islander Communities, Australia, 2006. 4710.0 Table 3.5 26.

---

481 For sole parent or couple households with more than four children the dwelling size in terms of bedrooms should be the same value as the total number of children in the household. Where more than one group is present, the needs of the two or more groups should be added together. For example, a sole parent with one child living with the sole parent's parents (three generations) would require 4 bedrooms, that is, 2 bedrooms for the sole parent and child and 2 bedrooms for the married couple.

On close inspection, and using a different measure of housing need, those living in temporary dwellings or requiring permanent housing (Figure 13), the shortage appears greatest in the very small, discrete Aboriginal communities of very remote regions.

It is clear that while small remote Aboriginal communities experience the greatest need, non-Indigenous households and individuals in the same regions were not similarly affected. For non-Indigenous households, the shortage of bedrooms declines with remoteness. There are two possible explanations. The first is that there is prejudice against Aborigines in the housing market unique to remote and very remote areas. Given that these areas are subject to Aboriginal housing control, this explanation is unlikely. A second explanation is that non-Aborigines are more likely to stay in remote regions when they have a job and are therefore able to afford sufficient accommodation; when they are not employed, or lack accommodation, they tend to leave the area (for example, mining and public sector jobs exhibit a quick turnover). To some extent the differing behavior is explained by tenure and income differences between Aborigines and non-Aborigines in remote areas.

Indigenous housing and land tenure (Figure 14) are significantly different to non-Indigenous tenure (Figure 15). There are fewer ownership and mortgage options for Indigenous people in all areas although they decline alarmingly for Aborigines in remote areas. The reason is the significant number of Indigenous people living on communally-owned or controlled land. Most housing on communally owned land is the property of community or cooperative housing organisations, which rent houses to families and individuals. Although some land in regional areas is communally-owned, most communally-owned land is located in remote and very remote areas. Generally, such land cannot be sold and the land itself cannot be mortgaged.[482]

---

482 DFCSIA, 2007, p. 16.

This ensures its continuing ownership by Aboriginal people, but it means that developments on the land, including home ownership and private sector financing, need to be pursued through sub-leasing arrangements.

Fortunately, both the current and previous Australian governments have been intent on establishing a more market friendly form of land tenure in discrete Aboriginal communities. Advisers to the Labor Government have written, 'in the absence of normalized tenure and some administrative system for managing tenure on communities, it seems inevitable that those residents with aspirations for greater economic security and better services will vote with their feet.'[483]

The legislation associated with the Emergency Response in the NT[484] was designed to enhance the likelihood of 99 year leases being made available through the Australian Government sub-leasing the land from Aboriginal owners. The idea was to give assurance to traditional owners that they could raise capital on their land and retain long-term ownership, although little headway has been made in convincing local traditional owners to engage in the arrangements.[485]

The desire to establish the preconditions for private ownership in remote communities[486] is laudable and establishing long-term leases

---

[483] Dillon and Westbury, 2007, p. 151.

[484] *ALR (NT)* A, 2006. The amendments to the Act only affect the Northern Territory. Land ownership in the states and other territories is determined by separate legislation in each jurisdiction. Long term leases for home ownership on Aboriginal communal land are possible under land tenure arrangements in some states and territories but are not common. As a result of these changes, Indigenous Business Australia offers a 'Home Ownership on Indigenous Land' loan for those living in communities located on Indigenous land.

[485] The Rudd Government has begun to negotiate shorter leases, for example, Groote Eylandt leaders were unwilling to sign up to a 99 year lease but agreed to a 40 year term with a 40 year option to renew over the three townships on Groote. Macklin J, 2008. 'Beyond Mabo: Native Title and Closing the Gap' *Mabo Lecture - James Cook University.*

[486] Pearson, N. 2007. 'Speech' *Housing in Cape York: The Role of Private Home Ownership Cape York Institute*, p. 1.

on collective title may attract some capital into the housing market, but it cannot do so in the absence of a labour market and the stream of income associated with work. Figure 11 demonstrates that most Aborigines throughout Australia have entered the housing market in the same way as other Australians, either renting or purchasing a home and paying for the property through their earnings. The data presented in Figure 14 and Figure 15 for Aborigines and non-Aborigines on a remoteness basis makes it clear that a sub-class of Aborigines, those in remote discrete Aboriginal communities, is worse off than other Indigenous Australians. The reason some Aborigines can enter the housing market is because they are participating in the labour market.

Mortgage obligations would involve a change in mind-set for Aborigines in remote communities. Tenancy or mortgage contracts will apply to them, as do the normal civic and legal obligations for the receipt of social services. This means that in order to pay for housing they must find work. If work is not available locally, they will need to move to find suitable employment. Those who do not relocate will continue to be unable to afford their own house and will suffer a lower standard of living. Although this is the case at present, making good the gap in living standards *in situ* would remove the incentive ever to take control of the situation, delaying the time when Aborigines can be free of government (including Aboriginal housing organisations) interference in their housing.

Figure 14: Indigenous tenure by remoteness areas, 2006

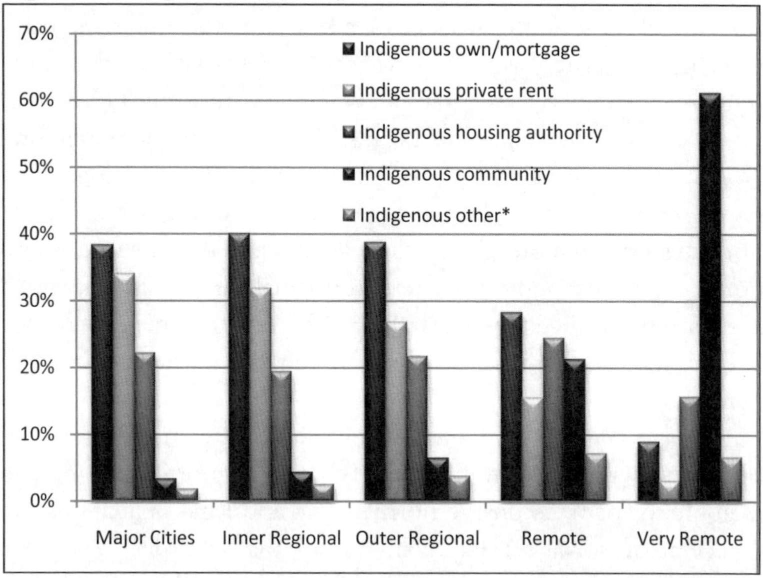

[Bar chart showing percentages across Major Cities, Inner Regional, Outer Regional, Remote, and Very Remote areas for the categories: Indigenous own/mortgage, Indigenous private rent, Indigenous housing authority, Indigenous community, Indigenous other*]

Note: Other* includes caravans, cabins, houseboats, tents and other improvised dwellings.
Data source: Australian Bureau of Statistics, 2008. Population Characteristics, Aboriginal and Torres Strait Islander Australians 2006. 4713.0 Table 9.1 138.

Some reasons for the difference between Indigenous and non-Indigenous uses of land can be gleaned by comparing the non-indigenous with the Indigenous 'other' category in Figure 14 and Figure 15. It is clear that non-Indigenous people take advantage of 'other' accommodation options in remote areas to a much greater degree than Indigenous people. This indicates greater use of temporary accommodation by non-Indigenous residents in remote areas. Non-Indigenous workers make temporary arrangements, for example, mobile homes and demountables, for accommodation where the market cannot supply permanent houses. Similar patterns of behaviour for Indigenous Australians could also be encouraged.

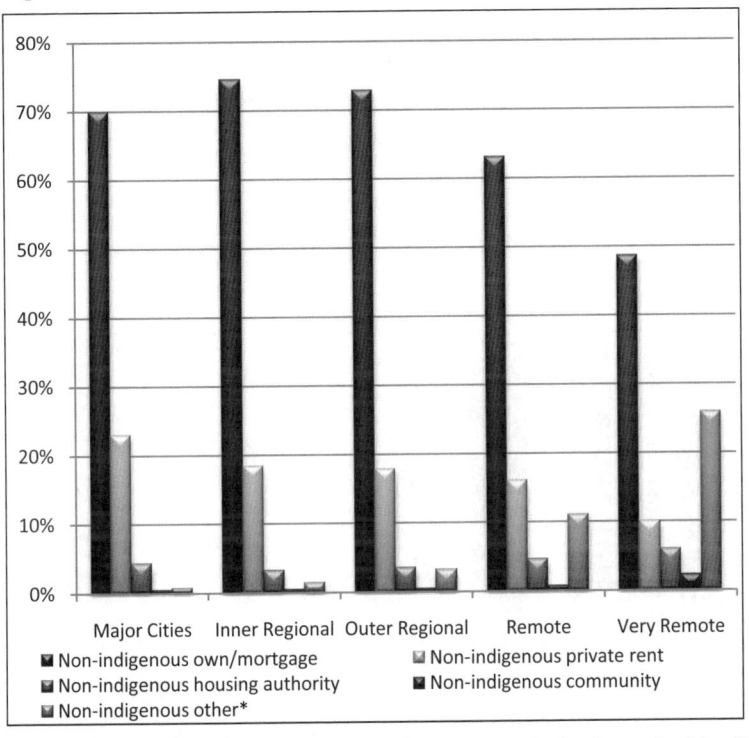

Figure 15: Non-Indigenous tenure by remoteness areas, 2006

[Bar chart showing percentages across Major Cities, Inner Regional, Outer Regional, Remote, and Very Remote areas for the following categories:
- Non-indigenous own/mortgage
- Non-indigenous private rent
- Non-indigenous housing authority
- Non-indigenous community
- Non-indigenous other*]

Note: Other* includes caravans, cabins, houseboats, tents and other improvised dwellings. Data source: Australian Bureau of Statistics, 2008. Population Characteristics, Aboriginal and Torres Strait Islander Australians 2006. 4713.0 Table 9.1 138.

Debates about Aboriginal housing policy are conducted on a similar basis to debates about Aboriginal income and employment policy.[487] The unstated assumption is that some Aborigines have a right to a lifetime income, based on an egalitarian dream that the government owes everyone a living, particularly as compensation, and

---

[487] Taylor J. and O. Stanley, 2005. 'The Opportunity Costs of the Status Quo in the Thamarrurr Region.' *Centre for Aboriginal Economic Policy Research Working Paper* No. 28/2005.

that earnings should be guaranteed. If earnings were guaranteed, there would be no need for Aborigines to seek other opportunities. The economic goal of income policy is to find the least expensive way to self-sufficiency. The same logic applies to housing. The economically strategic approach to Aboriginal housing is to consider housing and income together.

Figure 16: Main source of income, 2004-05

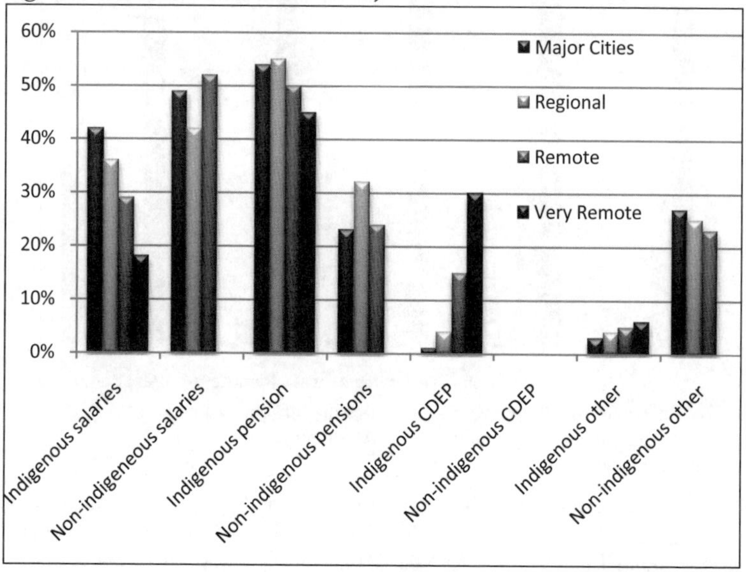

Note: Individual gross weekly income, people aged 18 years and over. 'Other' category includes 'other cash incomes' and source of income 'not stated/not known. 'Regional' includes inner and outer regional areas. Non Aboriginal data are not available for very remote areas as they were not collected in the 2004-05 NHS. The records for the very remote areas have been attributed appropriately to national estimates.
Data source: Productivity Commission, 2007. Overcoming Indigenous Disadvantage: Key Indicators. Chapter 3.

In 2004-05, 52 per cent of Aboriginal people received most of their individual income from government pensions and allowances, followed by salaries and wages (34 per cent) and CDEP (10 per cent). The proportion of Aboriginal people with salaries and wages as their main source of individual income decreased with remoteness, while the proportion with CDEP as the main source increased with remoteness. In contrast, 47 per cent of non-Aboriginal people received salaries and wages as their main source of individual income, followed by government pensions and allowances (26 per cent) and other cash income (20 per cent). Non-Aboriginal people in regional areas were more likely to receive government pensions and allowances as their main source of individual income (32 per cent) and less likely to receive salaries and wages (43 per cent), compared to those in major cities (24 and 49 per cent, respectively) and remote areas (21 and 53 per cent, respectively).

The broad pattern displayed in Fgure 16 is that non-Indigenous income holds up in remote areas whereas Indigenous income falls away and is replaced by CDEP and 'other' sources, including trust funds. Figure 17 shows that there is a gap in Indigenous income compared with non-Indigenous income, across all remoteness areas. Starkly, however, Indigenous income falls in remote areas but non-Indigenous income does not. In 2006, the mean equivalised[488] gross household income for Indigenous people was $460 a week, compared with $740 for non-Indigenous people. Mean equivalised household income was lower in remote areas compared with non-remote areas for Indigenous people ($539 a week in Major Cities and $329 a week in Very Remote areas). This pattern differed for non-Indigenous people, where mean income was highest in Major Cities ($779) and Very Remote areas ($812), probably reflecting both the strength of the labour market for highly skilled jobs in both, particularly mining in remote areas. Overall, the mean equivalised gross household income for Indigenous people is approximately 62 per cent of the corresponding figure for non-Indigenous people.

---

488 The equivalised income estimate for a household represents the amount of income that a single person household would require to maintain the same standard of living as that household. Household income is equivalised to allow households of different size and composition to be compared.

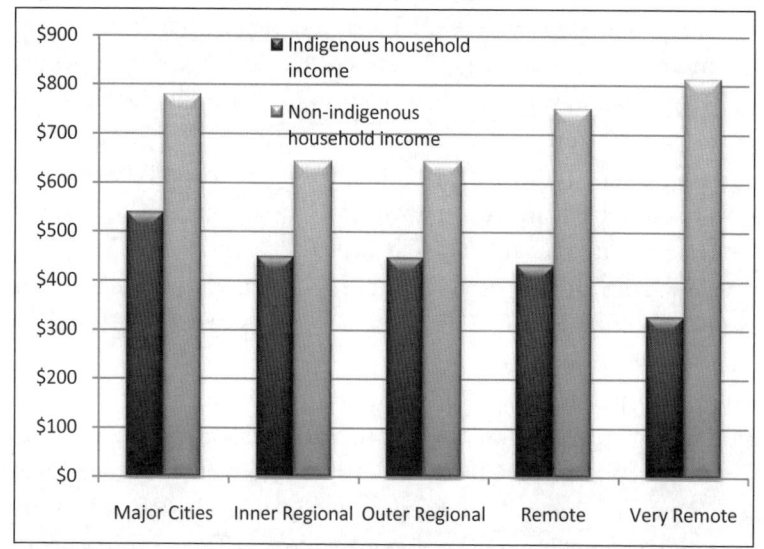

Figure 17: Gross household income, 2004-05

[Bar chart showing Indigenous household income and Non-indigenous household income across Major Cities, Inner Regional, Outer Regional, Remote, and Very Remote areas]

Note: Income based on mean equivalised. Residents of occupied private dwellings, which comprise persons in households in which there were no temporarily absent adults and all incomes were fully stated.
Data source: Australian Bureau of Statistics, 2008. Population Characteristics 2006, ATSI Australians. 4713.0 Table 8.1 110.

Taking a further measure of income, the proportion of people in the highest income quintile in very remote areas who are Indigenous is very small (Figure 18), but the proportion of Indigenous people in remote areas who are in the highest quintile is not insignificant (Figure 19). In other words, there are good incomes available in remote areas, but they are few, and held by those with the relevant skills.

The purchasing power and flexibility of non-Aboriginal people are the clues to solving the Aboriginal housing shortage. Purchasing power can only be solved through employment, and flexibility by changing behaviour and location. Non-Aboriginal people and, indeed, Aboriginal people with sufficient skills are more able to gain employment in all areas. In limited labour markets, by contrast, the least skilled are most likely to miss out on work and, having missed out, fail to provide for their housing needs.

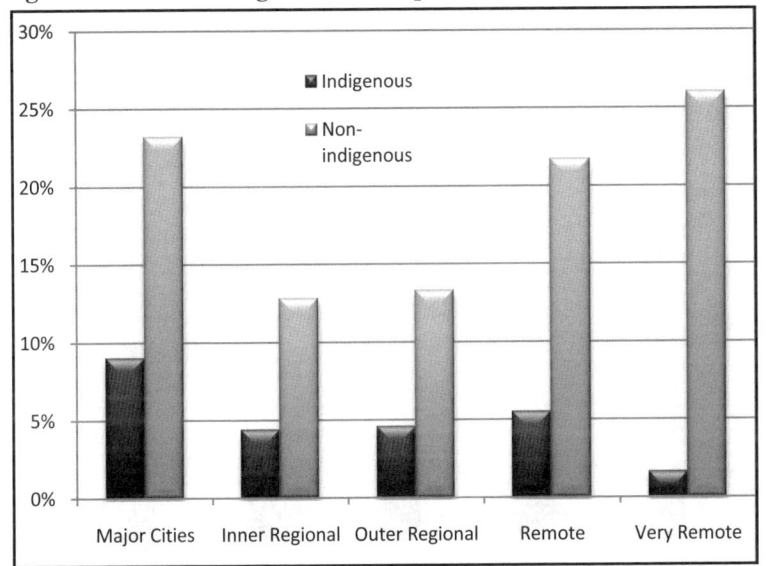

Figure 18: Persons in highest income quintiles, 2004-05

Data source: Australian Bureau of Statistics, 2008. Population Characteristics 2006, ATSI Australians. 4713.0 Table 8.1 110.

By comparing the distribution of discrete Indigenous communities (and their high need for housing) with projected employment growth, it is apparent that in a number of regions of Australia there are unlikely to be many jobs for Aborigines. The largest number of discrete communities is in northern and central Australia, particularly in Cape York, Top End and Central Desert Northern Territory and the Kimberley region in Western Australia. The projected jobs growth[489] indicates the bulk of new opportunities will emerge around the cities

---

[489] Johns, G. 2009. *No Job, No House: an Economically Strategic Approach to Remote Aboriginal Housing*. The Menzies Research Centre, p. 17.

and at discrete locations in remote Australia, particularly in mining areas. Cape York has employment growth in the region and, given the Herculean task of preparing people for these jobs, a housing market may be feasible. By contrast, the Kimberley and Northern Territory communities are bereft of future employment growth.

Figure 19: Persons in highest household income quintile, 2004-05

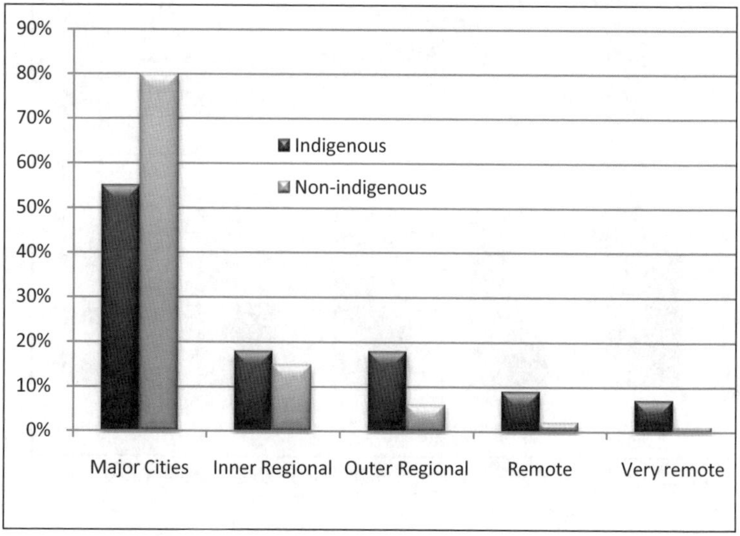

Note: based on equivalised gross household income per week.
Data source: Australian Bureau of Statistics, 2008. Population Characteristics 2006, ATSI Australians. 4713.0 Table 8.1 110.

There are few jobs in remote locations.[490] If Aborigines are to engage in the workforce, they will have to move to those areas where employment opportunities exist for their level of skill. By and large, this means a shift to town. Encouraging people to stay on their land

---

[490] Studies have identified some jobs but these are held by non-Aborigines and are not readily available to poorly trained Aborigines. See Department of Employment and Workplace Relations, 2006. *Audit of Employment Opportunities in Remote Communities in the Northern Territory*.

and outside the labour market means Aborigines will continue to face socio-economic disadvantages. Having people come to town will require substantial support for Aborigines who make that choice. So long as provision is made to help people to adapt, the long-held fear of problems caused by Aborigines 'coming to town'[491] can be allayed.

The ultimate solution to Aboriginal housing in remote areas is jobs. But a realistic assessment of employment prospects in remote areas is that they are bleak. One of the leading proponents of remote Aboriginal communities has suggested that even if Aborigines held all of the government-funded jobs on their land currently held by non-Aborigines, 'probably 80 per cent would [remain] ... in Work for the Dole or training ... unemployed or not in the labour force.'[492] The Commonwealth Government acknowledged this paucity of jobs by referring to regions in remote Australia 'where the development of a fully-fledged labour market ... may not be realistic.'[493]

The employment options beyond CDEP may revolve around substituting Aboriginal for non-Aboriginal labour, but these will harvest few jobs in remote regions.[494] Some mining industry jobs are located in remote areas and the industry has devoted considerable effort

---

[491] Etherington, S. 2007. 'Coming, Ready or Not: Aborigines are Heading for Town.' *The Bennelong Society Occasional Papers.*
[492] Altman, J. 2007. 'In the Name of the Market?' In Altman, J. and M. Hinkson, 2007. *Coercive Reconciliation: Stabilise, Normalise, Exit Aboriginal Australia.* Arena, p. 314. This is not to argue that no jobs exist, rather that the prospects are weakest in remote areas. For another view see Hughes, H. and M. Hughes, 2008. 'Location and Jobs: The Real Story.' *The Bennelong Society Conference.*
[493] Australian Government, 2008. *Increasing Indigenous Opportunity: Proposed Reforms to the CDEP and Indigenous Employment Programs,* p. 29.
[494] Studies have identified some jobs but these are held by non-Aborigines and are not readily available to poorly trained Aborigines.

to recruiting and training Aboriginal workers.[495] But drugs,[496] CDEP and royalties available to remote Aborigines add to disincentives to work,[497] contributing to a lack of job readiness among Aboriginal recruits and making them unreliable employees.

Figure 20: Models of Aboriginal economies

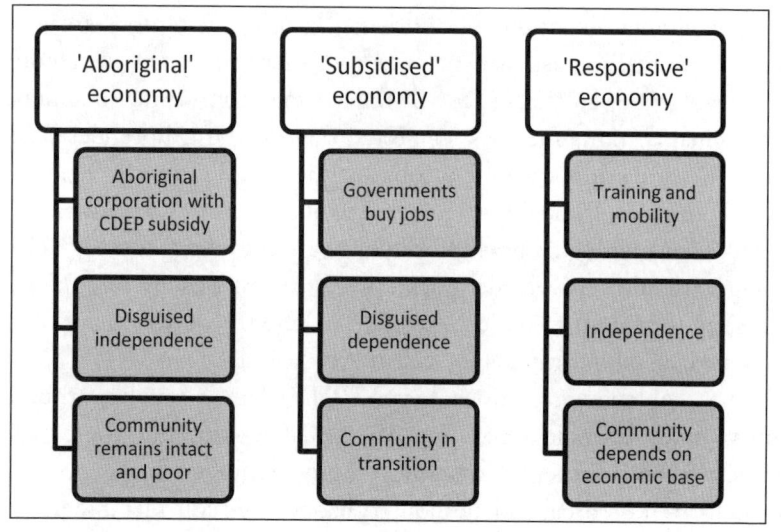

'Aboriginal' economy	'Subsidised' economy	'Responsive' economy
Aboriginal corporation with CDEP subsidy	Governments buy jobs	Training and mobility
Disguised independence	Disguised dependence	Independence
Community remains intact and poor	Community in transition	Community depends on economic base

Data source: Author

Economic development on-country is poor. Shallow labour markets with few opportunities will be insufficient to employ Aborigines in other than dead-end jobs, if at all. The stress of family obligations can ruin the prospects for Aboriginal on-country employment. Off-

---

495 Centre for Social Responsibility in Mining, 2007. *Indigenous Employment in the Australian Minerals Industry*. University of Queensland.
496 Personal communication with Woodside officials in the Pilbara, April 2005 and *Indigenous Land Corporation* officials August 2008.
497 The Indigenous Land Corporation welcomed the previous Australian Government proposal to move from CDEP to enhanced Structured Training and Employment Projects in strong labour markets. Australian Government, 2007. *Indigenous Land Corporation Annual Report 2006-07*, p. 22.

country employment is much more viable. It has the substantial advantage of deeper labour markets, especially for entry level jobs, but there are also considerable stresses of adjustment to new circumstances to be overcome (Figure 20 illustrates the issues).

The dearth of employment opportunities in remote areas is not the only factor leading to an Aboriginal housing shortage. Houses are often misallocated or destroyed by corruption and appalling tenant behaviour[498] or even misallocated owing to domestic violence.

> Men who perpetrate domestic violence or sexual abuse stay in the houses, forcing the women and children to leave to seek somewhere safe to live: there are men around here living in five bedroom homes by themselves. The women move and the blokes stay in the house.'[499]

The Aboriginal housing stock has been appallingly maintained. Aboriginal-controlled or inhabited housing lasts about ten years while other government housing lasts about 40 years.[500] In the past five years, the proportion of housing stock needing major repairs increased from 19 per cent to 23 per cent.[501] These are not the only problems. Aboriginal houses are abandoned as people move around. Often houses are located where there is no work and little prospect of earned income being applied to purchase or upkeep of houses. Proper planning of Aboriginal housing policy requires addressing tenant behaviour as well as land supply. Public housing policy should not prop up tenant decisions to locate to unviable areas.

In most cases, the housing stock in remote areas is managed by

---

498 DFCSIA, 2007, p. 16.
499 Cooper, L. and M. Morris, 2005. 'How to Help Indigenous Families into Stable Housing and Sustainable Tenancy.' *Australian Housing and Urban Research Institute Research and Policy Bulletin* 56, p. 3.
500 Brough M., 2007. 'Government tackles overcrowding in remote Indigenous communities.' Media release, 8 May.
501 Australian Bureau of Statistics, 2007b. *Housing and Infrastructure in Aboriginal and Torres Strait Islander Communities Australia 2006 (Reissue)* 4710.0 14.

Indigenous community housing organisations, but they alone are not to blame for shortages and damage. Many government houses are in poor condition because there is no one to supervise tenants or maintain accommodation.[502] There is a real danger that new houses, including those built under the supervision of housing authorities to replace those wrecked by tenants, will suffer the same fate. Replacement under the same rules creates a moral hazard by rewarding poor behaviour. More importantly, if replacement houses are located in areas with few employment prospects, the new accommodation will act as a disincentive to move to where the opportunities for work are greater.

Aboriginal housing policy is blighted by decades of poor behaviour inducing policies. There have been four major schools of thought surrounding Aboriginal housing policy: welfare, national interest transfer, self-sufficiency substitution, and population relocation. Each policy has an effect on Aboriginal behaviour. These effects are not always positive or have the intended consequences.

First, welfare dependency policies were supposed to be temporary but became permanent when Aborigines were exempted from the obligation to seek employment. Aborigines pursued land claims that left them stranded on uneconomic land seeking rent from mining companies, and practising self-determination. This left them at the mercy of those who controlled the purse strings within their own communities and a range of 'helpers'.

A related policy idea was that Aborigines in remote communities and in some regional and city communities be gifted housing.[503] Gifting a house does not solve the housing challenge; it can even exacerbate the problem. If the person gifted a house has little appreciation of its upkeep, gifting is a waste of resources. Gifting a house in a community

---

502 DFCSIA, 2007, p. 16.
503 Gifted in the sense that they have very low obligations to pay rent or care for the property, an observation from the CHIP review see DFCSIA, 2007, p. 16.

where there are few prospects for work creates an incentive to remain outside the workforce. The gift approach to the housing problem is naïve and unsustainable because it suffers from a belief that Aborigines should be provided houses without the firm conditions of tenure, behaviour and rental pay as apply elsewhere. As a result, Aboriginal housing has suffered from 'poor tenancy management and rent collections.'[504]

The second policy idea is a 'national interest transfer' model. Under this model, representatives of a community or individuals contract to carry out activities of regional or national interest such as land conservation and management programs. This seems to have been preferred by the Rudd Government with the announcement in the 2008-09 Budget of various programs such as Land and Sea Country Indigenous Partnerships, Indigenous Protected Areas, Indigenous Emissions Trading, and Working on Country.[505] Programs that are really in the national interest, rather than being in the interest of those who want to have Aborigines shepherded into a designated band of employment options, should be available to all Australians, not only Aborigines. While employment in mining or tourism is in the national interest, Aborigines are not employed in large numbers in these industries because CDEP provides disincentives to work, or the Aborigines are not job ready.

A 'self sufficiency substitution' model is sometimes floated as the answer to Aboriginal unemployment, where labour is substituted for capital through 'sweat equity'.[506] Part of this model was a feature of missions and government settlements and elements of this approach

---

504 Dillon and Westbury, 2007, p. 161.
505 Department of Families, Housing, Communities and Indigenous Affairs, 2009e. *2008-09 Indigenous Budget at a Glance*.
506 There are good examples of 'sweat equity': for example, *Habitat for Humanity* builds houses with people who would otherwise be unable to obtain finance. The secret to Habitat is that, in addition to 300 hours of sweat equity, the owner has to pay the mortgage, that is, carry the risk.

underpin such programs as the CDEP. This option is an 'import substitution' model and suffers from the same fate as the welfare model – it becomes a permanent substitute for engaging in real economy. Despite the widespread nature and longevity of these programs, the level of labour force participation by Aborigines in remote Australia has not lifted in decades.[507]

Finally, there is the 'population relocation' model under which continued location in remote areas is made so prohibitive that people in these communities have no option but to shift to regional localities where there are services and employment. As outlined below, it is clear that in addition to the prohibitive social and economic cost of preserving non-viable communities, people are already moving away to seek opportunities. While this is the preferred option, the risk, for policy-makers, is that people will move to such centres without the skills, knowledge or social capacity to operate independently and, as a consequence, will create underclass refugee communities whose various needs and behaviour are beyond the resources of the regional centre.

These development options have tended to oscillate between treating Aborigines as lower class and the apprehension that they would become 'white'. In the 'mission' era, the criticism was that Aborigines were only prepared for modest roles such as a labourer or domestic servant. In the self-determination period the tendency was that Aborigines should not be prepared for anything much, except perhaps as elders, artists and representatives. That Aborigines may have to start at the bottom is no different to any uneducated and poorly assimilated group (such as refugees). The idea that Aborigines should only work in culturally appropriate tasks, thereby preserving their culture, is debilitating. Policy-makers may have to make a bold assumption, that a modest start in the real economy is better than being held in a designated underclass on a permanent basis.

---

[507] Gregory, 2004, p. 4.

In developing policy the Government should distinguish four types of location:
- Outstations and homelands – no permanent accommodation unless a case for economic viability is proven
- Larger Indigenous settlements – land title changes are essential before any public and private investment. These settlements are not likely to be economically viable but regional stability dictates some public investment
- Country towns – experiencing stress due to influx of Aboriginal settlers should be better provided with services, including 'refugee' resources and facilities
- Major cities and regional centres – any shortfalls should be handled by mainstream services, including 'refugee' resources and facilities.

The Government should explore the location and eligibility for each form of accommodation. Such exploration should be undertaken on the basis that Aborigines when informed of their options may consider them and make decisions about where to live. The aim should be to house people in a sustainable fashion. The only way to do this is to encourage people to pursue opportunities and be rewarded. Those who will not or cannot seize the opportunity should not be housed in the same manner as those who do. Another issue in remote locations is the difficulty of protecting those who want to escape bad behaviour. The Government should encourage secure housing in large Aboriginal communities, country towns and regional centres to allow Aboriginal inhabitants to escape humbugging and other forms of violence and abuse.

Accommodation solutions will require a suite of other policies to reinforce the responsibilities attached to the housing market. These will range from welfare obligations, specifically income management as with the Emergency Response initiatives, land title changes, 'refugee' services to assist resettlement, and financial schemes such as 'sweat equity'[508], 'financial literacy'[509] and government special assistance[510] to encourage home ownership.

Finally, infrastructure expenditure should be approached with caution and incorporate discussion about future viability. In this regard, structural adjustment will be essential as many communities face change in their livelihood and location. Structural adjustment requires that governments assist people to move and establish themselves where prospects are better. If people choose to stay, however, they should be made aware of the consequences of remaining.

There are major barriers to adjustment of remote area Aborigines to the requirements of the modern economy. Governments can either ignore these barriers or continue to regard an absence of preparedness to engage in the modern economy as a gap to be filled with the gift of make-work schemes and government housing. The weight of evidence is that non-Aboriginal people can succeed in remote areas provided they live there only so long as they are employed. Aboriginal people in these areas have few job prospects because of language and skills difficulties. As Noel Pearson has argued, welfare programs that seek to save communities and ignore the needs of individuals are headed for a fall.[511] Housing programs should be based on employment and income prospects, and need to anticipate change, not fill old gaps. Anything other than a 'no job, no house' mindset will harm Aborigines.

Many remote communities are not economically viable. As some elements of support start to be withdrawn, the viability issue will become more acute, outmigration will intensify, and the indigeneity of

---

508 Habitat for Humanity model involves building a house using volunteer labour, donated material, 300 hours of owners' time and a mortgage.
509 Australian Bankers' Association Inc.
510 West Australia Government's *Keystart* program is exemplar of many state programs, and *Indigenous Business Australia* has a range of loan products.
511 Pearson, N. 2008. *What is Welfare?* Cape York Institute.

regional centres will rise. Housing will need to be built where people congregate and where there is economic opportunity. Policy-makers are not ready for the changes because so much intellectual investment has been devoted to the remote communities and land rights solutions to Aboriginal identity politics. Unfortunately, public policy-makers have created a dependent people with a joyless recreational lifestyle. The gap in living conditions, longevity and general well-being is stark and deteriorates with remoteness. The supposed beneficiaries of the progressive stance of Aboriginal policy of the past 40 years are those who suffer, while those who have escaped the land are best placed to prosper.

The response to Aboriginal housing problems must be based on an honest policy appraisal. A target to roll out houses or play catch-up with a housing deficit will not address the underlying problem. Policy-makers have three alternatives. Firstly, if the policy goal is to house Aborigines to a standard equal to other Australians, Aborigines will have to live like other Australians. Second, if the goal is to house Aborigines in a 'culturally' appropriate way, the result will be inadequate housing and continuing poor behaviour. Third, policy-makers may choose a neutral policy stance and allow Aborigines to choose their future in the full knowledge of the consequences of their choices. The housing policy that is most appropriate is one that allows people to choose where to live in the honest appraisal that if they remain in places where there is no economy, they will continue to suffer socio-economic disadvantage.

Using culture in education

The returns on education are real and measurable but, for a host of reasons, the results for Aboriginal children have not been good.

Evidence suggests a decline in outcomes in the past generation.[512] After decades of increased provision, the fact that Aboriginal elders can read and write and their grandchildren cannot is a direct result of the fact that educators have taught for self-determination and not integration. Education for integration places the child squarely in the mainstream, with outcomes measured the same as for non-Aboriginal students. The promise in the recent national measurement of education results is a very positive step.

There is, however, as for every other part of Aboriginal policy, reluctance to implement policies that actually achieve desired ends. There is a strong belief within policy circles that Aboriginal children should be taught their own culture and, at the very least, taught the general curriculum in their own language in the first instance. The Gordon Inquiry, for example, acknowledged that education was the most universal contact point between Aboriginal children and government services. In line with most inquiries, however, it suggested that 'increased Aboriginal "ownership" of the education system [was] likely to bring about the greatest changes in the education of young Aboriginal people.'[513] The Gordon Inquiry accepted evidence that,

> The Education Department doesn't understand about the need for kids to attend funerals, to stay home and care for sick relatives, and to do other stuff. Aboriginal people are willing to work to keep their children up to date with their learning but kids have other commitments too.[514]

And the Gordon Inquiry praised the Mooditj Noongar Community College Perth and the Djidi Djidi school for Aboriginal children, Bunbury, for their focus on Aboriginal culture, studies and language. But no evidence was forthcoming as to whether, measure for measure,

---

512 Collins, B. 1999. *Learning Lessons: An Independent Review of Indigenous Education in the Northern Territory.* Northern Territory Government, p. 14.
513 Gordon et al, 2002, p. 292.
514 Gordon et al, 2002, p. 284.

these schools have greater success than a mainstream school.[515] Nobody questioned whether these students succeeded or were less abused than others. There was simply an assertion that following the 'culture' trail was sufficient in itself. As with previous inquiries, there was no proof – simply an assertion that Aboriginal ownership solved problems of chronic underachievement in Aboriginal education. Such evidence as there is points to a contrary conclusion. Use of culture in Aboriginal education is complex, but the results are relatively straightforward. In so many ways the invocation of Aboriginal culture and cultural obligation (real or claimed) condemns the Aboriginal student to failure.

Aboriginal children entering school may be poorly prepared because Aboriginal culture has no base in formal education. There is no tradition of formal school education in Aboriginal culture and no tradition of mathematics, science, literature or commerce. Aborigines have little to draw upon, so the basis of utilising Aboriginal culture has to be viewed with scepticism. Education adds to what the parents provide by way of preparation of the child. In this regard, the picture is not promising.

> The simple fact is that we are not dealing with a community that gives a high value to learning, or at least the type of formal education offered by non-Aboriginal Australians. I have overheard a father extolling the value of education and telling his young daughters, of primary school age, that they should be in school. But these were just words (and probably for my benefit) for the children took no heed and the father made no attempt to compel them to go to school.
>
> In school children do not want to appear better than their peers. In many cases they do not want to learn, or they are embarrassed to learn, or they hide the fact that they are learning. They are well aware that it is mostly White people who are

---

515 Gordon et al, 2002, p. 284.

> teaching them. They know that they are politically dominated ... Like their parents they blame the Whites for everything that is wrong with their society ... Unfortunately, by blaming the Whites they do not get to grips with their problems and they are unable to face reality in later years that many of their immediate problems stem from their own choices.[516]

Aboriginal children may spend a great deal of time away from school in genuine cultural observance although, as noted earlier, the time taken for Aboriginal funerals seems to be growing but there is evidence that children use culture as an excuse to skive off. More worrying is that parents can use culture as an excuse to keep children out of school as was shown earlier in the story by Dr Steve Etherington at Oenpelli, NT.[517]

Aboriginal control is unlikely to be a remedy for the disadvantages implicit in coming from a different culture because Aboriginal control often results in hiring on the basis of political allegiance rather than competence, and leaves children with less than satisfactory assistance. Competence not race should be the only criterion for ownership.

Nor is it at all clear what exactly is to be taught as culture. Naturally the Aborigines are quite keen to have their culture included [in the school curriculum]. Just what this entails is sometimes a bit of a mystery but for the most part it appears to be language, songs and dances, art and bushcraft. Most of this should be acquired in the home or in the day-to-day interaction in the community. European teachers are not trained to teach Aboriginal culture nor do they know much about it. Hence if it is going to be taught it must be done by Aborigines ... Unfortunately, there is not much 'pure' Aboriginal culture to be taught and this is the case in many Aboriginal communities ...[518]

The case study from Wadeye is a stark illustration of a Catholic

---

516 McKnight, 2002, p. 140.
517 Etherington, above n.64.
518 McKnight, 2002, p. 142.

school run by Aboriginal people and a staff steeped in reverence for culture simply failing to educate children (see Box 6). How such a situation has been allowed to persist for a generation is a mystery, except that those who are most vocal about Aboriginal culture are those whose actions have undermined three essential ingredients for success – discipline, merit and compulsory attendance.

> **Box 6 - Our Lady of the Sacred Heart School, Wadeye, Northern Territory**
>
> At present, there are 500 to 600 school-aged children in the community of Wadeye who do not go to school. Most of them have never been to school. These children do not speak, read or write in English. They have no prospects of work and will spend the rest of their lives on welfare (as their parents did) many in various stages of addiction, most involved in petty crime and vandalism, many in serious violent crime. Many will live out their short lives in addiction recovery units (if there are any), jails and mental institutions. The young women will be forced to have babies as soon as possible to collect the baby bonus, and the young men will be amongst the most 'at risk' on earth. This is largely the legacy of a failed education.
>
> The two Co-principals of the school attended conferences all over Australia all year, the school went to the Garma festival, and there were cadet camps, excursions and funerals to such a large extent that the teaching programme was disrupted on a weekly basis. No child will learn to read and write under these conditions.
>
> Places such as Wadeye have fallen so far behind over the last 30 years (now in a second generation of illiteracy and welfare dependency) that they require a focused and lasting stimulus. Wadeye requires a significant intervention into the whole culture surrounding the school, including the aspects of tribal/traditional Aboriginal culture that in any way interfere with the process of children becoming numerate and literate in English. Teachers need to be sufficiently 'deprogrammed' from invasion, genocide, the stolen generation and the politics of apology enough to develop a 'teachers without borders' neutrality, from which they can command the respect of the students. Changes to traditional culture may be required unless the basic discipline of children, including adequate toilet training, can be maintained.
>
> There must be a programme to overcome the 'don't speak English, you're Aboriginal' mindset of many, if not most, Aboriginal people in Wadeye. This may include some serious discussions with whitefella linguistic philosophers who believe all languages must be saved no matter what the cost.
>
> Teacher Assistants (TAs) are unable to teach, and are used as translators and disciplinarians. This is counter-productive on a number of levels and actually hinders the students' progress in English. TAs should not be paid when they do not come to work. If they do not come to work, they should be sacked. TAs should not be employed along skin group/totem group/extended Aboriginal family lines. We have enough trouble with this sort of nepotism in our own society and it should not be encouraged in Indigenous culture
>
> Source: McCauley, P. 2009. 'A Proposal for Wadeye.' The Bennelong Society.

| Box 7 | Djarragun College, Gordonvale, north Queensland |

Through all the bad times students had been through, their spirits had survived. It struck me time and again that in spite of horrendous challenges many students had to face, they never lost their joy of life and their exuberant energy. We realised that this joy and energy needed to be nurtured and celebrated and so we dreamed up every excuse for days of celebration and feasting. Cultural performances became a feature of all these celebrations and relatives became involved in teaching students their traditional dances and music. As students' self esteem and belief in themselves grew, so the behaviour across the school improved. As behaviour improved, so we introduced a more rigorous curriculum and gradually minimised the amount of days of celebration. We got down to two days of celebration a term which allowed us to really spend quality time on delivering accredited courses and to follow the Queensland syllabus.

We must maintain our vigilance with the high standards in the delivery of the curriculum and watch carefully for well meaning but incredibly damaging people who think they are doing Indigenous students a favour by offering them sub standard educational programmes, false praise and contrived results. All this does is to belittle students and serve to diminish their confidence and self esteem.

Source: Illingworth, J. 2007. 'The Journey from Anger to Joy: the Djarragun College Story.' The Bennelong Society Conference, pages 3 and 10.

Aboriginal ownership is not a solution to Aboriginal success in education but strong leadership may be. In this regard, the debate between Chris Sarra,[519] an Aboriginal school principal from southern Queensland and Noel Pearson's Cape York Families Commission is a wholly positive one. It revolves around the most effective and least-cost method of having children attend school. This debate is a substantial advance on recent history when suggesting enforcement of compulsory attendance in education circles was almost forbidden. Most important is that culture be invoked in a positive way in combination with a clear and steely determination, as is Sarra's message to treat Aboriginal children the same as others and demand of them the effort of others.

The school principal at Djarragun College, Gordonvale (Box7),

---

519 Chris Sarra, *The Weekend Australian*, 3 October 2009.

explicitly used Aboriginal and Torres Strait Islander cultures as a means of attracting students and holding them at school. Once at school, regular regimes and expectations were imposed. Little by little the principal reduced the time devoted to culture and increased the time devoted to western studies. She sacked teachers who imposed lesser disciplines on Aboriginal students. By using culture in a utilitarian manner, she took a corrupt Aboriginal (and fellow traveler) run school and turned it around by imposing all of the disciplines of a western education.

Another case study was an attempt to establish a separate school for Aborigines outside Carnarvon (WA 1,000 kms north of Perth). It was a failure. This illustrates the confused objectives of the teachers and the community. The elders wanted the children schooled in traditional ways, but appreciated the need for their formal education. Younger Aborigines wanted a separate approach, not conforming to the needs of disciplined education. The problem was indiscipline on the part of a number of students.[520] The case illustrates the conflict inherent in a democratic approach to education, where a parent group have no background in formal education and, even with a desire to have their children taught, do not provide any example to them. Only lip service is paid by some parents to the need to educate. Others are openly hostile and not a little encouraged by some teachers who are ill at ease with the need to maintain discipline, either through romantic ideals or a view that it is too difficult to teach Aborigines. The answer: ordinary disciplines applied to non-Aboriginal students must be applied to Aboriginal students. Teachers must refuse to treat Aborigines as lesser people not deserving of western education.

The Northern Territory's education administrators of many years, and under both major parties, persisted in toying with obeisance to

---

520 Gray, D. and S. Saggers, 1990. 'Autonomy in Aboriginal Education: a Quest at Carnarvon.' In Tonkinson, R. and M. Howard (eds) 1990. *Going it Alone?: Prospects for Aboriginal Autonomy*. Aboriginal Studies Press, pp. 185-196.

culture. Northern Territory governments have struggled with two-way education.[521] A recent report of the NT Government into two-way schools offered mild support to two-way education (not surprising given this was the preference politically from its political masters at the time). It concluded, 'education research suggests that students demonstrate improved learning outcomes when there is connection between the home and school cultures.' But the figures presented in the report were not statistically significant and could not therefore be relied upon to sustain the case for two-way schooling.[522] The strongest conclusion was that 'a serious question for the review is in relation to the large numbers of students from both groups of schools that did not record any achievement in testing, and what educational benefit these students are gaining from school.'[523] In the bigger picture these matters are drowned out by the appalling results achieved by Aborigines in remote schools overall. They speak of much larger problems than the niceties of culture in the curriculum.

At the heart of the matter is school attendance, raised by Bob Collins in 1999 and politely ignored by education administrators since. Even Noel Pearson, while raising the importance of attendance targets in preference to year 12 success targets, does not indicate how these attendance rates are to be improved.[524] The official figures are appalling, as indicated in Table 7, but these poor figures may not be accurate. The official statistics that circulate in the education bureaucracy record student totals for enrolment, a figure measured on eight set days in each year. But enrolment figures are likely much higher than the true attendance rate and skew the picture completely. In a recent study in Wadeye, 890 children were of broad school-age range. Enrolment was almost 700, but only two-thirds of children were on the roll at some point each week, and only 122 were regulars,

---

521 Department of Employment, Education and Training, Northern Territory, 2006. *Indigenous Languages and Culture in Northern Territory School Report 2004-2005*.
522 DEET, 2006, pp. 34-5.
523 DEET, 2006, p. 35.
524 Pearson, N. *The Weekend Australian*, 27-28 March 2010.

attending for 151 days or more out of the total 189 school days in the year. If the total number of children who appeared at school in the year is taken as the measure, the attendance figure drops to 14 per cent. These are the well-masked facts on the ground.[525] There is no reason to think that Wadeye is a special case in the NT, and that the official figures for the NT do not, as with Wadeye, seriously underestimate attendance.

Table 7 Attendance at Northern Territory state schools, 2008 and 2009

	2008	2008		2009	2009	
Location	Indigenous	Non-Indigenous	Total	Indigenous	Non-Indigenous	Total
Provincial	81%	91%	89%	83%	92%	90%
Remote	82%	9%	88%	83%	93%	88%
Very Remote	66%	91%	69%	64%	90%	67%
Total	72%	91%	83%	71%	92%	83%

Data source: Northern Territory Department of Education and Training. These attendance figures include explained and unexplained absences. Explained absences include cultural events, illness, sorry business, community flooding etc.

At long last Aboriginal children will be tested and the results published alongside those of other students in all school systems by geographic location. Although these figures have been gathered for many years the states and territories refuse to publish them in a form that would allow the truth about Aboriginal results to be known. It has taken the Commonwealth many years successfully to demand the release of state and territory data. Only when compliance with the Commonwealth's wishes for data was made a condition of funding was the data finally revealed. As inaccurate as the data is, because it measures the performance of only those who attend school, it is nevertheless strong enough to indicate that the practice of leaving Aborigines in remote areas to play 'Aborigine', and in the hands of

---

525 Taylor, J. 2010. 'Demography as Destiny: Schooling, Work And Aboriginal Population Change At Wadeye.' *Centre for Aboriginal Economic Policy Research Working Paper* No. 64/2010.

teacher romantics, has real and damning consequences.

Figure 21 indicates, among other things, that Aboriginal children perform poorly against the national minimum standard when compared with all other students, in all states and all areas. Most concerning is that less than 15 per cent of Aboriginal children in very remote areas in the NT score at or above the national minimum standard for reading in year three, which is 56 per cent of the level of all students in very remote areas in the NT.[526]

National Assessment Program Literacy and Numeracy (NAPLAN) results must be published school-by-school so that parents and remote communities can evaluate their education options and identify the causes of non-performance for each school.[527] All children must be taught English from pre-school. Learning English is not optional in Australia.[528] It is up to parents and communities to decide whether they want to teach their children their native languages and cultural traditions at home, or whether they want native languages also taught at school. In the words of earlier calls in similar terms, 'the responsibility for teaching of culture and language rests with the Aboriginal community.'[529]

---

[526] Note the comparison is between Indigenous students and all students, which is the only comparison available at this time and understates the gap between the two groups, especially in the Northern Territory where the Indigenous constitutes a large proportion of remote students.
[527] Hughes H. and M. Hughes. 2009. 'Revisiting Indigenous Education.' *Centre for Independent Studies Policy Monograph* No. 94, p. vii.
[528] Hughes and Hughes, 2009, p. viii.
[529] Johns, G. 2006. *Aboriginal Education: Remote Schools and the Real Economy.* Menzies Research Centre, p. 22.

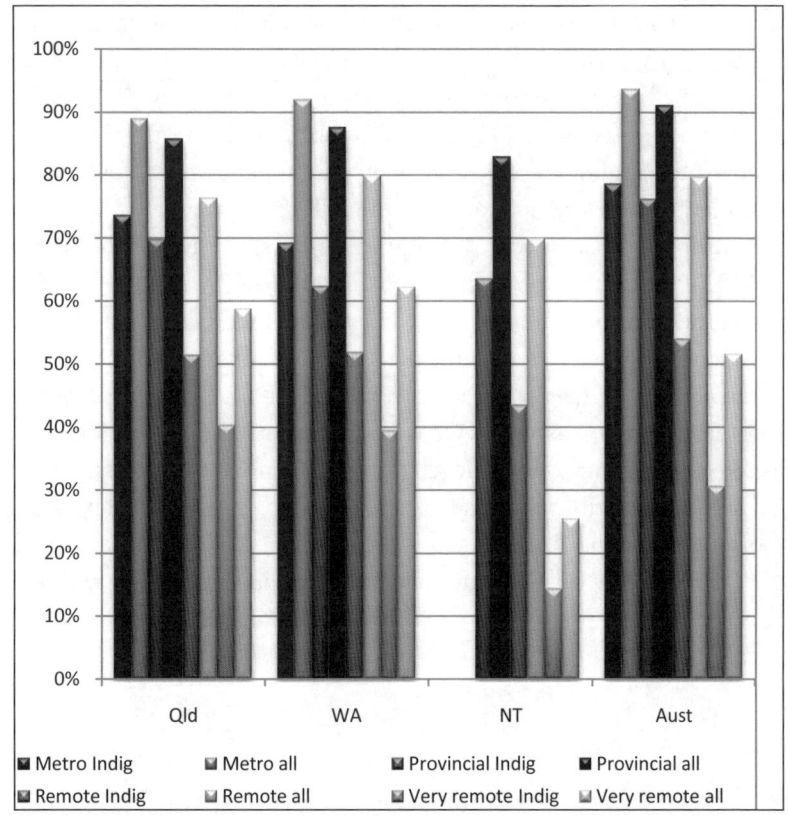

Figure 21: NAPLAN 2008, Indigenous and all students, reading year 3

Note: Students scoring at or above the national minimum standard. No Metropolitan category in NT, Darwin classed as provincial.
Data source: Ministerial Council for Education, Early Childhood Development and Youth Affairs, 2008. National Assessment Program Literacy and Numeracy.

Conclusion

Aborigines have had a hard time of it since the whiteman invaded Australia, or so the story goes. Curiously, it is only since all Aborigines won full citizens rights – with most obtaining the benefits of the modern world, gifted by the whiteman – that some of them and their supporters began to complain about their share of the gifts.

The problem is not with the complaint for a better deal. That is the stuff of democratic politics; complain and the politician will give you some more. The problem is that some Aborigines have wanted both the whiteman's gifts and that which is inconsistent with living in the whiteman's world. In an open and free society where every person is free to make their own way, there is a small group who want a special deal. These are Aborigines and their white advisers who want to preserve Aboriginal culture. They deny that aspects of Aboriginal culture are totally inconsistent with basic human decency in its resort to violence and in its appalling treatment of women. In so doing, they deny clear evidence to the contrary.

This minority mistakes bad behaviour for oppression rather than maladaption to modern society. This minority would rather spend the money of others in the pursuit of a foolish and damaging dream; that traditional Aborigines still live, and that traditional Aboriginal culture is defensible in modern liberal terms. They do not, and it is not defensible in these terms. People of Aboriginal descent live as free as any other Australian; free to pursue whatever life they desire within the broad bounds of Australian law. That is the long accepted settlement, the deal, although never sanctified by a formal document; it is nevertheless the reality, and a very decent one.

If I were an Aborigine I would take the deal and encourage all of my people to accept the long run integration into the open and modern and free Australian society. It does not get better than this. The false hope of the 'other' world where the noble savage roamed is dead and buried, and for good reason.

Bibliography

Aboriginal Child Sexual Assault Taskforce, 2006. *Breaking the Silence: Creating the Future. Addressing child sexual assault in Aboriginal communities in NSW*, New South Wales Government.
Aboriginal Land Rights (Northern Territory) Act 1976.
Aboriginal Land Rights (Northern Territory) Amendment Act 2006.
Aboriginals Benefit Account, *Annual Reports.*
ACIL Tasman, 2007. *Bring Forward Discovery: Review of NT Exploration Investment Attraction Programs 1999–2007.*
Albrecht, P. 2008. *Relhiperra: Aboriginal Issues.* The Bennelong Society.
Altman, J.C., Gray, M.C and R. Levitus, 2005. Policy Issues for the Community Development Employment Scheme in Rural and Remote Australia, *Centre for Aboriginal Economic Policy Research Discussion Paper* No. 271/2005.
Altman, J.C. 2007. 'In the Name of the Market?' In Altman, J. and M. Hinkson, 2007. *Coercive Reconciliation: Stabilise, Normalise, Exit Aboriginal Australia.* Arena.
Anderson, C. 1989. 'Aborigines and Conservationism: the Daintree–Bloomfield Road.' *Australian Journal of Social Issues*, August.
Auditor-General, 2009. 'Performance Audit Administration of Job Network Outcome Payments Department of Education, Employment and Workplace Relations.' *Audit Report* No.17 2008–09.
Australian Bureau of Statistics, 1999. 'Population Issues, Indigenous Australians 1996.' *Occasional Paper* 4708.0.
Australian Bureau of Statistics, 2002. 'Population Special Article: A Profile of Australia's Indigenous People.' *Year Book Australia.*
Australian Bureau of Statistics, 2004. *National Aboriginal and Torres Strait Islander Social Survey, 2002* 4714.0.
Australian Bureau of Statistics, 2006. Population Characteristics, Aboriginal and

Torres Strait Islander Australians, 2006. 4713.0.
Australian Bureau of Statistics, 2007a. *Population Distribution, Aboriginal and Torres Strait Islander Australians, 2006* 4705.0
Australian Bureau of Statistics, 2007b. *Housing and Infrastructure in Aboriginal and Torres Strait Islander Communities Australia 2006 (Reissue)* 4710.0 14.
Australian Bureau of Statistics, 2008a. *Population Characteristics 2006, ATSI Australians*, 4713.0.
Australian Bureau of Statistics, 2008b. *Australian Historical Population Statistics*, 3105.0.65.001.
Australian Council of Social Services, 2004. *Congress Selected Papers*.
Australian Crime Commission, 2009. Task Force *Picture of Criminality in Indigenous Communities*, interim report.
Australian Government, 1992. *Aboriginal Deaths in Custody: Response by Governments to the Royal Commission*. Australian Government Publishing Service.
Australian Government, 2007. *Secretaries' Group on Indigenous Affairs Annual Report 2005-06*.
Australian Government, 2007. *Indigenous Land Corporation Annual Report 2006-07*.
Australian Government, 2008. *Increasing Indigenous Employment Opportunity; Proposed Reforms to the CDEP and Indigenous Employment Programs*.
Australian Government, 2009. *Closing the Gap on Indigenous Disadvantage: The Challenge for Australia*.
Australian Government, undated. *Achieving Indigenous Economic Independence: Indigenous Economic Development Strategy*.
Australian Human Rights Commission, 2006. *Native Title Report 2005*.
Australian Human Rights Commission, 2009. *Our Future in Our Hands: Creating a Sustainable National Representative Body for Aboriginal and Torres Strait Islander Peoples*.
Australian Institute of Health and Welfare, 2006. *Family Violence among Aboriginal and Torres Strait Islander Peoples*.
Bardon, G. and J. 2004. *Papunya: A Place Made After the Story, the Beginnings of the Western Desert Painting Movement*. The Miegunyah Press.
Bath, H. and D. Boswell, 2007. *Northern Territory Community Services High Risk Audit, Executive Summary and Recommendations*. Northern Territory Department of Health and Families.
Bauman, T. 2006. *Final Report of the Indigenous Facilitation and Mediation Project July 2003-June 2006: Research Findings, Recommendations and Implementation*, Australian Institute of Aboriginal and Torres Strait Islander Studies Report No. 6.

Berndt R.M. and C.H. 1987. *End of an Era: Aboriginal Labour in the Northern Territory.* Australian Institute of Aboriginal Studies.

Berndt, R. M. and C. H. 1988. 'Body and Soul.' In Swain, T. and D.B. Rose, *Aboriginal Australians and Christian Missions: Ethnographic and Historical Studies.* The Australian Association for the Study of Religions.

Biddle N. and B.H. Hunter, 2005. Factors associated with internal migration: A comparison between Indigenous and non-Indigenous Australians. *Centre for Aboriginal Economic Policy Research Working Paper* No. 32/2005.

Biles, D. and D. McDonald, 1992. 'Overview of the Research Program and Abstracts of Research Papers.' *Australian Institute of Criminology Research Paper* No. 22.

Biles, D. and D. McDonald, (eds) 1992. *Deaths in Custody Australia, 1980-1989: The Research Papers of the Criminology Unit of the Royal Commission into Aboriginal Deaths in Custody.* Australian Institute of Criminology.

Blagg, H. 2007. 'Zero Tolerance or Community Justice? The Role of the Aboriginal Domain in Reducing Family Violence.' *Indigenous Family Violence Prevention Forum*, Queensland Centre for Domestic Family Violence and Research.

Blainey, G. 1983. *Triumph of the Nomads.* Macmillan.

Bolger, A. 1991. *Aboriginal Women and Violence.* Australian National University, North Australian Research Unit, Darwin, NT.

Briskman, L. 2003. *The Black Grapevine: Aboriginal Activism and the Stolen Generations.* The Federation Press.

Brunton, R, 1993. *Black Suffering, White Guilt: Aboriginal Disadvantage and the Royal Commission into Deaths in Custody*, Institute of Public Affairs.

Brunton, R. 1998. 'Betraying the Victims: The Stolen Generations' Report.' *IPA Backgrounder*, Institute of Public Affairs.

Brunton, R. 2007. 'A Bombshell in the Centre of Perth: An Anthropologist Considers the Single Noongar Judgment.' *The Bennelong Society Occasional Papers.*

Burgess, C.P. and F.H. Johnston, 2007, 'Healthy Country: Healthy People: Stakeholder Debriefing Paper.' Menzies School of Health Research, Northern Territory.

Burridge, K. 1988. 'Aborigines and Christianity.' In Swain, T. and D.B. Rose, *Aboriginal Australians and Christian Missions: Ethnographic and Historical Studies.* The Australian Association for the Study of Religions.

Central Land Council, 2005. 'Communal Title and Economic Development.' *CLC Policy Paper.*

Central Land Council, 2008. Annual *Report 2007-2008*.
Centre for Social Responsibility in Mining, 2007. *Indigenous Employment in the Australian Minerals Industry*. University of Queensland.
Chapman v Luminis Pty Ltd (No 5) [2001] FCA 1106.
Chapman v Tickner and ors [1995] FCA 1068.
Charter of Human Rights and Responsibilities Act 2006 (Vic).
Children's Protection (Implementation of Report Recommendations) Amendment Act 2009 (SA).
Collins, B. 1999. *Learning Lessons: An Independent Review of Indigenous Education in the Northern Territory*. Northern Territory Government.
Commonwealth Grants Commission, 2001. *Report on Indigenous Funding 2001*.
Coombs, H.C. 1976. *Aboriginal Australia 1967-1976: A Decade of Progress?* Murdoch University.
Cooper, L. and M. Morris, 2005. 'How to Help Indigenous Families into Stable Housing and Sustainable Tenancy.' *Australian Housing and Urban Research Institute Research and Policy Bulletin*.
Council for Aboriginal Reconciliation, 1994. 'Agreeing on a Document: Will the Process of Reconciliation be Advanced by a Document or Documents of Reconciliation?' *Key Issues* Paper 7, Australian Government Publishing Service.
Crime and Misconduct Commission Queensland, 2009. *Restoring Order: Crime Prevention, Policing and Local Justice in Queensland's Indigenous Communities*.
Cubillo v. Commonwealth [2000] FCA 1084.
Cubillo v Commonwealth of Australia and *Gunner v Commonwealth of Australia, Commonwealth Submissions*, undated. The Bennelong Society.
Dagmar, H. 1990. 'Development and Politics in an Interethnic Field.' In Tonkinson, R. and M. Howard *Going it Alone?: Prospects for Aboriginal Autonomy*. Aboriginal Studies Press.
Davis, W. 2010. 'The Wayfinders: why ancient wisdom matters in the modern world.' *Massey lectures*. Canadian Broadcasting Corporation.
Deeble, J., Agar J. S. and J. Goss, 2008. 'Expenditures on Health for Aboriginal and Torres Strait Islander Peoples 2004 - 05.' *Australian Institute of Health and Welfare*.
Department of Employment and Workplace Relations, 2003. 'Indigenous Employment Policy Evaluation Stage Two: Effectiveness Report.' *Evaluation and Programme Performance Branch Report* 1/200.
Department of Employment and Workplace Relations, 2006. *Audit of Employment Opportunities in Remote Communities in the Northern Territory*.

Department of Employment, Education and Training, Northern Territory, 2006. *Indigenous Languages and Culture in Northern Territory School Report 2004-2005.*

Department of Families, Community Services and Indigenous Affairs, 2007. *Housing Assistance Act: 1996 Annual Report 2005-06.*

Department of Families, Community Services and Indigenous Affairs, 2007. *Living in the Sunburnt Country - Indigenous Housing: Findings of the Review of the Community Housing and Infrastructure Programme.*

Department of Families, Housing, Community Services and Indigenous Affairs, 2009a. *Submission of Background Material to the Northern Territory Emergency Response Review Board* and *Future Directions for the Northern Territory Emergency Response: Discussion Paper.*

Department of Families, Housing, Community Services and Indigenous Affairs, 2009b. *Native Title Discussion Paper.*

Department of Families, Housing, Communities and Indigenous Affairs, 2009c. *Portfolio Budget Statement 2008-09.*

Department of Families, Housing, Community Services and Indigenous Affairs, 2009d. *Increasing Indigenous Economic Opportunity: a Discussion Paper on the Future of the CDEP and Indigenous Employment Programs.*

Department of Families, Housing, Communities and Indigenous Affairs, 2009e. *2008-09 Indigenous Budget at a Glance.*

Department of Families, Housing, Community Services and Indigenous Affairs, 2010. *Evaluation of the Child Protection Scheme of Income Management and Voluntary Income Management Measures in Western Australia.*

Department of Finance and Deregulation, 2009. *Evaluation of the Community Development Employment Projects Program.*

Department of Indigenous Affairs, Western Australia, undated. *Overcoming Indigenous Disadvantage.*

Department of the Chief Minister (Northern Territory), undated. *Detailed Joint Submission to the Commonwealth. Workability Reforms of the Aboriginal Land Rights (Northern Territory) Act 1976.*

Desert Knowledge Australia 2008. 'remoteFOCUS: Revitalising Remote Australia', *Prospectus.*

Diamond, J. 1998. *Guns, Germs and Steel.* Vintage.

Dillon, M. and N. Westbury, 2007. *Beyond Humbug: Transforming Government Engagement with Indigenous Australia.* Seaview Press.

Dodson, M. 2003. 'Violence, Dysfunction, Aboriginality.' *Address to the National Press Club*, 11 June.

Elferink, J. 2001. 'Land Rights: Why the Potential Hasn't Been Reached and What To Do About It.' *The Bennelong Society Conference.*

Etherington, S. 2007. 'Coming, Ready or Not: Aborigines are Heading for Town.' *The Bennelong Society Occasional Papers.*

Family Responsibilities Commission Act 2008 (Qld).

Ferguson, N. 2003. *Empire: How Britain Made the Modern World.* Penguin.

Flannery, T., Kendall, P. and K. Wynn-Moylan, 1990. *Australia's Vanishing Mammals: Endangered and Extinct Native Species.* RD Press.

Flood, J. 2006. *The Original Australians: Story of the Aboriginal People*, Allen and Unwin.

Folds, R. 2001. *Crossed Purposes: the Pintupi and Australia's Indigenous Policy.* UNSW.

Foley, D. 2006. 'Indigenous Australian Entrepreneurs: Not all Community Organisations, Not all in the Outback.' *Centre for Aboriginal Economic Policy Research Discussion Paper* No. 279/2006.

Gardiner-Garden, J. 1998a. 'From Dispossession to Reconciliation.' *Research Paper* No. 27. Department of the Parliamentary Library.

Gardiner-Garden, J. 1998b. 'Identifiable Commonwealth Expenditure on Aboriginal and Torres Strait Islander Affairs.' *Current Issues Brief,* No. 18. Department of the Parliamentary Library.

Gennochio, B. 2008. *Dollar Dreaming: Inside the Aboriginal Art World.* Hardie Grant Books.

Gordon, S., Hallahan, K. and D. Henry, 2002. *Putting the Picture Together, Inquiry into Response by Government Agencies to Complaints of Family Violence and Child Abuse in Aboriginal Communities,* Department of Premier and Cabinet, Western Australia.

Government of Western Australia, 2002. Putting People First: *The Response to the Inquiry into Response by Government Agencies to Complaints of Family Violence and Child Abuse in Aboriginal Communities.*

Gray, D. and S. Saggers, 1990. 'Autonomy in Aboriginal Education: a Quest at Carnarvon.' In Tonkinson, R. and M. Howard (eds) 1990. *Going it Alone?: Prospects for Aboriginal Autonomy.* Aboriginal Studies Press.

Gregory, B. 2004. 'Asking the Right Questions?' in Austin-Broos D. and G. Macdonald (eds) 2004. *Aborigines, Culture and Economy.* ANU.

Haebich, A. 2000. *Broken Circles: Fragmenting Indigenous Families 1800-2000.* Fremantle Arts Centre Press.

Hansen v Northern Land Council [1999] NTSC 69.

Hardy, F. 1968. *The Unlucky Australians.* One Day Hill.

Harris, S. 1979. 'It's Coming Yet...: An Aboriginal Treaty Within Australia Between Australians.' *Aboriginal Treaty Committee.*

Haveman, R. 1996. 'Reducing Poverty While Increasing Employment: a Primer on Alternative Strategies and a Blueprint.' *OECD Economic Studies* No. 26. 1996/1.

Heckman, J. 2003. 'Human Capital Policy'. *National Bureau of Economic Research Working Paper* No. 9495.

Hindmarsh Island Bridge Royal Commission, 1995. South Australia.

Hughes H. and M. Hughes, 2008.'Location and Jobs: The Real Story.' *The Bennelong Society Conference.*

Hughes H. and M. Hughes, 2009. 'Revisiting Indigenous Education.' *Centre for Independent Studies Policy Monograph* No. 94.

Human Rights Act 2004 (ACT).

Human Rights and Equal Opportunities Commission, 1997. *Bringing Them Home, Report of the National Inquiry into the Separation of Aboriginal and Torres Strait Islander Children from Their Families.*

Human Rights and Equal Opportunity Commission, 2005. *Native Title Report 2005.*

Iles, S. and G. Johns, 2010. 'An Economic Unravelling of the Precautionary Principle: the Queensland Wild Rivers Act 2005.' *Agenda* 17(4).

Illingworth, J. 2007. 'The Journey from Anger to Joy: the Djarragun College Story.' *The Bennelong Society Conference.*

Indigenous Land Corporation, 2009. *Annual Report 2008-09.*

Jacobs, J. et al 1988. 'Pearls from the Deep: Re-evaluating the Early History of Colebrook Home for Aboriginal Children.' In Swain, T. and D.B. Rose, *Aboriginal Australians and Christian Missions: Ethnographic and Historical Studies.* The Australian Association for the Study of Religions.

Jarrett, S. 2009. 'Violence: An Inseparable Part of Traditional Aboriginal Culture.' *The Bennelong Society Occasional Papers.*

Jarrett, S. *Aboriginal Violence.* forthcoming 2011.

Johns, G. 2006. *Aboriginal Education: Remote Schools and the Real Economy.* Menzies Research Centre.

Johns, G. 2008. 'The Northern Territory Intervention in Aboriginal Affairs: Wicked Problem or Wicked Policy?' *Agenda* 15(2).

Johns, G. 2009. *No Job, No House: an Economically Strategic Approach to Remote Aboriginal Housing.* The Menzies Research Centre.

Johnston, E. 1991. *Royal Commission into Aboriginal Deaths in Custody, National Report.*

Jones, R. 1969. 'Fire-stick Farming.' *Australian Natural History*, (16)7.
Joudo, J. and M. Veld, 2005. 'Deaths in Custody in Australia: National Deaths in Custody Program Annual Report 2004.' *Australian Institute of Criminology Technical and Background Paper Series* No. 19.
Joudo, J. and Curnow, J. 2006. 'Deaths in Custody in Australia: National Deaths in Custody Program Annual Report 2006.' *Australian Institute of Criminology Research and Public Policy Series* No. 85.
Kenny, C. 1996. *It Would Be Nice If There Was Some Women's Business: The Story Behind the Hindmarsh Island Affair*. Duffy and Snellgrove.
Kimberley Indigenous Management Support Services, 2008. *September Quarterly Report*, Noonkanbah Station.
Kolig, E. 1990. 'Government Policies and Religious Strategies: Fighting With Myth at Noonkanbah.' In Tonkinson, R. and M. Howard (eds) 1990. *Going It Alone: Prospects for Aboriginal Autonomy*. Aboriginal Studies Press.
Lambert-Pennington, A.K. 2005. 'Being in Australia, Belonging to the Land: The Cultural Politics of Urban Aboriginal Identity.' Doctoral thesis, Department of Cultural Anthropology Duke University.
Latz, P. 1995. *Bushfires and Bushtucker: Aboriginal People and Plant use in Central Australia*. IAD Press.
Latz, P. 2007. The Flaming Desert : Arid Australia: a Fire Shaped Landscape. Alice Springs.
Laynhapuy Homelands Association Incorporated, 2008. *Submission to Northern Territory Government on the CDEP Discussion Paper*.
Lloyd, J. 2008. 'Domestic Violence Related Homicide Cases in Central Australia.' *International Conference on Homicide: Domestic Related Homicide*. Australian Institute of Criminology.
Macklin J, 2008. 'Beyond Mabo: Native Title and Closing the Gap' *Mabo Lecture - James Cook University*.
McCallum, D. 2005. 'Law and governance in Australian Aboriginal communities: liberal and neo-liberal political reason.' *The International Journal of Children's Rights* Vol 13.
McCauley, P. 2009. 'A Proposal for Wadeye.' *The Bennelong Society*.
McKnight, D. 2002. *From Hunting to Drinking: The Devastating Effects of Alcohol on an Australian Aboriginal Community*. Routledge.
McKnight, D. 2004. *Going the Whiteman's Way: Kinship and Marriage among Australian Aborigines*. Aldershot.

McKnight, D. 2005. *Of Marriage, Violence and Sorcery: the Quest for Power in Northern Queensland*. Aldershot.

Maddock, K. 1982. *The Australian Aborigines: A Portrait of Their Society*. Penguin. Second edition.

Martin, D. 1995. 'Money, Business and Culture: Issues for Aboriginal Economic Policy.' *Centre for Aboriginal Economic Policy Research Discussion Paper* No. 101.

Martin, B. 2007. 'Customary Law.' *Judicial Conference of Australia Colloquium 2007*.

Memmott, P., Stacy, R., Chambers, C. and C. Keys, 2001. *Violence in Indigenous Communities*. Report to Crime Prevention Branch of the Attorney-General's Department.

Ministerial Council for Education, Early Childhood Development and Youth Affairs, 2008. *National Assessment Program Literacy and Numeracy*.

Morley, R. 2005. 'The Pitjanjatjara Land Rights Amendment Act: Addressing Governance on APY Lands.' *Indigenous Law Bulletin* 6(15).

Morphy, F. (ed) 2007. 'Agency, Contingency and Census Process: Observations of the 2006 Indigenous Enumeration Strategy in Remote Aboriginal Australia.' *Research Monograph* No. 28. ANU E Press.

Morphy, F. 2008. 'The future of the homelands in north-east Arnhem Land', quoted in Laynhapuy Homelands Association Incorporated *Submission to Northern Territory Government on the CDEP Discussion Paper*.

Mullighan, E. P. 2008. *Children on Anangu Pitjantjatjara Yankunytjatjara Lands Commission of Inquiry: a Report into Sexual Abuse*.

National Native Title Tribunal, 2009. *Native Title in Australia*.

Neville, A.O. 1947. *Australia's Coloured Minority: Its Place in the Community*. Currawong.

New South Wales Government, 2007. *New South Wales Interagency Plan to Tackle Child Sexual Assault in Aboriginal Communities 2006 – 2011*.

Northern Land Council, 2008. *Annual Report 2007-2008*.

Northern Territory Emergency Response Taskforce, 2008. *Final Report to Government*.

Northern Territory Government, 2008. *Maningrida Study*. Department of Regional Development, Primary Industry, Fisheries and Resources.

Northern Territory Government, 2009. *Indigenous Development Strategy 2009-2012*. Department of Regional Development, Primary Industry, Fisheries and Resources.

Northern Territory Government, 2010. *Inquiry into the Child Protection System in the Northern Territory 2010*. Department of Health and Families.

Northern Territory Treasury, 2006. *Indigenous Expenditure Review*.

O'Dea, D.J. 1991. *Regional Report of Inquiry into Individual Deaths in Custody in Western Australia*.

Partington, G. 2003. 'Hindmarsh Island and the Fabrication of Aboriginal Mythology.' *Samuel Griffith Society*, volume15.

Pearson, N. 2007. 'Speech' *Housing in Cape York: The Role of Private Home Ownership Cape York Institute*.

Pearson, N. 2008. *What is Welfare?* Cape York Institute.

Phillpot, S. 2007. 'The Future Of Remote Aboriginal Communities: A Series of Relic Settlements of People Created by the Ebb and Flow of Contact with non-Aboriginals.' *The Bennelong Society Conference*.

Productivity Commission, 2002. *Independent Review of the Job Network Inquiry Report*. Number 21.

Productivity Commission, 2007a.*Overcoming Indigenous Disadvantage*.

Productivity Commission, 2007b. *Report on Government Services 2007 - Indigenous Compendium*.

Productivity Commission, 2007c. 'Men Not at Work: An Analysis of Men Outside the Labour Force.' *Staff Working Paper*.

Productivity Commission, 2009. *Overcoming Indigenous Disadvantage: Key Indicators 2009*.

Queensland Government, 2009. *Lockhart Basin Wild River Declaration*. Department of Environment and Resource Management.

Queensland Government, 2009. *Stewart Basin Wild River Declaration*. Department of Environment and Resource Management. Queensland Government.

Queensland Government, 2007. *Wild Rivers Code*. Department of Natural Resources and Water.

R v KU& Ors; ex parte A-G (Qld) [2008] QCA 154 (13 June 2008).

Reconciliation Australia, 2006. *Annual Report 2005-06*.

Reeves, J. 1998. *Building on Land Rights for the Next Generation: The Review of the Aboriginal Land Rights (Northern Territory) Act 1976*, Aboriginal and Torres Strait Islander Commission.

Roberts R. G. and B. W. Brook, 2010. 'Paleontology: And Then There Were None?' *Science* 22 Vol. 327. No. 5964.

Robertson, B. 1999. *Aboriginal and Torres Strait Islander Women's Task Force on Violence Report*, Queensland Department of Aboriginal and Torres Strait Islander Policy.

Rowley, C. 1972. *The Destruction of Aboriginal Society*. Pelican.

Royal Commission into Aboriginal Deaths in Custody, 1991.

Sandall, R. 2001. *The Culture Cult: Designer Tribalism and Other Essays*. Westview.

Smith, K. 2001. *Bennelong: the coming in of the Eora: Sydney Cove 1788-1792*.

Kangaroo Press.
Smith, T. 2002. 'Indigenous Accumulation and the Question of Land in the Kimberley Region of Western Australia: Pre 1968-1975.' *International Economic History Association, XIII Congress.*
South Australian Government Response to the Children in State Care Commission of Inquiry Report 2009.
Sowell, T. 2005. *Black Rednecks and White Liberals*, Encounter.
Stanner, W.E.H. 1960. 'Durmugam: A Nangiomeri' in Casagrande, J. B. (ed.), *In the Company of Man*, Harper.
Sullivan, I., Hunt, J. and D. Smith, 2007. 'Indigenous community governance project: Year Two Research Findings.' *Centre for Aboriginal Economic Policy Research Working Paper* No. 36/2007.
Sullivan, P. 2007. 'Indigenous Governance: The Harvard Project, Australian Aboriginal Organisations and Cultural Subsidiarity.' *Desert Knowledge CRC Working Paper* No. 4.
Sutton, P. 2009. *The Politics of Suffering: Indigenous Australia and the End of the Liberal Consensus.* Melbourne University Press.
Sutton, P. 2007. 'The worst of good intentions?' *ABC The Drum Unleashed.* 11 December.
Swain, T. and D. B. Rose, (eds.) 1988. *Aboriginal Australians and Christian Missions: Ethnographic and Historical Studies.* Australian Association for the Study of Religions.
Taylor, J. and B. Scambary, 2005. 'Indigenous People and the PilbaraMining Boom: A Baseline for Regional Participation.' *Research Monograph* No. 25. Australian National University E Press.
Taylor J. and O. Stanley, 2005. 'The Opportunity Costs of the Status Quo in the Thamarrurr Region.' *Centre for Aboriginal Economic Policy Research Working Paper* 28/2005.
Taylor, J. 2010. 'Demography as Destiny: Schooling, Work And Aboriginal Population Change At Wadeye.' *Centre for Aboriginal Economic Policy Research Working Paper* No. 64/2010.
The Queen and GJ (Sentence) [2005] SCC 20418849 (NT).
Thomson, D. 1949. *Economic Structure and the Ceremonial Cycle in Arnhem Land*, Macmillan.
Tonkin, D. and Landon, C. 1999. *Jackson's Track: Memoir of a Dreamtime Place*, Penguin.
Tonkinson. R. 1990. 'The Changing Status of Aboriginal Women: Free Agents at Jigalong.' In Tonkinson, R. and M. Howard (eds) 1990. *Going It Alone:*

Prospects for Aboriginal Autonomy. Aboriginal Studies Press.

Vickery, D. 2007. 'Culture of Work and Community: Consultations on the Anangu Pitjantjatjara Yankunytjatjara Lands in South Australia.' *Report prepared for the Department of Education, Employment & Workplace Relations*.

Wells, E. 1982. *Reward and Punishment in Arnhem Land*, Australian Institute of Aboriginal and Torres Strait Islander Studies.

Wild R. and P. Anderson, 2007. *Inquiry into the Protection of Aboriginal Children from Sexual Abuse*. Northern Territory Government.

Windschuttle, K. 2009. *The Fabrication of Aboriginal History Volume Three: The Stolen Generations 1881-2008*. Macleay Press.

Woodward A.E. 1974. *Aboriginal Land Rights Commission*, Second Report, Australian Government Publishing Service.

Wootten, J.H. 1989. *Report of the Inquiry into the Death of Thomas William Murray*, Royal Commission into Aboriginal Deaths in Custody.

Wright, J. 1985. *We Call for a Treaty*, Collins/Fontana.

Yunupingu, G. 2008. *The Monthly*, December 2008-January 2009, No. 41.

Index

1967 Referendum, 8

A Working Future (NT), 255

Aboriginal
- corporations, 91-3, 246
- culture, 9, 18-19, 23, 26, 31, 46, 52-57, 62-3, 68, 71, 73, 75, 99, 102-9, 118, 122, 128, 140, 147, 165, 171, 176, 184, 192, 248-9, 290-4, 301
- customs, 82, 212, 214-5, 251
- Deaths in Custody, 23, 31, 34, 45-8, 77, 92, 107, 131-41, 148, 160, 162, 165,191, 196
- estate, 66, 221, 230-2
- language, 19, 22, 42, 46-7, 58, 62-4, 66, 81, 92, 182, 184, 202, 239, 250, 262, 288, 290, 292, 300
- race, 36, 42, 51, 72, 76-7, 79, 97, 136, 155, 205-6, 292
- self-determination, 20, 32, 40-67, 86-7, 90, 95, 131, 135, 165, 174, 188, 202, 239, 258, 264, 284, 286, 290

Aboriginal Affairs Planning Authority Act 1972, (WA), 210

Aboriginal and Torres Strait Islander Commission (ATSIC),13, 47, 51, 77, 89, 91, 212

Aboriginal and Torres Strait Islander Land Holding Act 1985 (Qld), 210

Aboriginal and Torres Strait Islander Women's Task Force on Violence (Robertson), 108, 165-7, 169

Aboriginal Areas Protection Authority, 228

Aboriginal Child Placement Principles, 47-8, 166, 177, 192, 200, 202-3

Aboriginal Child Sexual Assault Taskforce (Ella-Duncan), 104, 175-9, 201

Aboriginal Land Act 1991 (Qld), 210

Aboriginal Land Act 1992 (NT), 225

Aboriginal Land Fund, 222, 263

Abbott, Tony, 55, 230

Anderson, Patricia, See Wild and Anderson
Anglican Church, 56, 59-61
- Anglicare, 60
Apology to Stolen Generations, 27, 31, 60, 152, 161-64, 294
Assimilation, 17, 41, 46, 150-55, 163
Atkinson, Judy, 180, 182
Australian Aborigines League, 89
Australian Broadcasting Corporation, 107
Australian Citizenship Council, 58
Bad behavior, 33, 42, 50, 52, 67-72, 86, 99, 104, 108, 110, 123, 173, 202, 287, 301
Bandler, Faith, 8
Bardon, Geoffrey, 102-3
BasicsCard, 197, 199
Bath, Howard, 202-3
Bawinanga (Aboriginal corporation), 93-4
Bennelong, 19, 66
Bennelong Society, 1, 11, 50-1, 53
Berndt, Ronald and Catherine, 145, 250
Bevan, Phil, 265
Blackburn, Richard, 220
Blainey, Geoffrey, 101
Board of Inquiry into the Protection of Aboriginal Children from Sexual Abuse, See Wild and Anderson (Little Children are Sacred)
Bonaparte Gulf pipeline, 96
Brewarrina, 47
Bringing Them Home report, See Stolen Generations
Brisbane Catholic Justice and Peace Commission, 61
Brough, Mal, 13, 179, 192-3
Brunton, Ron, 1
Bungala (Aboriginal corporation), 94-5
Bush, George W., 70-1
Cannington, 257
Cape York Heads of Agreement, 233-4
Cape York Welfare Reform Trials, 233, 247, 257
Cape York Wild Rivers, 230-6
Caring for Country, 96, 102
Cattle Station Industry (Northern Territory) Award 1951, 239
Centre for Aboriginal Economic and Policy Research, Australian National University (CAEPR), 54
Centre for Anthropological Research, University of Western Australia, 172
Centre for Restorative Justice, South Australia, 189
Centrelink, 44, 51, 196-9, 263
Chaney, Fred, 50, 52
Chapman, Tom and Wendy, 141, also see Hindmarsh Island Royal Commission
Child Placement Principles, 47-8, 166, 166, 177, 192, 200-3

Children and Young Persons (Care and Protection) Act 1998 (NSW), 201

Children on Anangu Pitjantjatjara Yankunytjatjara Lands Commission of Inquiry: a Report into Sexual Abuse, (Mullighan), 188-192

Children's Protection (Implementation of Report Recommendations) Amendment Act 2009 (SA), 191

Closed culture, 62
- society, 65

Closing the Gap, 20, 40, 53, 55, 68, 71

Coalition Opposition, 53

Colebrook Home, 58

Collins, Bob, 133, 297

Colonisation, 62, 124, 129, 171, 177, 182

Comalco, See Mapoon

Commonwealth expenditure in Aboriginal affairs, 83-4

Commonwealth Grants Commission, 266

Community Development Employment Projects (CDEP), 21, 25, 43, 47, 93-4, 96, 168, 195, 221-2, 237-47, 253, 263, 276-7, 281-2, 285-6

Community Living Areas, 208

Community Services (Aborigines) Act 1984 (Qld), 211

Constitution Act 1889 (WA), 125

Coombs, H. C. (Nugget), 11-2, 35-6

Cooper, William, 90-1

Corporations (Aboriginal and Torres Strait Islander) Act 2006 (Cth), 91

Council for Aboriginal Affairs, 9-10

Council for Aboriginal Reconciliation 12, 60, 124, 148

Croker Island, 163

Cubillo and Gunner, 12, 154, 156-7, 161-2, 177

Cubillo, Lorna, See Cubillo and Gunner

Customary law, 124-30, 172

Daguragu Land Trust, 226

Daly River, 30

Davis, Wade, 100

Dawson, John, 1

Deed of Grant in Trust Community (DOGIT), 219, 232

Derby Aboriginal Health Service Council (Aboriginal corporation), 94

Diamond, Jared, 24

Dillon, Michael, 183

Dispossession, 171, 182

Djarragun College, 295

Dodson
- Mick 45, 61, 89-90, 106-7, 148
- Model, 45, 48-9, 54, 56
- Pat, 45, 54, 60

Doomadgee, 110, 197, 259

Ella-Duncan, Marcia, See Aboriginal Child Sexual Assault Taskforce

Elcho Island, 210, 256

Etherington, Steve, 1, 292

Exit strategy, 37, 67-74, 179

Families, Community Services and Indigenous

Affairs and Other Legislation Amendment (Northern Territory National Emergency Response and Other Measures) Act 2007 (Cth), 194

Family Responsibility Commission, 140, 197

Federal Council for Aboriginal Advancement, 89

Federal Council of the Aborigines and Torres Strait Islanders, 8

Fejo, Nungala, 162

Folds, Ralph, 74-5

French, Robert, 21

Galatians Group, 11

Genocide, 61, 69, 150, 154, 156, 162, 294

Giese, Harry, 6, 11

Gnibi College, 180

Goolwa, 147

Gordon, Sue, 153, See also Inquiry into Response by Government Agencies to Complaints of Family Violence and Child Abuse in Aboriginal Governance

Gregory, Bob, 238, 240

Guardian for Children and Young People South Australia, 198

Gunner, Peter, see Cubillo and Gunner

Gurindji, 219-20, 257

Hagan, Stephen, 123

Half-caste, 58, 79, 145, 156

Halls Creek, 172, 259

Hand, Gerry, 132

Hasluck, Paul, 12, 157

Havnen, Olga, 181

Hawke, Bob, 12, 59

Health and Community Services Complaints Commissioner South Australia, 192

Hermannsburg, 1, 156-7, 102, 111, 122, 257

Herne Hill, 170

Herron, John, 12

Hindmarsh Island Royal Commission 131, 141-2

Hooker Creek, 6, 257

Howard, John (Government), 12-3, 96-7, 125, 152, 193, 254-5

Howson, Peter, 1, 5

Human Rights and Equal Opportunity Commission, 89, 131, 148, 210

Humbugging, 63, 198, 242, 265, 287

Hunter-gatherer, 12, 19-20, 62, 117, 243, 249

Identity, 19-20, 32, 44, 46-7, 52-3, 72-3, 75-6, 81-2, 86, 124, 168, 192, 289

Incest, 114, 168, 181

Income Management, 51, 192, 196-99, 247, 257, 287

Indigenous Emissions Trading, 285

Indigenous Land Use Agreements, 215-7, 232

Indigenous Protected Areas, 285

Inquiry into Response by Government Agencies to Complaints of Family Violence and Child Abuse in Aboriginal Communities, (Gordon), 170-74, 200, 290

Integration, 7, 20, 26, 28-9, 32, 40-3, 50, 53, 55, 67-8, 71, 82, 131, 151, 168, 258, 290, 302

Intermarriage, 42, 62, 66, 79, 80-1

Intervention, See Northern Territory Emergency Response

Ferguson, Martin, 222

Jackson's Track, 28

Jarrett, Stephanie, 1, 104, 124

Jigalong, 111

Joint Investigation Response Teams, 178

Julalikari Council (Aboriginal corporation), 93-4

Kaarta-Moorda (Aboriginal corporation), 94

Kartinyeri, Doreen, 144-8

Kenny, Chris, 141

Kilgariff, Bernie, 58

Kimberley Land Council, 223

Kipling, Rudyard, 27

Kurra (Aboriginal corporation), 94

Land Act 1994 (Qld), 211

Land Administration Act 1997 (WA), 210

Land and Sea Country Indigenous Partnerships, 285

Land rights, 7-8, 10, 12, 23, 28, 32, 42, 48, 51, 59, 68, 82, 87, 116, 206-7, 209, 212, 214-8, 223, 240, 247, 253, 219

Land Rights Act 1981 (SA), 95

Latz, Peter, 101

Lingiari, Vincent, 220

Link-Up, 152

Lion Nathan, See Brewarrina

Little Children are Sacred, See *Wild and Anderson Mabo judgement*, See *Native Title Act 1993 (Cth)*

Macklin, Jenny, 183

Maddock, Kenneth, 99, 209

Majurey, Tony, 77

Maningrida, 82, 93-4, 256, 260

Manne, Robert, 58-9

Mapoon, 218-9

Marra Worra Worra (Aboriginal corporation), 94

Martin, Brian, See also Queen and GJ 127, 129

McEwen, John, 157

McHughes, John, 147

McKnight, David, 57, 88, 107, 110-11, 115, 117-18, 126, 170, 181, 207, 238, 251-2

Memmott, Paul, 108-9

Menzies School of Health Research, 208

Mer, 82

Milirrpum and Others v Nabalco Pty

Ltd and the Commonwealth of Australia, 220

Milliken, Ted, 6

Miscegenation, 41-2

Missions, 7, 10, 31, 56-8, 67, 112, 117, 134, 162, 196, 218, 254-5, 260, 264, 285

Missionaries, 15, 19, 30, 42, 54, 56-8, 60, 104, 109, 111, 114, 117, 156, 157, 207, 218, 250, 256-7

Mixed descent, 79-80

Modern economy, 26, 33, 45, 49-50, 64, 67, 118, 164, 196, 206, 249, 252, 288

Moriarty, John, 59

Mornington Island, 88, 110-11, 115, 120, 197, 252

Muckaty Station, 223

Mullighan, E.P., See Children on Anangu Pitjantjatjara Yankunytjatjara Lands Commission of Inquiry: a Report into Sexual Abuse

Multilingualism, 63

Murri Court, 141

Nabalco, See Yirrkala

Namatjira, Albert, 102

Napperby Station, 59

National Assessment Program Literacy and Numeracy (NAPLAN), 299

National Council of Churches, 61

National Indigenous Violence and Child Abuse Intelligence Task Force, 180

National Native Title Tribunal, 50, 218

National nuclear waste dump, 223

National Partnership on Remote Indigenous Housing, 255-6, 259-60

National Representative Body Native Title Act 1993 (Cth), 211-4

Nethercote, John, 1

Neville, A.O., 34, 36, 55, 148, 163

Newmont Asia-Pacific, 96

Newstart, 83

Noonkanbah, 218, 221-3

Northern Land Council (NLC) 45, 95-6, 208

Northern Territory National Emergency Response Act 2007 (Cth), 194

Northern Territory Emergency Response, (Intervention), 55, 192

Northern Territory Law Reform Committee's Report on Aboriginal Customary Law, 129

Nyerere, 35-6

Obama, Barack, 70-1

O'Donoghue, Lowitja, 90

O'Loughlin, Maurice, 157-8, 160, 162

Oenpelli, 1, 292

Open society, 49-50, 62-3, 67, 76, 123

Our Lady of the Sacred Heart School,

Wadeye, 257, 294

Outmigration, 288

Outstations, 85, 196, 198, 207-8, 222, 253-4, 256, 259, 287

Papunya, 36, 102-3

Parliamentary Voting Rights Committee, 5-6

Partington, Geoffrey, 11, 144, 146-7

Pastoral Land Act 1992 (NT), 210

Payback, 108-10, 187, 189

Pearson, Noel, 15, 51, 54, 197, 263, 288, 297

Penhall, Les, 5

Perkins, Charles, 59

Phillips, David (Werther effect), 137

Pornography, 3, 42, 185, 193-4, 197, 199

Possum, Clifford, 59, 102

Prescribed Bodies Corporate, 215

Pretend economy, 76, 205-6, 247

Protection and Integration of Indigenous and other Tribal and Semi-Tribal Populations ILO convention, 151

Punmu, 33

Quadrant, 11

Queen v GJ, 128

Queensland Crime and Misconduct Commission, 140-1

Reconciliation, 27-8, 45, 59, 103

Reconciliation Australia, 51, 54

Reeves, John, 221, 224

Re-missionise, 258

Remote communities, 6, 11, 13, 19, 23, 40, 42-3, 46, 55, 58, 62, 72, 76, 168, 174, 179-80, 195-6, 246-7, 255, 260, 265, 273, 284, 288-9

Rent-seeking, 73

Ridley College, 61

Robertson, Boni, See Aboriginal and Torres Strait Islander (ATSI) Women's Task Force on Violence

Rogers, Nanette, 193

Rowley, Charles, 25, 205-6

Royal Commission into Aboriginal Deaths in Custody (RCADC), 34, 45, 47, 77, 131-41, 162

Rudd, Kevin
- government, 32, 55, 89, 196-7, 214, 255, 285

Samson and Delilah, 18, 254

Saunders, Cheryl, 142-4

Schools, 7, 43, 62, 64, 155-6, 190, 208, 212, 284, 291, 297

Sebastion, Frank, 223

Self-determination, 15, 20, 32, 40-55, 59, 62, 66-7, 86-7, 90, 95, 131, 135, 165, 174, 188, 205, 239, 258, 264, 284, 286, 290

Self-identify, 78

Skelton, Russell, 186

Smith, Percy, 59

Social Security and Other Legislation Amendment (Welfare Payment Reform) Act 2007 (Cth), 194

Southern (Aboriginal corporation), 94

Sowell, Thomas, 65, 70-1

Stanner, W.E.H., 29-30

Stephen, Ninian, 58

Stevens, I.E., See Hindmarsh Island Royal Commission

Stewart Basin, 236

Stolen Generations, (Bringing Them Home report), 12, 23, 31, 45, 58, 61, 92, 131, 135, 148, 151-4, 158, 160-2, 165

Stone Age, 17, 49

Strehlow, T.G.H., 27

Sutton, Peter, 17-8

Swan Valley, 170

Tanzania, 35-6

Taylor, Susan, 170-2

Tennant Creek, 82, 93-4, 162, 195, 223, 257, 265

Thomson, Donald, 249

Tickner, Robert, 142-4, 181

Tonkin, Daryl, 28

Tonkinson, Robert, 111, 126

Toohey, John, 218

Traditional authority, 86, 88, 207, 217

Tribal Aborigines, 16-17, 151

Truancy (non-attendance), 47, 172

United Nations Convention on the Rights of the Child, 153

United Nations Convention on Genocide, 150, 156

United Nations Declaration on the Rights of Indigenous Peoples
United Nations' Millennium Development Goals, 61

United Nations Special Rapporteur, 15

Vesteys, See Wave Hill

Violence, 4, 19, 26, 42-3, 46, 72, 103-18, 124, 126, 128, 132, 140-53, 160, 166-8, 170-4, 177, 180-2, 186-8, 198, 265, 283, 287, 301

Wadeye, 197, 255, to 57, 293-4, 297-8

Walker, Jenny, 187

Warlpiri, 96, 257

Wattie Creek, 219-20

Wave Hill, 210, 218-9, 257

Weipa, 218-9

Wentworth, Bill, 8

Werther effect, See Phillips

Westbury, Neil, 183

Whitlam, Gough, 219-20, 223

Wild, Rex, See Wild and Anderson Wild and Anderson, (Little Children are Sacred), 52, 129, 179, 181, 88, 192-3, 206

Wild Rivers (Environmental Management) Act 2005 (QLD), 230

Wilson, Ronald, 148

Windschuttle, Keith, 153

Woodward, A.E., 223

Working on Country, 285

Yamatji Marlpa (Aboriginal corporation), 94

Yunupingu, Galarrwuy, 16, 49